The District Controller's
THE PEAK DISTI
Derby/Sheffield - Chinley - Manchester

New Mills South Junction was one of the key locations on the Midland system; the left hand fork being the main line to Manchester Central via Cheadle Heath and the right hand the much busier Midland & Great Central joint line giving access to North Lancashire, Heaton Mersey and Ancoats goods yard. 5MT 4-6-0 44776 of Derby attacks the 1 in 90 gradient to Chinley and Peak Forest with an up express on July 8th 1950.

Previous books in this series have dealt with the quieter main lines of 1950's British Railways and have been of a proportionate size.

The route covered by this book falls into a completely different category and in order to describe the train service and the volume of traffic conveyed over the Derbyshire heights, the number of pages has been expanded to double the norm for the series.

The public timetables - the most frequently consulted guides to the line - have never done the routes justice. (The plural is justified since the transpennine route from Chinley to Sheffield has been included in the narrative).

Bradshaw and the British Railways timetables have given a picture of half a dozen London expresses between Manchester and Derby, a similar number of stopping trains and a service barely worthy of the name between Chinley and Sheffield. Why, one may wonder, was such an elaborate system necessary for such a small number of trains?

The answer lies in goods and mineral traffic which up to the 1950's brought in nearly 70% of the railway's revenues and occupied 95% of their energies. (For every passenger locomotive based in the area, there were four goods engines).

This is hardly to be wondered at. Manchester and Liverpool jointly formed the largest industrial conurbation in the country whilst access to the huge Nottingham and North Derbyshire coalfield was controlled almost entirely by the Midland whose trains continuously occupied almost every block section north of

Thanks for assistance with text and illustrations are due to:

C. Bentley, N. K. Harrop, N. Knight, John Morten, E.R. Morten, Norman Jones, Jack Cat, F. Morton, W.S.Becket, D. Collins, J. Suter, G. Waite.

Ambergate and West of Hathersage. Passenger services were in a minority because there was not the capacity to absorb them.

Operating freight traffic over the Peaks was far from easy. Northbound trains entered the district on easy gradients which leant themselves to far greater tonnages than could be conveyed over Peak Forest. Consequently

facilities had to be constructed at Rowsley which allowed heavy trains to be broken down into manageable units which still needed the assistance of a second engine in order to surmount the heights.

Traffic, including the huge tonnage which arrived via the Hope Valley, also needed segregating on the outskirts of Manchester. Some went west over the Cheshire Line to Merseyside whilst the rest continued northwards to the mills and factories of North Manchester. For this, a second marshalling yard was built at Gowhole, near Chinley.

Several devices are employed to describe the activities of the line during its postwar heyday and these include an hourly narrative of event during a typical 1950's day, locomotive allocations and engine workings for the sheds in the district, a 24-hour traffic graph which will allow an appreciation of line occupation and, in the centre section of the book, a reproduction of the 1954 working timetables for passenger and goods traffic.

To the spectator and railwayman alike, it was a fascinating line to watch or work and we hope this book will rekindle many memories of trains blasting their way over the Peak.

1

To most people other than those resident in Manchester, the Central station was the city's Midland Terminus and therefore part of the LMS arrangement in Manchester. In fact the Midland Railway terminated at Chorlton Junction where it made an end-on junction with the Cheshire Lines Committee; a joint system with operational leanings towards the LNER; the locomotive fleet being provided by the Great Central Railway. In 1953 B1 4-6-0 61317 of Sheffield (Darnall) prepares to depart with the 09.30 Liverpool (Central) - Hull whilst an N5 0-6-2T works as the station pilot. In the lower view D11 4-4-0 62666 'Zeebrugge' pulls away with a Northwich service. Shortly after this view was taken, 62666 was transferred from Trafford Park to Immingham

The handsome 5XP 'Jubilee' 4-6-0's held dominion for almost a quarter of a century on the Manchester - St Pancras express and although they were relieved by class 7 Britannia's and Royal Scots from 1957, the 5XP's could be found in and around Manchester Central until the very final days of steam. 45576 'Bombay' of Millhouses strikes an oft-seen pose as it waits to depart for St Pancras in 1955.

Displaced from the expresses by the 5XP's and 5MT 4-6-0's, the Compound 4-4-0's survived in significant numbers at Trafford Park until 1957, much of their work involving the stopping trains between Derby and Manchester and from Manchester to Sheffield via the Hope Valley. Their demise came as post-nationalisation standard engines released 5MT 4-6-0's to take over 4-4-0 duties. One of their more interesting duties concerned the Derby engine which arrived with the 16.10 stopping train from Derby. Instead of returning with an up stopping service, the engine worked to Cheadle Heath with the 22.10 suburban service - one of the few such trains not to be worked by a 3P 2-6-2T - before running light to Marple where it took over the 20.35 Bolton - Leicester Parcels from a Newton Heath 'Crab' 2-6-0. In the above 1948 scene, Compound (4)1052 has been released from a Sheffield train and is making its way to the turntable.

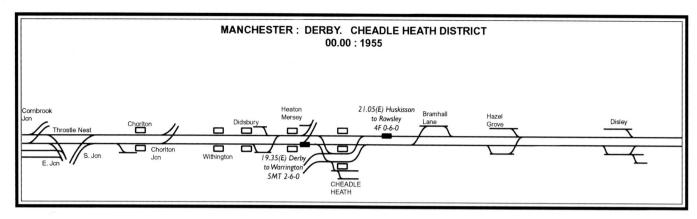

MANCHESTER : DERBY. CHEADLE HEATH DISTRICT
00.00 : 1955

CONTROLLER'S LOG : The former Gowhole and Rowsley districts, now combined and controlled from Derby, are areas of extremes. On the one hand they are amongst the most sparsely populated sections of line served by the Midland (or indeed any other railway in the country) whilst on the other, they are well to the fore in terms of traffic movements.

On some sections of the line, traffic is so dense that special trains are not at all easy to fit in whilst even the windswept wilderness of the Hope Valley route - generally supposed to be the quietest of all the trans-Pennine lines - caters for no less than 103 trains per day: an

presses, five stopping trains to Derby, two through Manchester - Buxton services and a handful of trains at the southern end of the district.

Traffic flows vary from one part of the section to another but in the area round Monsal Dale, for example, there are 131 booked daily movements of which only 27 are passenger or parcels services. Even the Manchester suburban service runs no further up the line than Cheadle Heath, eight miles out of Central, and is made up of no more than thirteen departures: not much for a city the size of Manchester.

Coal rather than commuters is the business

Mills South Junction. Parcels trains do not normally arouse much excitement but by virtue of a non-stop run between Marple to Derby together with the associated engine diagrams, the Bolton - Leicester rises from the ranks of the ordinary. Both engines booked to the train are unusual; the locomotive working the train as far as Marple - by no means a normal engine-changing point - being a Newton Heath 'Crab' 2-6-0 whilst the relieving engine is the Derby-based Compound 4-4-0 that worked down on the 16.10 Derby - Manchester slow.

The 4-4-0 makes its way to the relieving point by working the 22.10 local from Man-

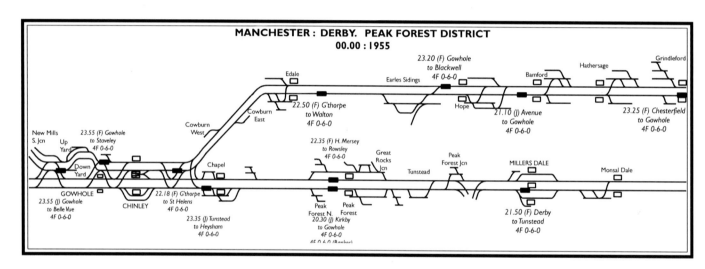

MANCHESTER : DERBY. PEAK FOREST DISTRICT
00.00 : 1955

average of one every fourteen minutes. Of these less than a quarter are passenger services - hence the reputation as a backwater - and most of the workings are unfitted mineral services worked, like so many other trains in the district, by standard 4F 0-6-0's.

The ratio of passengers to goods is even lower on the Derby main line where the volume of freight traffic limits passenger movements to scarcely more than a dozen trains in each direction. These include six London ex-

of the line.

At the moment, however, the line is in the unusual position of hosting a pair of express services which about to drive a swathe through the unfitted goods workings and some attention has to be given to the task of ensuring both a clear run.

The first of the pair is an express parcels service which runs through from the Lancashire & Yorkshire - 20.37 ex Bolton - via Belle Vue and Marple to join the main line at New

chester to Cheadle; the displaced 2-6-0 then running light to Tiviot Dale to wait for the Victoria portion of the 19.40 ex St Pancras.

Hard on the heels of the Bolton Parcels will be the overnight express to St Pancras which, having reduced its load at Derby, will merge with the former at Leicester bringing into the terminus the unaccustomed sight of two fish vans from Wyre Dock (Fleetwood), a pair of parcels vehicles from Bolton and one from Burscough Bridge.

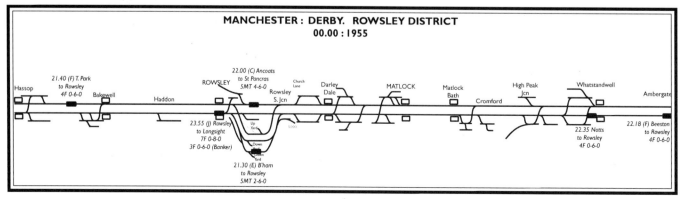

MANCHESTER : DERBY. ROWSLEY DISTRICT
00.00 : 1955

ALLOCATION & MOVEMENTS : TRAFFORD PARK

Loco	Class	Aug-50	Sep-50	Oct-50	Nov-50	Dec-50	Jan-51	Feb-51	Mar-51	Apr-51	May-51	Jun-51	Jul-51
48411	8F 2-8-0 (1935)												
48440	8F 2-8-0 (1935)								To Willesden	X	X	X	X
48680	8F 2-8-0 (1935)												
48698	8F 2-8-0 (1935)												
45553	5XP 4-6-0 (1934)											To Longsight	X
45618	5XP 4-6-0 (1934)												
45622	5XP 4-6-0 (1934)												
45628	5XP 4-6-0 (1934)												
45629	5XP 4-6-0 (1934)												
45652	5XP 4-6-0 (1934)												
45655	5XP 4-6-0 (1934)	X	X	X	X	X	X	X	X	X	X	Ex Longsight	
44717	5MT 4-6-0 (1934)	X	X	X	X	X	X	X	Ex Crewe (N)				
44938	5MT 4-6-0 (1934)												
64723	5F : J39 0-6-0 (1926)								To Colwick	X	X	X	X
64823	5F : J39 0-6-0 (1926)								To Colwick	X	X	X	X
64901	5F : J39 0-6-0 (1926)									To Stockport	X	X	X
64954	5F : J39 0-6-0 (1926)									To Stockport	X	X	X
40900	4P 4-4-0 (1924)												
40910	4P 4-4-0 (1924)												
40936	4P 4-4-0 (1924)												To M. Lane
41052	4P 4-4-0 (1924)												
41055	4P 4-4-0 (1924)								To L'dno Jcn	X	X	X	X
41066	4P 4-4-0 (1924)												
41076	4P 4-4-0 (1924)								To Crewe (N)	X	X	X	X
41111	4P 4-4-0 (1924)	X	Ex M. Lane						To L'dno Jcn	X	X	X	X
41112	4P 4-4-0 (1924)	X	X	X	X	X	X	X	Ex Crewe (N)				
41154	4P 4-4-0 (1924)												
41161	4P 4-4-0 (1924)	X	X	X	X	X	X	X	Ex L'dno Jcn				
41173	4P 4-4-0 (1924)	X	X	X	X	X	X	X	Ex L'dno Jcn				
41181	4P 4-4-0 (1924)												
42064	4MT 2-6-4T (1945)	X	X	X	X	X	X	X	Ex Stoke				
42065	4MT 2-6-4T (1945)	X	X	X	X	X	X	X	Ex Stoke				
44236	4F 0-6-0 (1924)												
43896	4F 0-6-0 (1911)								To Upperby	X	X	X	X
43908	4F 0-6-0 (1911)												
68064	4F : J94 0-6-0T (1943)		To Gorton	X	X	X	X	X	X	X	X	X	X
68064	4F : J94 0-6-0T (1943)	X	X	X	X	X	X	X	Ex Gorton				
68067	4F : J94 0-6-0T (1943)	X	X	Ex Gorton									
68071	4F : J94 0-6-0T (1943)	X	X	X	Ex Gorton	To Brunswick	X	X	X	X	X	X	X
40093	3P 2-6-2 (1935)												
40094	3P 2-6-2 (1935)							To Heaton M	X	X	X	X	X
40118	3P 2-6-2 (1935)		To Heaton M.	X	X	X	Ex Heaton M						
62532	3P : D16 4-4-0 (1923)												
62535	3P : D16 4-4-0 (1923)												
62536	3P : D16 4-4-0 (1923)												
62568	3P : D16 4-4-0 (1923)												
62587	3P : D16 4-4-0 (1923)												
62588	3P : D16 4-4-0 (1923)												
62599	3P : D16 4-4-0 (1923)												
62609	3P : D16 4-4-0 (1923)												
62660	3P : D11 4-4-0 (1920)	X	X	X	X	X	X	X	Ex Immingham				
62661	3P : D11 4-4-0 (1920)	X	X	X	X	X	X	X	Ex Immingham				
62662	3P : D11 4-4-0 (1920)	X	X	Ex Immingham									
62664	3P : D11 4-4-0 (1920)	X	X	X	X	X	Ex Immingham						
62666	3P : D11 4-4-0 (1920)	X	X	Ex Immingham									
62667	3P : D11 4-4-0 (1920)	X	X	X	X	X	Ex Immingham						
62668	3P : D11 4-4-0 (1920)	X	X	X	Ex Immingham								
62669	3P : D11 4-4-0 (1920)	X	X	X	Ex Immingham								
62670	3P : D11 4-4-0 (1920)												
62651	3P : D10 4-4-0 (1913)								To Northwich	X	X	X	X
62653	3P : D10 4-4-0 (1913)												
62654	3P : D10 4-4-0 (1913)												
62656	3P : D10 4-4-0 (1913)												
62657	3P : D10 4-4-0 (1913)												
62658	3P : D10 4-4-0 (1913)												
62659	3P : D10 4-4-0 (1913)												
69252	2MT : N5 0-6-2T (1891)												
69255	2MT : N5 0-6-2T (1891)												
69304	2MT : N5 0-6-2T (1891)												
69326	2MT : N5 0-6-2T (1891)												
69336	2MT : N5 0-6-2T (1891)												
69343	2MT : N5 0-6-2T (1891)												
69347	2MT : N5 0-6-2T (1891)	X	Ex Gorton										
69361	2MT : N5 0-6-2T (1891)												
69364	2MT : N5 0-6-2T (1891)												
69370	2MT : N5 0-6-2T (1891)												
68540	2F : J67 0-6-0T (1890)												
68583	2F : J67 0-6-0T (1890)												
68595	2F : J67 0-6-0T (1890)												
68598	2F : J67 0-6-0T (1890)												
65137	2F : J10 0-6-0 (1892)												
65141	2F : J10 0-6-0 (1892)												
65142	2F : J10 0-6-0 (1892)	X	Ex Brunswick	To Brunswick	X	X	X	Ex Brunswick	To Brunswick	X	X	X	X
65143	2F : J10 0-6-0 (1892)	X	Ex Northgate	To Northgate	X	X	X	Ex Northgate	To Northgate	X	X	X	X
65144	2F : J10 0-6-0 (1892)	X	Ex Heaton M	Ex Heaton M	X	X	X	Ex Heaton M	Ex Heaton M	X	X	X	X
65145	2F : J10 0-6-0 (1892)	X	Ex Heaton M	Ex Heaton M	X	X	X	Ex Heaton M	Ex Heaton M	X	X	X	X
65146	2F : J10 0-6-0 (1892)	X	Ex Heaton M	Ex Heaton M	X	X	X	Ex Heaton M	Ex Heaton M	X	X	X	X
65147	2F : J10 0-6-0 (1892)	X	Ex Northwich	To Northwich	X	X	X	Ex Northwich	To Northwich	X	X	X	X
65148	2F : J10 0-6-0 (1892)	X	Ex Heaton M	Ex Heaton M	X	X	X	Ex Heaton M	Ex Heaton M	X	X	X	X
65154	2F : J10 0-6-0 (1892)												
65161	2F : J10 0-6-0 (1892)												
65168	2F : J10 0-6-0 (1892)												
65179	2F : J10 0-6-0 (1892)												
65183	2F : J10 0-6-0 (1892)												
65184	2F : J10 0-6-0 (1892)												
65186	2F : J10 0-6-0 (1892)												
65201	2F : J10 0-6-0 (1892)												
65204	2F : J10 0-6-0 (1892)												
67366	1P : C12 4-4-2T (1898)												
67369	1P : C12 4-4-2T (1898)												

LOCO MOVEMENTS : Trafford Park's principal role lay with CLC services to Liverpool and Chester and its contribution to Midland workings went little further than a share in the London, Sheffield and Cheadle Heath passenger services.

At the beginning of the decade LNER engines outnumbered those of the LM by two to one although the imbalance was not allowed to last. The first to go were a quartet of J39 0-6-0's which had been allocated to the shed for the anachronistic 20.22 Deansgate - Colwick: an express goods which ensured that premium LNER traffic - mainly meat and other perishable matter for the London Docks - did not get tied up in the Midland system. The service finished in 1952 and the engines concerned - normally two of the four were engaged with the Colwick duty - were returned to their home metals.   Other returns to the ex-LNER included the eight Great Eastern D16 4-4-0's which had been sent to share the Manchester - Liverpool CLC passenger workings.   At the time the allocation of engines exceeded actual requirements by a handsome margin and not only were the D16's not replaced but the strength of D10 4-4-0's was reduced from six to two by withdrawals and transfers.

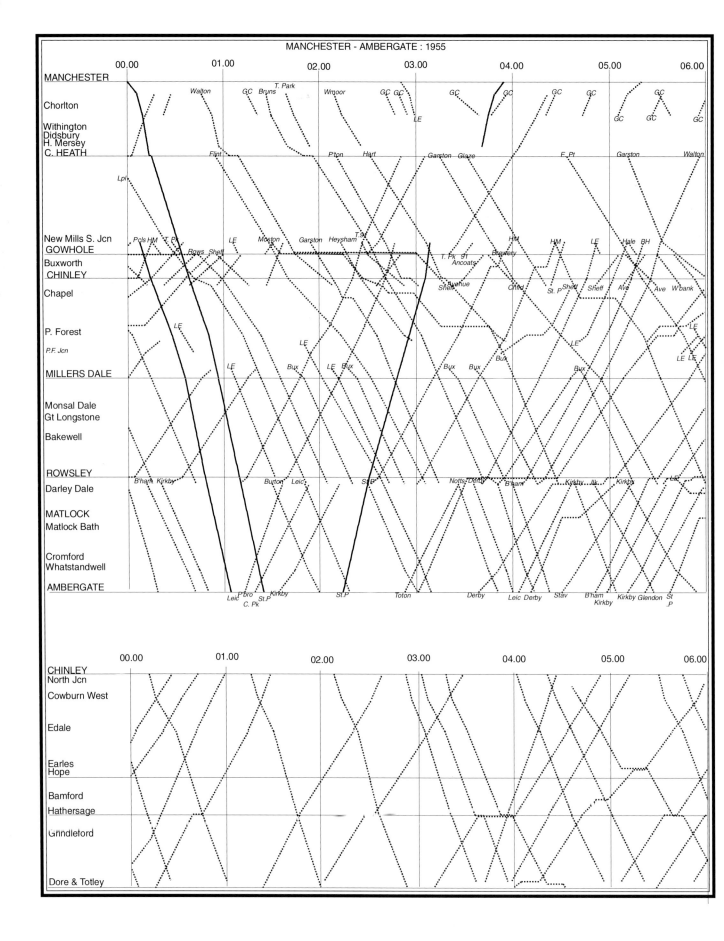

MANCHESTER - AMBERGATE : 1955

ALLOCATION & MOVEMENTS : TRAFFORD PARK

Loco	Class	Aug-51	Sep-51	Oct-51	Nov-51	Dec-51	Jan-52	Feb-52	Mar-52	Apr-52	May-52	Jun-52	Jul-52
48342	8F 2-8-0 (1935)	X	X	X	X	X	X	X	X	X	X	Ex Mold Jcn	
48411	8F 2-8-0 (1935)												
48680	8F 2-8-0 (1935)							To Northwich	X	X	Ex Northwich		
48698	8F 2-8-0 (1935)												
45618	5XP 4-6-0 (1934)												
45622	5XP 4-6-0 (1934)												
45628	5XP 4-6-0 (1934)												
45629	5XP 4-6-0 (1934)												
45652	5XP 4-6-0 (1934)												
45655	5XP 4-6-0 (1934)												
44717	5MT 4-6-0 (1934)												
44938	5MT 4-6-0 (1934)												
40900	4P 4-4-0 (1924)											To Nottingham	X
40910	4P 4-4-0 (1924)												
41052	4P 4-4-0 (1924)												
41066	4P 4-4-0 (1924)												
41112	4P 4-4-0 (1924)												
41154	4P 4-4-0 (1924)												
41161	4P 4-4-0 (1924)												
41173	4P 4-4-0 (1924)												
41181	4P 4-4-0 (1924)											To Nottingham	X
42064	4MT 2-6-4T (1945)												
42065	4MT 2-6-4T (1945)												
42676	4MT 2-6-4T (1945)	X	X	X	X	X	X	X	X	X	X	Ex Stoke	
42683	4MT 2-6-4T (1945)	X	X	X	X	X	X	X	X	X	X	Ex Stoke	
42452	4MT 2-6-4T (1935)	X	X	X	X	X	X	X	Ex Walsall				
42466	4MT 2-6-4T (1935)	X	X	X	X	X	X	X	Ex Walsall				To Brunswick
42469	4MT 2-6-4T (1935)	X	X	X	X	X	X	X	Ex Walsall				
44236	4F 0-6-0 (1924)												
43908	4F 0-6-0 (1911)												
68067	4F : J94 0-6-0T (1943)												
40093	3P 2-6-2 (1935)												
40118	3P 2-6-2 (1935)												
62532	3P : D16 4-4-0 (1923)											To Cambridge	X
62535	3P : D16 4-4-0 (1923)											To Cambridge	X
62536	3P : D16 4-4-0 (1923)											To Cambridge	X
62568	3P : D16 4-4-0 (1923)											To Norwich	X
62587	3P : D16 4-4-0 (1923)											To Cambridge	X
62588	3P : D16 4-4-0 (1923)											To Norwich	X
62599	3P : D16 4-4-0 (1923)											To Norwich	X
62609	3P : D16 4-4-0 (1923)											To Cambridge	X
62660	3P : D11 4-4-0 (1920)												
62661	3P : D11 4-4-0 (1920)												
62662	3P : D11 4-4-0 (1920)												
62664	3P : D11 4-4-0 (1920)												
62666	3P : D11 4-4-0 (1920)												
62667	3P : D11 4-4-0 (1920)												
62668	3P : D11 4-4-0 (1920)												
62669	3P : D11 4-4-0 (1920)										To Northwich	X	X
62670	3P : D11 4-4-0 (1920)												
62653	3P : D10 4-4-0 (1913)												
62654	3P : D10 4-4-0 (1913)												
62656	3P : D10 4-4-0 (1913)												
62657	3P : D10 4-4-0 (1913)												
62658	3P : D10 4-4-0 (1913)												
62659	3P : D10 4-4-0 (1913)												
69252	2MT : N5 0-6-2T (1891)	W/D	X	X	X	X	X	X	X	X	X	X	X
69255	2MT : N5 0-6-2T (1891)												
69304	2MT : N5 0-6-2T (1891)												
69326	2MT : N5 0-6-2T (1891)												
69336	2MT : N5 0-6-2T (1891)												
69343	2MT : N5 0-6-2T (1891)												
69347	2MT : N5 0-6-2T (1891)												
69358	2MT : N5 0-6-2T (1891)	X	Ex Neasden										
69361	2MT : N5 0-6-2T (1891)												
69364	2MT : N5 0-6-2T (1891)												
69370	2MT : N5 0-6-2T (1891)												
68540	2F : J67 0-6-0T (1890)												
68583	2F : J67 0-6-0T (1890)												
68595	2F : J67 0-6-0T (1890)												
68598	2F : J67 0-6-0T (1890)												
65137	2F : J10 0-6-0 (1892)										W/D	X	X
65141	2F : J10 0-6-0 (1892)												
65142	2F : J10 0-6-0 (1892)	X	X	X	X	X	X	Ex Brunswick	To Brunswick	X	X	X	X
65143	2F : J10 0-6-0 (1892)	X	X	X	X	X	X	Ex Chester	To Chester	X	X	X	X
65144	2F : J10 0-6-0 (1892)	X	X	X	X	X	X	Ex Wigan	To Wigan	X	X	X	X
65145	2F : J10 0-6-0 (1892)	X	X	X	X	X	X	Ex Heaton M.	To Heaton M	X	X	X	X
65146	2F : J10 0-6-0 (1892)	X	X	X	X	X	X	Ex Heaton M.	To Heaton M	X	X	X	X
65147	2F : J10 0-6-0 (1892)	X	X	X	X	X	X	Ex Northwich	To Northwich	X	X	X	X
65148	2F : J10 0-6-0 (1892)	X	X	X	X	X	X	Ex Heaton M.	To Heaton M	X	X	X	X
65154	2F : J10 0-6-0 (1892)												
65161	2F : J10 0-6-0 (1892)												
65168	2F : J10 0-6-0 (1892)												
65179	2F : J10 0-6-0 (1892)												
65183	2F : J10 0-6-0 (1892)										W/D	X	X
65184	2F : J10 0-6-0 (1892)												
65186	2F : J10 0-6-0 (1892)												
65201	2F : J10 0-6-0 (1892)												
65204	2F : J10 0-6-0 (1892)												
65205	2F : J10 0-6-0 (1892)	X	X	X	X	X	X	X	X	X	Ex Northwich		
67366	1P : C12 4-4-2T (1898)												
67369	1P : C12 4-4-2T (1898)												

In 1953 the trend towards working the CLC trains by LMS rather than LNER power accelerated as the diminishing ranks of the latter were augmented by no less than eight Midland Compounds. Many CLC services were also handed over to LMS 2-6-4T's; the number swelling from two engines in 1951 to eight, five years later.

Hopes that the allocation of fifteen Compound 4-4-0's during the middle part of the decade would prove something of a renaissance for the class where short-lived and most disappeared as quickly as they had arrived, the last of the class leaving the shed in 1958. The period of decline for the Compounds saw a slow growth in the number of 5MT 4-6-0's; a class used in tandem with the 2-6-4T's on the majority of services to Liverpool Central. (Continued p.10)

7

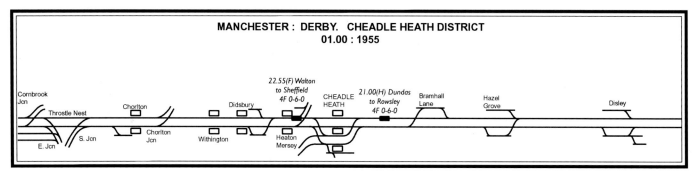

MANCHESTER : DERBY. CHEADLE HEATH DISTRICT
01.00 : 1955

CONTROLLER'S LOG : With the Bolton Parcels and the Manchester - London at Cromford and Monsal Dale respectively, almost everything else on the up line has come to a standstill in order to allow the two services a clear path.   The disparity in running between passenger and goods services is illustrated by watching the gap that grows between midnight ex Manchester and the 21.05 Huskisson - Rowsley goods.   The latter ran slow line from New Mills South to Chinley while being overtaken and returned to the main line immediately behind the express. Twenty minutes later, the goods is barking its way through Dove Holes Tunnel whilst the express is approaching Monsal Dale, ten miles further on. By the time the goods gets to Rowsley in fifty minutes time, the express will have been in been in Derby for almost fifteen minutes. The

issued in the Working Timetable for each train. Some, for example, are booked slow between Chinley and New Mills South whilst other are shown to run main line.

The answer is that such detail is not taken into account nor is it expected to be since the timetable - so far as goods trains are concerned - is a guide rather than an absolute and in practise a number of common rules are applied to services in general.

So far as it is possible, through trains via Peak Forest and Disley are run main/fast line throughout whilst services from the Sheffield direction for the Disley line are brought onto the fast line at Chinley. Conversely, trains from the Sheffield line for either Gowhole or the GC are kept to the slow line; those for the Cheadle Heath line being turned slow to main north of Chinley station.

of the system is going to appear in twenty minutes time - it does not carry the highest priory and one is expected to monitor the regulation of trains as a matter of routine whilst attending to more important matters such as the loading of trains and the utilisation of engines and crews.

The measure of the Midland is often taken to be the well known Wellingborough - Brent services on which Garratt engines plod up to London with as many as 87 wagons of coal.

If only such things applied to the system as a whole since between Rowsley and Cheadle Heath the same Garratt would be limited to a paltry twenty-six vehicles: the standard single-engine load over Peak Forest. (Those who believe that the solution to severe gradients lies in the provision of larger engines might like to reflect on the fact that a Garratt and a 4F are

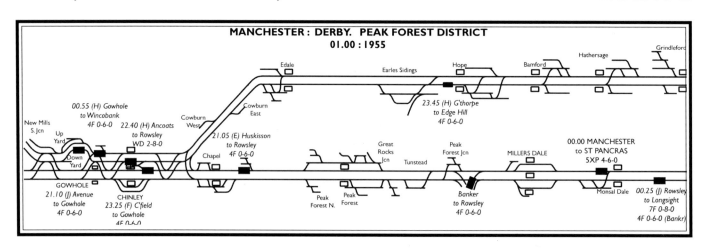

MANCHESTER : DERBY. PEAK FOREST DISTRICT
01.00 : 1955

havoc that express workings cause to the system can be gauged from the fact that the up main line has been completely denuded of trains whilst the vacuum to the south extends back almost to Chinley.   Frankly, the less passenger trains there are over Peak Forest, the better one likes it since they achieve little more than putting a stop on goods movements.

With such a variety and volume of trains approaching from and going to all directions, it might be wondered how it is possible to remember the individual regulating instructions

Trains from the Peak Forest direction for Gowhole tend to go inside at Chinley South although if there is a string of services coming off the Hope Valley, it may be expedient to loop the main line train at Chapel to avoid congestion at Chinley.

Passenger trains are dealt with quite differently and generally keep to the paths shown in the timetable.

Whilst the regulation of trains can vary from the interesting to the exciting - one has to develop the habit of visualising how any part

restricted to the same loadings north of Rowsley: a circumstance that explains why Garratts tend to be uncommon in North Derbyshire).

The severity of the gradients either side of Peak Forest and the strain they impose upon wagon couplings impose an absolute limit of twenty-six loaded mineral wagons the 4F 0-6-0 loading - on any northbound working from Rowsley and also place severe restrictions on the length of trains that can be worked downhill from Peak Forest towards Manchester. Little in the Peaks is straightforward.

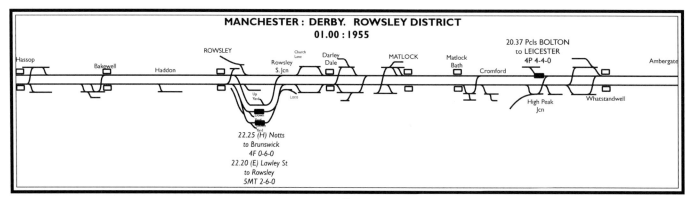

MANCHESTER : DERBY. ROWSLEY DISTRICT
01.00 : 1955

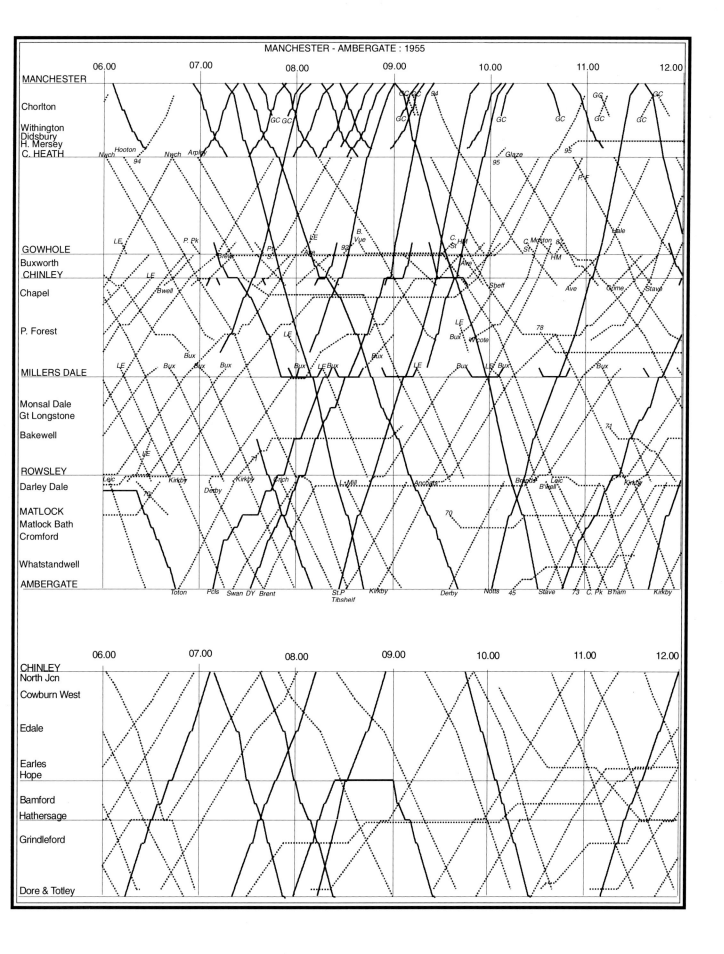

MANCHESTER - AMBERGATE : 1955

ALLOCATION & MOVEMENTS : TRAFFORD PARK

Loco	Class	Aug-52	Sep-52	Oct-52	Nov-52	Dec-52	Jan-53	Feb-53	Mar-53	Apr-53	May-53	Jun-53	Jul-53
48342	8F 2-8-0 (1935)												To Buxton
48411	8F 2-8-0 (1935)												
48680	8F 2-8-0 (1935)												
48698	8F 2-8-0 (1935)												
48741	8F 2-8-0 (1935)	X	X	X	X	X	X	X	X	X	X	X	Ex Buxton
45604	5XP 4-6-0 (1934)	X	X	X	X	X	X	X	X	X	Ex Crewe (N)		To Crewe (N)
45617	5XP 4-6-0 (1934)	X	X	X	X	X	X	X	X	X	Ex Crewe (N)	To Crewe (N)	X
45618	5XP 4-6-0 (1934)												
45622	5XP 4-6-0 (1934)												
45628	5XP 4-6-0 (1934)												
45629	5XP 4-6-0 (1934)												
45652	5XP 4-6-0 (1934)												
45655	5XP 4-6-0 (1934)												
44717	5MT 4-6-0 (1934)												
44938	5MT 4-6-0 (1934)												
45239	5MT 4-6-0 (1934)	X	X	X	X	X	X	X	X	X	X	Ex Crewe (S)	
45347	5MT 4-6-0 (1934)	X	X	X	X	X	X	X	X	X	X	Ex Edge Hill	
40910	4P 4-4-0 (1924)												
41052	4P 4-4-0 (1924)									W/D	X	X	X
41066	4P 4-4-0 (1924)												
41098	4P 4-4-0 (1924)	X	X	X	X	X	X	X	X	X	X	Ex Chester	
41112	4P 4-4-0 (1924)												
41154	4P 4-4-0 (1924)												
41161	4P 4-4-0 (1924)												
41170	4P 4-4-0 (1924)	X	X	X	X	X	X	X	Ex Brunswick				
41173	4P 4-4-0 (1924)												
42064	4MT 2-6-4T (1945)												
42065	4MT 2-6-4T (1945)												
42676	4MT 2-6-4T (1945)												
42683	4MT 2-6-4T (1945)			To Bangor	X	X	Ex Bangor						
42452	4MT 2-6-4T (1935)												
42469	4MT 2-6-4T (1935)												
44236	4F 0-6-0 (1924)												
44275	4F 0-6-0 (1924)	X	X	X	X	X	X	X	X	X	X	X	Ex Sheffield
44350	4F 0-6-0 (1924)	X	X	X	X	X	X	X	X	X	X	X	Ex Aston
44392	4F 0-6-0 (1924)	X	X	X	X	X	X	X	X	X	X	Ex Brunswick	
43908	4F 0-6-0 (1911)												To Mold Jn
68067	4F : J94 0-6-0T (1943)												
40093	3P 2-6-2 (1935)			To Warwick	X	X	X	X	X	X	X	X	X
40118	3P 2-6-2 (1935)			To Brunswick	X	X	X	X	X	X	X	X	X
40009	3P 2-6-2 (1930)	X	X	X	X	X	Ex Willesden						
40017	3P 2-6-2 (1930)	X	X	X	X	X	Ex Willesden						
62660	3P : D11 4-4-0 (1920)												
62661	3P : D11 4-4-0 (1920)												
62662	3P : D11 4-4-0 (1920)												
62664	3P : D11 4-4-0 (1920)												
62666	3P : D11 4-4-0 (1920)							To Immingham	X	X	X	X	X
62667	3P : D11 4-4-0 (1920)							To Immingham	X	X	X	X	X
62668	3P : D11 4-4-0 (1920)												
62670	3P : D11 4-4-0 (1920)												
62653	3P : D10 4-4-0 (1913)												
62654	3P : D10 4-4-0 (1913)												
62656	3P : D10 4-4-0 (1913)												
62657	3P : D10 4-4-0 (1913)							W/D	X	X	X	X	X
62658	3P : D10 4-4-0 (1913)												
62659	3P : D10 4-4-0 (1913)							To Northwich	X	X	X	X	X
69255	2MT : N5 0-6-2T (1891)												
69304	2MT : N5 0-6-2T (1891)												
69326	2MT : N5 0-6-2T (1891)												
69336	2MT : N5 0-6-2T (1891)												
69343	2MT : N5 0-6-2T (1891)												
69347	2MT : N5 0-6-2T (1891)												
69358	2MT : N5 0-6-2T (1891)												
69361	2MT : N5 0-6-2T (1891)												
69364	2MT : N5 0-6-2T (1891)												
69370	2MT : N5 0-6-2T (1891)												
68499	2F : J67 0-6-0T (1890)	X	Ex Brunswick	To Brunswick	X	X	X	X	X	X	X	X	X
68540	2F : J67 0-6-0T (1890)							To Lincoln	X	X	X	X	X
68559	2F : J67 0-6-0T (1890)	X	X	X	X	X	X	X	X	X	Ex Brunswick		
68583	2F : J67 0-6-0T (1890)												
68595	2F : J67 0-6-0T (1890)												
68598	2F : J67 0-6-0T (1890)												
65138	2F : J10 0-6-0 (1892)	X	X	X	X	X	X	Ex Northwich					
65141	2F : J10 0-6-0 (1892)		W/D	X	X	X	X	X	X	X	X	X	X
65146	2F : J10 0-6-0 (1892)	X	X	X	X	X	X	X	X	X	X	Ex Heaton M.	
65153	2F : J10 0-6-0 (1892)	X	Ex Brunswick										
65154	2F : J10 0-6-0 (1892)										W/D	X	X
65156	2F : J10 0-6-0 (1892)	X	X	X	X	X	X	X	Ex Northwich				
65157	2F : J10 0-6-0 (1892)	X	X	X	X	X	X	X	X	X	X	Ex Heaton M.	
65161	2F : J10 0-6-0 (1892)		W/D	X	X	X	X	X	X	X	X	X	X
65164	2F : J10 0-6-0 (1892)	X	X	X	X	Ex Wigan					W/D	X	X
65167	2F : J10 0-6-0 (1892)	X	X	X	X	X	X	X	X	X	X	Ex Northgate	X
65168	2F : J10 0-6-0 (1892)					W/D	X	X	X	X	X	X	X
65170	2F : J10 0-6-0 (1892)	X	X	X	Ex Wigan								
65179	2F : J10 0-6-0 (1892)					W/D	X	X	X	X	X	X	X
65181	2F : J10 0-6-0 (1892)	X	Ex Heaton M.										
65184	2F : J10 0-6-0 (1892)												
65186	2F : J10 0-6-0 (1892)												
65191	2F : J10 0-6-0 (1892)	X	X	X	X	X	X	X	X	X	Ex Northwich		
65197	2F : J10 0-6-0 (1892)	X	X	X	X	X	X	X	X	X	X	Ex Heaton M.	
65198	2F : J10 0-6-0 (1892)	X	X	X	X	X	X	X	X	X	X	Ex Heaton M.	
65201	2F : J10 0-6-0 (1892)									W/D	X	X	X
65204	2F : J10 0-6-0 (1892)				W/D	X	X	X	X	X	X	X	X
65205	2F : J10 0-6-0 (1892)												
65209	2F : J10 0-6-0 (1892)	X	X	X	X	X	X	X	X	X	X	Ex Heaton M.	
67366	1P : C12 4-4-2T (1898)							To Spital B.	X	X	X	X	X
67369	1P : C12 4-4-2T (1898)							To N. England	X	X	X	X	X

The period from 1957 to 1959 saw the greatest change with respect to express passenger motive power when the 5XP Jubilee 4-6-0's which had monopolised the London services for over twenty years were abruptly replaced by Britannia and Royal Scot locomotives, the latter operating initially from the London end of the route. At the same time the last LNER locomotive left the shed with the departure of J10 0-6-0 65166 in December 1959.

By the end of the decade almost all the colour had gone from Trafford Park. Ten years earlier no less than fifteen varieties of engine had been housed at the depot; by 1960 this had dwindled to eight classes with over a third of the allocation consisting of 2-6-4T's. Diesel locomotives started appearing on the London services in 1959 in the form of Derby-based Metrovick Co-Bo's and by 1961 it was all but impossible to ride from Manchester to St Pancras behind a steam locomotive.

The high degree of standardisation reached by the LMS was not always apparent in the Manchester area and although a 5XP could usually be relied upon for the London expresses, holiday periods often produced an interesting variety of types as engine workings broke down under the pressure of an abnormally high volume of work. Crewe-based engines were not over-common on the Midland and 2-6-0 'Crab' 42939, which somehow became stranded in Manchester is being returned to Crewe South via the 13.05 Manchester Central - Derby in 1953. In the lower view Ivatt 2-6-0 43042 of Sheffield, seen at Chinley, has replaced the usual 4-4-0 on a Hope Valley Service.

Compound 4P 4-4-0 41056 of Holbeck approaches Heaton Mersey with the 16.10 Derby - Manchester (Central) on the 26th July 1952.   The train has come via Stockport (Tiviot Dale); the direct route from Chinley via Disley coming in on the right.

Having only recently moved from Liverpool (Brunswick) to Trafford Park, Compound 41118 leaves ~~Cheadle Heath~~ Didsbury with the 14.05 Manchester Central to Derby on 25th July 1954.   This service was unusual in that it recessed in a loop between Rowsley and Darley Dale to let the 16.00 Manchester - St Pancras overtake.

Three BR 4MT 2-6-0's were delivered new to Trafford Park during the summer of 1957, intended as replacements for the shed's 4P Compound 4-4-0's; the complement of the latter falling from eleven to six during the twelve months from September 1956. Exactly what role the 4MT 2-6-0's were supposed to play as a whole was never fully clarified and far from replacing a specific class of engine, the 115 examples were distributed between no less than twenty-two sheds (January 1958); every region other than the Western having a quota. 76089 is seen running into Heaton Mersey in July 1961 with the 13.50 Manchester Central to Sheffield. This service was worked as far as Chinley by the Buxton men who had arrived with the 08.00 Buxton - Manchester Central.

5MT 4-6-0 pauses at Cheadle Heath in July 1952 with the 11.30 (Saturdays only) Llandudno - Sheffield Midland

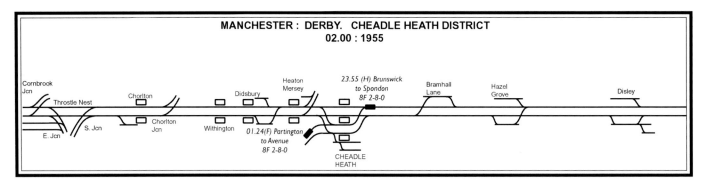

MANCHESTER : DERBY. CHEADLE HEATH DISTRICT
02.00 : 1955

Cornbrook Jcn · Throstle Nest · Chorlton · S. Jcn · E. Jcn · Chorlton Jcn · Withington · Didsbury · Heaton Mersey · 01.24(F) Partington to Avenue 8F 2-8-0 · CHEADLE HEATH · 23.55 (H) Brunswick to Spondon 8F 2-8-0 · Bramhall Lane · Hazel Grove · Disley

CONTROLLER'S LOG : Goods traffic having been restored in the up direction, it is time to curtail matters on the down line for the 19.40 St Pancras - Manchester Parcels, an express service which has left Derby and will come onto the district at Ambergate at 02.14.

Booked non-stop between Derby and Stockport (TD), it is a fast service with portions for both Manchester Central and Victoria. The latter is worked forward from Tiviot Dale by the Newton Heath 2-6-0 which arrived on the 20.37 Bolton parcels.

The first thing to check is that the Derby - Ambergate section has not despatched any slow moving services ahead of it. The running time for a mineral service from Ambergate to Church Lane loop is thirty-five min-

into Church Lane loop.

Similar precautions have to be taken for train leaving Rowsley for the north and calculations have to be made to ensure that the last down train out of the yard can get to the loop at Millers Dale without delaying the 19.40. The margin for the section is forty-two minutes.

" - *Spondon goods up at one-thirty: Chorlton Junction.*" is a reminder that not all the goods services on the district are based on either Gowhole or Rowsley and where it is possible - usually because of known regular traffic flows - through workings are maintained between the Nottingham/Derby areas and the North West. The greater part of such workings operate between Kirkby Colliery near

the sake of good timekeeping, important though that is, but because serious delay would waste the crew waiting to work the train forward from Rowsley.

The Spondon is unusual in that it works over the section of line between Chorlton Junction and Cheadle Heath; a stretch of line not much used by goods services since most trains from the CLC leave the Liverpool - Manchester line at Grazebrook to join the Midland at Cheadle Heath. This slight diversion avoids a clash with the 01.24 Partington - Avenue which is coming off the CLC, bringing coal empties from the West Manchester area to Avenue sidings near Chesterfield. Routed via the Hope Valley the train is relieved at Chinley and it is essential to make certain that the relieving crew

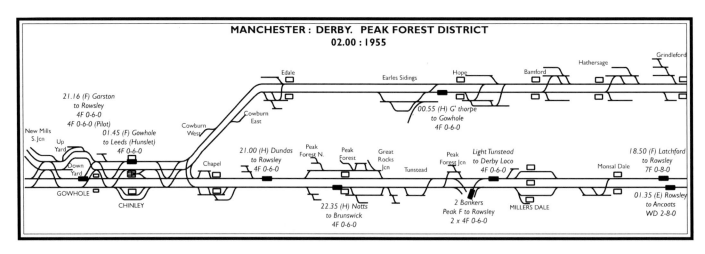

MANCHESTER : DERBY. PEAK FOREST DISTRICT
02.00 : 1955

21.16 (F) Garston to Rowsley 4F 0-6-0 · 4F 0-6-0 (Pilot) · 01.45 (F) Gowhole to Leeds (Hunslet) 4F 0-6-0 · New Mills S.Jcn · Up Yard · Down Yard · GOWHOLE · CHINLEY · Chapel · Cowburn West · Cowburn East · Edale · 21.00 (H) Dundas to Rowsley 4F 0-6-0 · 22.35 (H) Notts to Brunswick 4F 0-6-0 · Peak Forest N. · Peak Forest · Great Rocks Jcn · Tunstead · Earles Sidings · 00.55 (H) G'thorpe to Gowhole 4F 0-6-0 · Hope · Peak Forest Jcn · 2 Bankers Peak F to Rowsley 2 x 4F 0-6-0 · Light Tunstead to Derby Loco 4F 0-6-0 · Bamford · Hathersage · Grindleford · Monsal Dale · MILLERS DALE · 18.50 (F) Latchford to Rowsley 7F 0-8-0 · 01.35 (E) Rowsley to Ancoats WD 2-8-0

utes - double the time booked for the 19.40 - and in order to guarantee the parcels a clear run to Rowsley, the last mineral train to leave Ambergate must do so not later than one-fifty.

A train short of a margin can - in theory - be shunted at most of the intermediate stations but the Midland had a dread of facing points and in order to recess at points such as Whatstandwell and Matlock, trains have to run ahead of the crossover and reverse in. Usually it is quicker to keep a service moving until it gets to Darley Dale at which point it can run straight

Chesterfield and various points in Manchester although the 23.55 Brunswick - Spondon is an ICI service conveying imported matter for a chemical dye works on the outskirts of Derby.

Considering the distance covered - Merseyside to the East Midlands - it is quite a notable working since it makes no more than two stops - Cheadle Heath and Rowsley - aggregating twelve minutes; both being for water with the crew being changed at the second.

Considerable importance is placed on the punctual working of such trains, not simply for

are in position before letting it pull away from Cheadle Heath. One of the worst positions to get yourself into is to have a train standing at Chinley (or anywhere else), blocking the main line because there is no-one to work it forward.

It is easy to forget that a train is relieved half way through its journey and to minimise the chance of such things happening, one of the 'back desk' controllers has the responsibility of ensuring that crews are in position to relieve through trains, irrespective of whether or not they are on time.

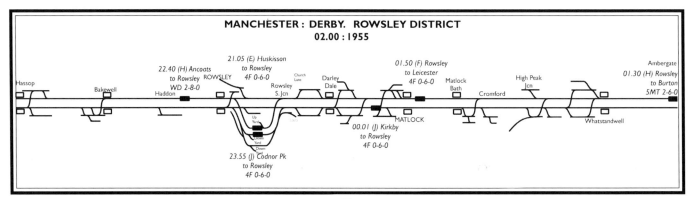

MANCHESTER : DERBY. ROWSLEY DISTRICT
02.00 : 1955

Hassop · Bakewell · Haddon · 22.40 (H) Ancoats to Rowsley WD 2-8-0 · ROWSLEY · Up Yard · Down Yard · 23.55 (J) Codnor Pk to Rowsley 4F 0-6-0 · Rowsley S.Jcn · 21.05 (E) Huskisson to Rowsley 4F 0-6-0 · Church Lane · Darley Dale · 00.01 (J) Kirkby to Rowsley 4F 0-6-0 · MATLOCK · 01.50 (F) Rowsley to Leicester 4F 0-6-0 · Matlock Bath · Cromford · High Peak Jcn · Whatstandwell · Ambergate · 01.30 (H) Rowsley to Burton 5MT 2-6-0

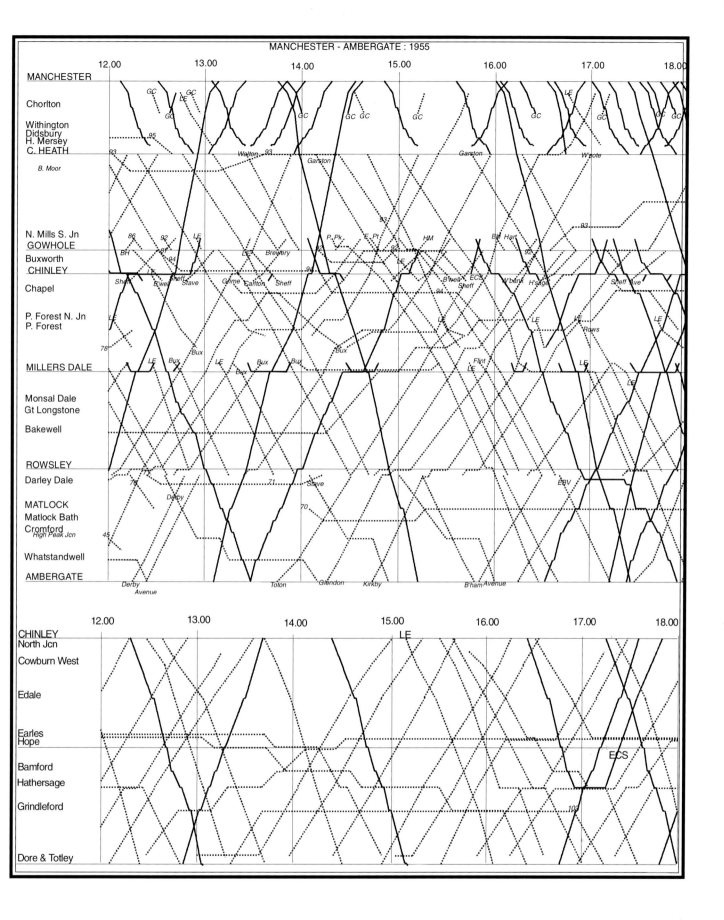

MANCHESTER - AMBERGATE : 1955

ALLOCATION & MOVEMENTS : TRAFFORD PARK

Loco	Class	Aug-53	Sep-53	Oct-53	Nov-53	Dec-53	Jan-54	Feb-54	Mar-54	Apr-54	May-54	Jun-54	Jul-54
48411	8F 2-8-0 (1935)												
48680	8F 2-8-0 (1935)												
48698	8F 2-8-0 (1935)												
48741	8F 2-8-0 (1935)												
45618	5XP 4-6-0 (1934)												
45622	5XP 4-6-0 (1934)												
45628	5XP 4-6-0 (1934)												
45629	5XP 4-6-0 (1934)												
45652	5XP 4-6-0 (1934)												
45655	5XP 4-6-0 (1934)												
45689	5XP 4-6-0 (1934)	Ex Crewe (N)	To Longsight	X	X	X	X	X	X	X	X	X	X
44717	5MT 4-6-0 (1934)												
44938	5MT 4-6-0 (1934)												
45006	5MT 4-6-0 (1934)	X	X	X	X	X	X	Ex Crewe (N)					
45239	5MT 4-6-0 (1934)												
45347	5MT 4-6-0 (1934)												
40910	4P 4-4-0 (1924)												
41066	4P 4-4-0 (1924)												
41098	4P 4-4-0 (1924)												
41112	4P 4-4-0 (1924)												
41114	4P 4-4-0 (1924)	X	X	X	X	X	X	X	X	X	Ex L'dno Jcn		
41118	4P 4-4-0 (1924)	X	X	X	X	X	X	X	X	X	X	X	Ex Brunswick
41123	4P 4-4-0 (1924)	X	X	X	X	X	X	X	X	X	Ex L'dno Jcn		
41150	4P 4-4-0 (1924)	X	X	X	X	X	X	X	X	X	Ex L'dno Jcn		
41151	4P 4-4-0 (1924)	X	X	X	X	X	X	X	X	X	X	X	Ex Brunswick
41154	4P 4-4-0 (1924)												
41161	4P 4-4-0 (1924)												
41163	4P 4-4-0 (1924)	X	X	X	X	X	X	X	X	X	Ex Chester		
41169	4P 4-4-0 (1924)	X	X	X	X	X	X	X	X	X	Ex Chester		
41170	4P 4-4-0 (1924)												
41173	4P 4-4-0 (1924)												
42064	4MT 2-6-4T (1945)												
42065	4MT 2-6-4T (1945)												
42676	4MT 2-6-4T (1945)												
42683	4MT 2-6-4T (1945)												
42452	4MT 2-6-4T (1935)												
42469	4MT 2-6-4T (1935)												
44236	4F 0-6-0 (1924)												
44275	4F 0-6-0 (1924)												
44350	4F 0-6-0 (1924)												
44392	4F 0-6-0 (1924)												
68065	4F : J94 0-6-0T (1943)	X	Ex Bidston										
68067	4F : J94 0-6-0T (1943)								To Immingham	X	X	X	X
40009	3P 2-6-2 (1930)												
40017	3P 2-6-2 (1930)												
62660	3P : D11 4-4-0 (1920)				To Lincoln	X	X	X	X	X	X	X	X
62661	3P : D11 4-4-0 (1920)												
62662	3P : D11 4-4-0 (1920)												
62664	3P : D11 4-4-0 (1920)												
62668	3P : D11 4-4-0 (1920)												
62670	3P : D11 4-4-0 (1920)				To Immingham	X	X	X	X	X	X	X	X
62653	3P : D10 4-4-0 (1913)							To Northwich	X	X	X	X	X
62654	3P : D10 4-4-0 (1913)	W/D	X	X	X	X	X	X	X	X	X	X	X
62656	3P : D10 4-4-0 (1913)		To Northwich	X	X	X	X	X	X	X	X	X	X
62658	3P : D10 4-4-0 (1913)										To Northwich	X	X
69255	2MT : N5 0-6-2T (1891)												
69304	2MT : N5 0-6-2T (1891)												
69326	2MT : N5 0-6-2T (1891)												
69336	2MT : N5 0-6-2T (1891)												
69343	2MT : N5 0-6-2T (1891)												
69347	2MT : N5 0-6-2T (1891)												
69358	2MT : N5 0-6-2T (1891)												
69361	2MT : N5 0-6-2T (1891)												
69364	2MT : N5 0-6-2T (1891)												
69370	2MT : N5 0-6-2T (1891)												
68559	2F : J67 0-6-0T (1890)	To Brunswick	X	X	X	X	X	X	X	X	X	X	X
68583	2F : J67 0-6-0T (1890)												
68595	2F : J67 0-6-0T (1890)												
68598	2F : J67 0-6-0T (1890)												
65138	2F : J10 0-6-0 (1892)											To Widnes	X
65146	2F : J10 0-6-0 (1892)												
65153	2F : J10 0-6-0 (1892)												
65156	2F : J10 0-6-0 (1892)												
65157	2F : J10 0-6-0 (1892)												
65167	2F : J10 0-6-0 (1892)											To Widnes	X
65170	2F : J10 0-6-0 (1892)												
65181	2F : J10 0-6-0 (1892)												
65184	2F : J10 0-6-0 (1892)												
65186	2F : J10 0-6-0 (1892)												
65191	2F : J10 0-6-0 (1892)												
65197	2F : J10 0-6-0 (1892)												
65198	2F : J10 0-6-0 (1892)						To Widnes	X	X	X	X	X	X
65205	2F : J10 0-6-0 (1892)												
65209	2F : J10 0-6-0 (1892)											To Widnes	X

Jubilee 5XP 4-6-0 45618 ' New Hebrides' was a long-term resident of Trafford Park, remaining at the shed until July 1958 when, displaced by Britannia Pacifics, it and four others of the class were transferred to Kentish Town. The engine is seen near Didsbury on the 5th July 1952 with the 09.00 Manchester (Central) - St Pancras.

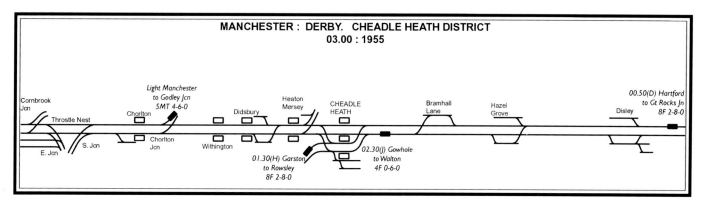

MANCHESTER : DERBY. CHEADLE HEATH DISTRICT
03.00 : 1955

CONTROLLER'S LOG : Although a large proportion of the traffic dealt with at Rowsley consists of coal travelling northwards and mineral empties in the opposite direction, goods traffic is not inconsiderable; much of it arriving during the first half of the night shift, being worked in from stations in the South that lack an express service to Manchester. Much also comes in from East Anglia on the 20.55 goods from Peterborough East.

Under the normal rules of movement, these wagons would be staged from Rowsley to Gowhole to connect with a local Manchester

can be worked under Class H condition unassisted - irrespective of the engine provided - up the bank to Peak Forest.

The loading of each train working into the district is telephoned forward well in advance by the neighbouring Controller and it is therefore usually possible to arrive at a fairly accurate estimate of the traffic to be dealt with long before it reaches Rowsley.

The capacity of the goods departures is 240 wagons and if it appears that one or more of them is going to be oversubscribed, an arrangement will be made to either move the overspill

Forest complex to the ICI plants at Hartford, Northwich and Wallerscote on the Cheshire Lines system.

Operated by Northwich-based LMS 8F 2-8-0's, there are six scheduled workings in each direction; each train consisting of sixteen vacuum braked hoppers and covering the forty-two mile distance to Northwich in about three hours which just allows a set of men to encompass a round trip in the course of a shift.

The benefit of the vacuum-fitted working is not so much speed - an H class goods takes only ten or fifteen minutes more from Peak

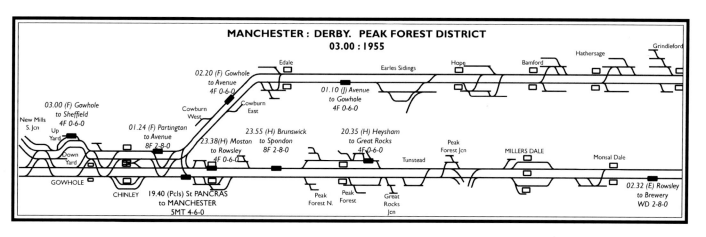

MANCHESTER : DERBY. PEAK FOREST DISTRICT
03.00 : 1955

or Liverpool service but since goods is more time-sensitive that mineral traffic, time is of the essence and a series of five goods workings leaves Rowsley at intervals from 02.32 to 04.15 running direct to Brewery Yard (North-East Manchester L&Y), Heaton Mersey, Ancoats (Manchester, Midland), Brindle Heath (Manchester West, L&Y) and Liverpool (Walton). The first of these trains can be seen approaching Monsal Dale whilst the second is on the point of pulling out of Rowsley Down Yard.

A close eye is kept on the level of goods traffic as it builds up since none of the five trains is booked for a banker and each is therefore limited to 48 wagons; the maximum that

on another service, run a special train or arrange to have the overloaded service banked to Peak Forest.

This last option is not the casual matter it appears. The section to Peak Forest is fifteen miles and a single banking trip can very often occupy a crew and an engine for an entire shift. If a guard is available, it is just as economical to run a relief service.

The priority accorded goods traffic as opposed to mineral is high and is extended to the type of working now approaching New Mills South: the 00.50 Hartford to Great Rocks class D.

This is part of a service which works limestone from the extensive quarries in the Peak

Forest to Northwich - as certainty of arrival since a fully-braked class D is guaranteed a clear run through the district whereas a conventional class H or J would have to take its turn with everything else and is as likely to end up without an engine or crew at Gowhole or Cheadle as it is arriving at Northwich. The vacuum hoppers are also much easier to unload than ordinary flat-bottomed wagons.

There is not much difference in capacity between the hoppers and a conventional service. The former conveys a payload of just under 700 tons whilst that taken by a convention train of thirty-one 21-ton flats, the maximum allowed a class 8F 2-8-0, is only fifty tons less.

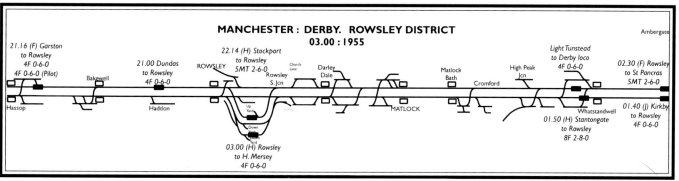

MANCHESTER : DERBY. ROWSLEY DISTRICT
03.00 : 1955

At the time of nationalisation control of the line had been shared between Liverpool (CLC) who took the section from Manchester Central to Chorlton Junction, Gowhole (Chorlton Junction to Chapel en le Frith), Rowsley (Chapel to Ambergate) and Derby. During the late 1940's the control rooms were amalgamated into a single organisation at Derby. Whatever the gains in efficiency, the new order never came as close to the running of trains as the former Gowhole controller, whose office is about to be overshadowed by a 5MT-hauled excursion from the L&Y.

Unusually for the Midland whose secondary running lines were normally for goods trains only, the additional pair of lines from New Mills South Jcn to Chinley were signalled for passenger trains and allowed considerable flexibility in the regulation of trains. A 5MT 2-6-0 'Crab' runs through Gowhole on the up slow line with a special train from the Lancashire & Yorkshire.

Although the service between Euston and Manchester (London Rd) was reckoned to be the principal route, in fact during the 1950's the Midland and the North Western operated an identical service; each having six trains from London to Manchester. With class 7P locomotives available, the LNW services tended to be heavier and faster; two services from Euston running to Manchester in three hours and thirty minutes. Handicapped by Class 6P engines and a mountainous line through the Peaks, the best the Midland could offer was four and a quarter hours. Jubilee 4-6-0 45557 'New Brunswick' of Kentish Town accelerates the 16.00 Manchester Central - St Pancras past Gowhole Yard on 2nd May 1953.

A view of Gowhole taken from the Down Sidings, looking across the slow lines to 8F 2-8-0 48709 on the up yard headshunt.

19

Jubilee 4-6-0's were retained for the St Pancras services but on 8th July 1950 the booked engine for the 13.04 Manchester - Sheffield slow failed and Trafford Park had to substitute 45628 'Somaliland'. The service is seen coming off the GC/Midland Joint line from Tiviot Dale and running up the slow line of the Midland main line at New Mills South Junction. Normally the train would have run on the up fast line but being about eight minutes late, it was put inside for the 13.45 Manchester - St Pancras which passed a few minutes later behind 45650 'Blake'.

4F 0-6-0 44162 of Hasland passes round the back of Buxworth station (platforms on the fast lines only) with the 09.40 Gowhole - Avenue mineral empties. There was a temptation to ridicule the Midland for its adherence to elderly 0-6-0's although, as in the case of the Hope Valley line, the limits on train loadings had very little to do with the type of engine employed. A class 8F was capable of working 64 empty wagons over much of the route yet the operating characteristics of the line limited trains to 43 vehicles which was the limit for a 4F. Why, it was asked, use anything larger?

Chinley was busy enough to become exciting at times; traffic from the Stockport and Sheffield lines joining that of the Midland main line for the four mile section to New Mills South Junction. The majority of movements were by goods trains with passenger services consisting largely of infrequent stopping trains to Derby and Sheffield. A dozen times a day the temperature would rise as a London express ran in behind a 5XP Jubilee 4-6-0, pausing briefly to connect with a stopping train before continuing its journey. Jubilee 5XP 45665 'Lord Rutherford of Nelson' of Kentish Town arrives at Chinley with the 10.15 St Pancras - Manchester Central in 1952. A few weeks after the photograph was taken 45665 disappeared to the far end of the system when it was transferred to Corkerhill, Glasgow.

8F 2-8-0 48533 of Barrow Hill is given the unusual luxury of being turned slow to main at Chinley North Junction whilst working the 10.05 ex Staveley. Normally this train ran slow line in order to terminate at Gowhole but on this occasion the service has been given a block train of coal for the CLC and has been extended to Cheadle Exchange Sidings. Running it down the fast line will keep it clear of the usual congestion on the slow lines around Gowhole.

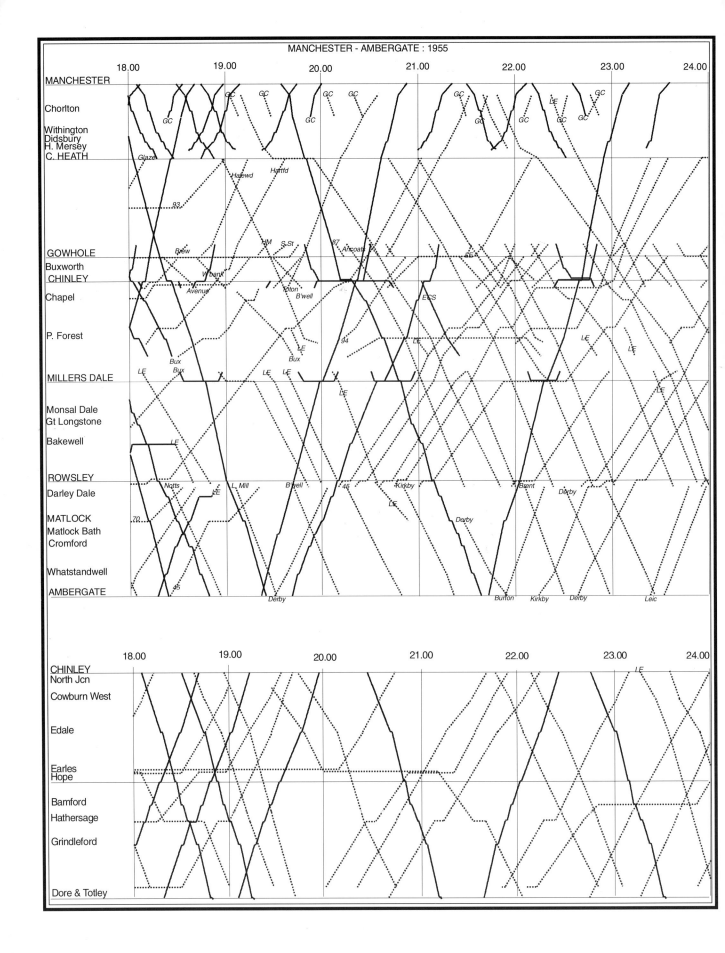

MANCHESTER - AMBERGATE : 1955

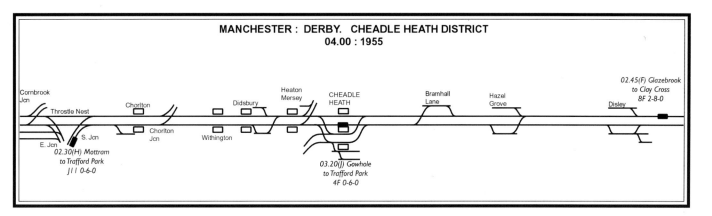

MANCHESTER : DERBY. CHEADLE HEATH DISTRICT
04.00 : 1955

CONTROLLER'S LOG : Attention moves from the main line to the Hope Valley whose regular flow of coal trains to and from the North Erewash Valley is being interrupted by a rather higher form of life.

"- Hope. London down at oh-three."

The 'London' referred to is the overnight fitted goods from Somers Town to Ancoats and by general consent is the most important train

free of slow trains and is booked via Derby although one suspects that the decision to route the down service via Chesterfield would not survive cross examination. Whichever way a class C approaches Manchester, there will be some disruption to other services and the volume of traffic over the Hope Valley is no less dense than that via Peak Forest.

"- Where do you want 48155?"

This routine question appears every time a

such as that of 48155 which has arrived at Great Rocks with ICI fitted empties from Northwich, the answer is usually a matter of routine although occasionally the engine is taken out of the working and replaced by another, sent light perhaps from Buxton.

"- As booked. Turn and light to Tunstead for the five twenty-three Northwich."

Peak Forest is probably best known for the

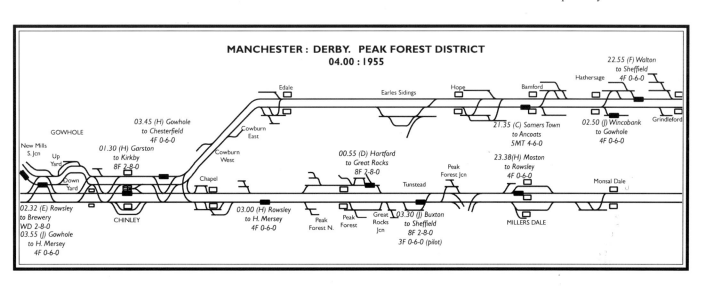

MANCHESTER : DERBY. PEAK FOREST DISTRICT
04.00 : 1955

of the day. Routing it via the Hope Valley and adding five miles to its running may seem a little strange until it is realised that the line via Trent and Chesterfield is almost entirely four-tracked whereas that via Derby is only two and the presence of a high speed class C would result in the recessing of a great many other trains at an awkward time of night between Trent and Chinley. The routing via Chesterfield makes no difference to the loading since the number of vehicles hauled by class C services (45 for a 5MT locomotive) applies throughout the London Midland, irrespective of gradient.

The up working, 22.00 from Ancoats, runs at a time when the Rowsley line is relatively

This routine question appears every time a train terminates - which means that a fair proportion of ones working life is spent telling people what to do with engines. Although all locomotive movements are meticulously programmed, the number of workings is so large that no-one outside can be expected to remember the minutiae of return workings and it falls to the Controller therefore to see that incoming engines are directed to wherever they are needed. To facilitate matters all shunters and yard inspectors are required to call up as soon as an engine is released from an inward working rather than making an assumption or - folly of follies - asking the driver. In some cases,

fully-fitted vacuum hopper trains which operate six times daily to and from Northwich but the degree of other traffic is sufficient to warrant the provision of two trip engines; a pair of 3F 0-6-0's which shunt the surrounding yards and assist the departing hopper trains up the hill from Tunstead to Peak Forest North. Both engines are supplied by Buxton loco, the first running to Peak Forest by piloting the 03.30 Buxton - Sheffield. Upon arrival the 3F will uncouple and run light to Tunstead to pilot the 05.23 Northwich hoppers. Its companion, Target 79, leaves Buxton at 05.25 and comes down coupled to the engine for the 07.09 Chinley - Rotherham passenger.

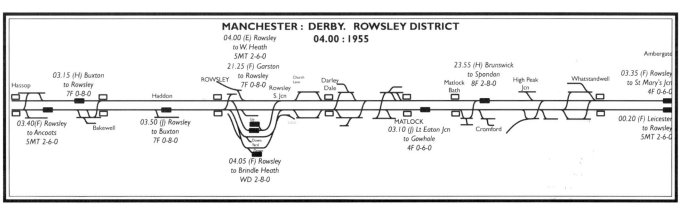

MANCHESTER : DERBY. ROWSLEY DISTRICT
04.00 : 1955

ALLOCATION & MOVEMENTS : TRAFFORD PARK

Loco	Class	Aug-54	Sep-54	Oct-54	Nov-54	Dec-54	Jan-55	Feb-55	Mar-55	Apr-55	May-55	Jun-55	Jul-55
48411	8F 2-8-0 (1935)												
48680	8F 2-8-0 (1935)												
48698	8F 2-8-0 (1935)												
48741	8F 2-8-0 (1935)												
45618	5XP 4-6-0 (1934)												
45622	5XP 4-6-0 (1934)												
45628	5XP 4-6-0 (1934)												
45629	5XP 4-6-0 (1934)												
45652	5XP 4-6-0 (1934)												
45655	5XP 4-6-0 (1934)												
44717	5MT 4-6-0 (1934)												
44938	5MT 4-6-0 (1934)												
45006	5MT 4-6-0 (1934)												
45132	5MT 4-6-0 (1934)	X	Ex Chester		To Aston	X	X	X	X	X	X	X	X
45239	5MT 4-6-0 (1934)												
45347	5MT 4-6-0 (1934)											To Wigan	X
40910	4P 4-4-0 (1924)												
41066	4P 4-4-0 (1924)												
41098	4P 4-4-0 (1924)												
41112	4P 4-4-0 (1924)												
41114	4P 4-4-0 (1924)												
41118	4P 4-4-0 (1924)												
41123	4P 4-4-0 (1924)												
41150	4P 4-4-0 (1924)												
41151	4P 4-4-0 (1924)												
41154	4P 4-4-0 (1924)												W/D
41161	4P 4-4-0 (1924)												
41163	4P 4-4-0 (1924)												
41169	4P 4-4-0 (1924)												W/D
41170	4P 4-4-0 (1924)												
41173	4P 4-4-0 (1924)												
42064	4MT 2-6-4T (1945)												
42065	4MT 2-6-4T (1945)												
42676	4MT 2-6-4T (1945)												
42683	4MT 2-6-4T (1945)												
42452	4MT 2-6-4T (1935)												
42469	4MT 2-6-4T (1935)												
42423	4MT 2-6-4T (1927)	X	X	X	X	X	X	X	X	Ex Wigan			
44236	4F 0-6-0 (1924)												
44275	4F 0-6-0 (1924)												
44350	4F 0-6-0 (1924)												
44361	4F 0-6-0 (1924)	X	X	X	X	X	Ex M. Lane						
44392	4F 0-6-0 (1924)												
40088	3P 2-6-2 (1935)	X	X	X	X	X	X	Ex Birk'hd					
40009	3P 2-6-2 (1930)												
40017	3P 2-6-2 (1930)					To Hull (BG)	X	X	X	X	X	X	X
40018	3P 2-6-2 (1930)	X	X	X	X	X	Ex Willesden						
40052	3P 2-6-2 (1930)	X	X	X	X	Ex Willesden							
40053	3P 2-6-2 (1930)	X	X	X	X	Ex Willesden	To Willesden	X	X	X	X	X	X
40055	3P 2-6-2 (1930)	X	X	X	X	Ex Willesden							
62661	3P : D11 4-4-0 (1920)								To Northwich	X	X	X	X
62662	3P : D11 4-4-0 (1920)												
62664	3P : D11 4-4-0 (1920)								To Northwich	X	X	X	X
62668	3P : D11 4-4-0 (1920)												
69255	2MT : N5 0-6-2T (1891)									To Northwich	X	X	X
69255	2MT : N5 0-6-2T (1891)	X	X	X	X	X	X	X	X	X	X	X	Ex Northwich
69304	2MT : N5 0-6-2T (1891)								W/D	X	X	X	X
69326	2MT : N5 0-6-2T (1891)												
69336	2MT : N5 0-6-2T (1891)					W/D	X	X	X	X	X	X	X
69343	2MT : N5 0-6-2T (1891)												
69347	2MT : N5 0-6-2T (1891)												
69358	2MT : N5 0-6-2T (1891)												
69361	2MT : N5 0-6-2T (1891)												
69364	2MT : N5 0-6-2T (1891)												
69370	2MT : N5 0-6-2T (1891)												
68583	2F : J67 0-6-0T (1890)												
68595	2F : J67 0-6-0T (1890)	To Wrexham	X	Ex Wrexham		To Wrexham	X	X	X	X	X	X	X
68598	2F : J67 0-6-0T (1890)					To Brunswick	X	X	X	X	X	X	X
65146	2F : J10 0-6-0 (1892)												
65153	2F : J10 0-6-0 (1892)												
65156	2F : J10 0-6-0 (1892)												
65157	2F : J10 0-6-0 (1892)									To Widnes	X	X	X
65167	2F : J10 0-6-0 (1892)	X	Ex Widnes										
65170	2F : J10 0-6-0 (1892)												
65181	2F : J10 0-6-0 (1892)												
65184	2F : J10 0-6-0 (1892)												
65186	2F : J10 0-6-0 (1892)									To Widnes	X	X	X
65191	2F : J10 0-6-0 (1892)												
65197	2F : J10 0-6-0 (1892)												
65205	2F : J10 0-6-0 (1892)												
65209	2F : J10 0-6-0 (1892)	X	Ex Widnes										

THROUGH FREIGHT SERVICES

UP			DOWN		
Train	Route	Destination	Train	Route	Destination
01.30 Liverpool (Garston)	Peak Forest	Kirkby	02.35 Birmingham (W. Heath)	Peak Forest	Liverpool (Brunswick)
03.29 Chester (Hooton)	Peak Forest	Kirkby	18.00 Kettering (Glendon)	Peak Forest	Manchester (Glazebrook)
08.02 Manchester (B. Vue)	Peak Forest	Kirkby	00.57 London (Brent)	Peak Forest	Liverpool (Brunswick)
09.35 Chester (Dundas)	Peak Forest	Kirkby	03.35 Kettering (Glendon)	Peak Forest	Manchester (Glazebrook)
22.00 Manchester (Ancoats)	Peak Forest	St Pancras	10.23 Alfreton (Codnor Park)	Peak Forest	Manchester (Agecroft)
01.24 Manchester (Partington)	Hope Valley	Avenue	10.30 Kirkby	Peak Forest	Manchester (Ashton Rd)
22.55 Liverpool (Walton)	Hope Valley	Sheffield	13.17 Kirkby	Peak Forest	Manchester (Ashton Rd)
02.45 Manchester (Glazebrook)	Hope Valley	Clay Cross	04.35 Kettering (Corby)	Peak Forest	Manchester (Glazebrook)
09.20 Manchester (Glazebrook)	Hope Valley	Clay Cross	20.30 Kirkby	Peak Forest	Manchester (Ashton Rd)
13.17 Liverpool (Garston)	Hope Valley	Danesmoor (Clay Cross)	22.35 Nottingham	Peak Forest	Liverpool (Brunswick)
18.50 Liverpool (Halewood)	Hope Valley	Avenue	23.45 Sheffield (Grimesthorpe)	Hope Valley	Liverpool (Edge Hill)
			21.35 London (Somers Town)	Hope Valley	Manchester (Ancoats)
			03.35 Barnsley (Carlton)	Hope Valley	Manchester (Trafford Pk)

The majority of services arriving on the district terminated at either Rowsley or Gowhole and were remarshalling before proceeding towards Manchester or Liverpool. In a number of cases, which included certain mineral and iron ore trains, block workings were arranged which allowed intermediate yards to be avoided.

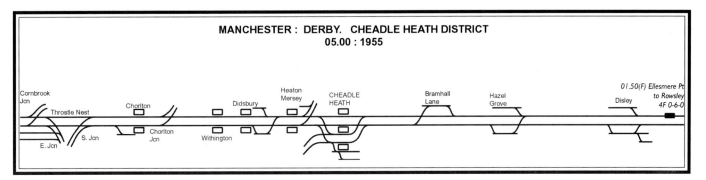

MANCHESTER : DERBY. CHEADLE HEATH DISTRICT
05.00 : 1955

CONTROLLER'S LOG : One might think that the closer one gets to Manchester, the denser traffic would become but in contrast to the usual rule, the nearer one gets to the city, the quieter things become. This reversal can be gauged from the traffic maps which show the area north of Disley as being relatively underused. South of New Mills Junction there are trains at almost every block section yet the area around Cheadle Heath is almost clear of trains.

The reason for this is that much of the traffic worked through Chinley is directed either to North Manchester via Belle Vue or else is destined for the Cheshire Lines Committee and has to be remarshalled in Heaton Mersey yard,

call at either Heaton Mersey or Gowhole. Convenient as such workings are, they call for the presence of an engine and men who are in a position to work through as opposed to staging the train in the normal way.

The appearance of a suitable engine at the right time is not a coincidence but a product of the central timing and diagramming office who have managed to get a Kirkby 4F 0-6-0 as far from home as Heaton Mersey, the engine thus being well positioned to run light to Cheadle and take over the 01.50 from Ellesmere Port. The arrival of the train at Rowsley does nothing to get the travel-stained 0-6-0 back to its home shed since it is then used to bank the 11.15 goods to Buxton, returning to Rowsley

does - for the 11.15 and a Rowsley engine will be put into the working until another Kirkby engine can be found to take forward the diagram.

The use of an 0-6-0 on such a long working appears strange until it is realised that replacing it with an 8F 2-8-0 would give no greater benefit than an extra five wagons in the train. The maximum number of empties permitted on any up service between Cheadle and Rowsley is sixty vehicles which is very close to the 55 limit allowed to a 4F 0-6-0, making the use of a much larger engine rather difficult to justify.

Some additional and equally irksome restrictions apply on the downhill sections in both

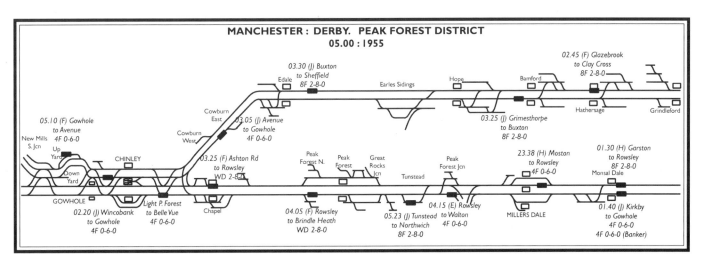

MANCHESTER : DERBY. PEAK FOREST DISTRICT
05.00 : 1955

Stockport. A certain amount of CLC traffic is moved in block loads to avoid Heaton Mersey and is taken to the Cheshire Lines via Disley and Cheadle Heath. Such workings are in the minority and the majority leave the district at New Mills South for either the Cheshire Lines or the Lancashire & Yorkshire.

One of these exceptions has just passed Disley and is a through train of mineral empties from Ellesmere Port (Chester) to Rowsley. Empties need less remarshalling than loaded traffic and thus there is no need for them to

with the 09.35 ex Mold Junction. In theory the engine returns to Kirkby on the 20.50 from Rowsley although in practice the diagram is so convoluted that the chances of the engine remaining in the working is remote. It is, for example, quite possible that the Nottingham district needs more mineral empties than can be moved by the booked service in which case a set of men will be sent to Rowsley station to relieve the Ellesmere Port and take its empties to wherever they are needed. The engine will almost certainly not reappear in time - if it ever

directions from Peak Forest where, because of their limited braking powers, Garratts, Austerity 2-8-0's and Super-D 0-8-0's have to be regarded as 4F 0-6-0's for loading purposes.

The limit on Garratts explains why the class is rarely if ever seen over Peak Forest whilst the one trial made on the line with the type ended with the brake blocks all but fused onto the wheels after the engine ran away downhill from Peak Forest to Cheadle Heath.

In the meantime 4F's 0-6-0's work a very high proportion of the service.

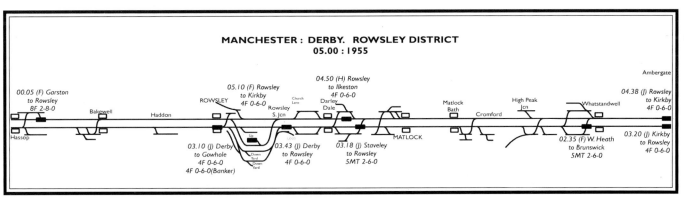

MANCHESTER : DERBY. ROWSLEY DISTRICT
05.00 : 1955

The Midland conveyed a large volume of traffic from the East Midlands to Industrial Lancashire as did its associate, the Cheshire Lines Committee, whose function was to collect traffic from Mottram and Guide Bridge and work its across to Merseyside.   Strangers to the area were often surprised to see the LNER so well represented.   O4 2-8-0 67313 of Gorton overtakes a train of passenger stock at Stockport (Tiviot Dale) with a Gorton - Brunswick goods on the 26th September 1959

Great Central 2-8-0's could also be seen on the section of line between Throstle Nest South and Chorlton Junction as they worked services between Guide Bridge and the Manchester Ship Canal Yards at Trafford Park.   A rather indistinct O4 2-8-0 runs through Chorlton-cum-Hardy, slowing up for Chorlton Junction and the Wilbraham Road line to Guide Bridge.

Halfway between Chinley station and Chinley North Junction, 8F 2-8-0 48711 of Northwich heads the 17.00 vacuum empties from Hartford to Great Rocks. The engine and wagons returned north the same evening with the 22.00 Tunstead - Hartford. Standard LMS 8F locomotives from Northwich were the booked engines for the ICI workings and in the northbound (loaded) direction could take 16 hoppers by the normal route (Disley) or 14 if the train was diverted via Stockport. If a 4F 0-6-0 had to be substituted, it was limited to 11 and 9 hoppers respectively whilst the 9F 2-10-0's were permitted to handle 19 and 17.

A few minutes after the upper view was taken, 48711 and its train cross Chapel Milton Viaduct and approach Chinley South Junction. The arms of the junction signal ahead of the engine refer to the down Chapel loop and the main line. As the arms indicate, the hopper trains were used to getting a clear run and enjoyed a high priority.

LMS Standard 8F 2-8-0 48213 of Staveley passes Chinley North Junction with a Gowhole - Barrow Hill class H service of empties. The distinction between an 0-6-0 and a 2-8-0 was far more marked on the Hope Valley line than over Peak Forest. On the former an 8F 2-8-0 was allowed to take 76 vehicles as opposed to 52 for a 4F 0-6-0. Class J trains - rough services made up with a minimum of supervision - were rather more restricted and were limited to 43 wagons except during the night when no passenger trains were running.

The balance of 5XP 4-6-0's at Trafford Park was rather fine and it was by no means unusual to find 5MT 4-6-0's having to cover some of the London trains. 44938 passes Chinley South Junction and attacks the 1 in 90 gradient on Chapel Milton viaduct with the 13.45 Manchester Central - St Pancras on May3rd 1953. Mindful of the hard climb up to Peak Forest and the conditions in Dove Holes, the fireman is evidently filling the box before entering the gloom of the tunnel

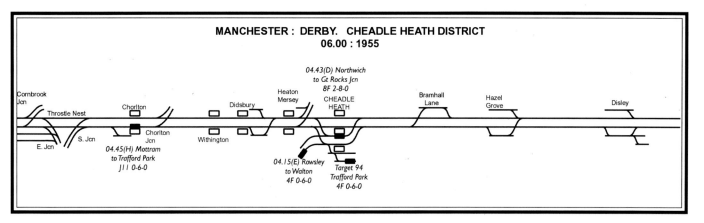

CONTROLLER'S LOG : Although, as ever, goods traffic continues to dominate the system, there are signs of life in the passenger field as Rowsley's two Compound 4-4-0's ring off shed. The first of the pair leaves at 05.42 and runs to Darley Dale where it collects its stock before working the 06.25 local to Nottingham whilst the second rings off at 06.48 for Bakewell for the 07.35 to Derby. The regular engines for these jobs - Rowsley's only passenger diagrams - are 40929 and 40931; nei-

shunt engine, returning home with the 17.57 Spondon - Darley Dale. It is interesting to note that the engine and stock of the Darley Dale working returns as the Bakewell service and vice versa.

Although a 4F 0-6-0 could be used as a substitute in the event of a failure, 2P 4-4-0 40520 is held at Rowsley as the spare engine which is no bad thing given that both Compounds tend to be first choice as replacements for anything that fails on the main line whilst

The Midland Manchester rush-hour is not the busiest in the country and is made up of no more than nine arrivals: four coming from Cheadle Heath and one each from Stockport and Sheffield. They do, however, enjoy an unrivalled line occupation and with most goods services leaving the main line at New Mills South, there is very little to get in their way.

The major concern is ensuring that the engines get from Heaton Mersey loco to Cheadle Heath in time, without getting lost on the

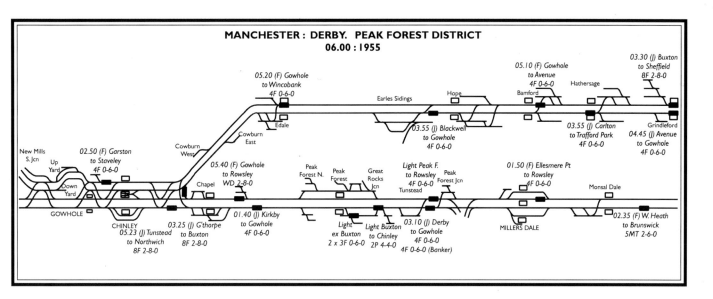

ther putting in a particularly exacting day.

The Darley Dale service terminates at Nottingham, the engine and stock forming the 11.05 local to Derby and the 17.05 to Bakewell; the engine, during its long stay at Derby, running light engine to St Mary's Yard and back at 13.50 in order to change the men on the local shunting engines: targets 15 and 16. The 4-4-0 which works the 07.35 Bakewell - Derby spends most of the day as the Park Sidings

they are shunting at Derby and Nottingham.

The are also signs of stirrings in the passenger camp at the Northern end of the line; three 3P 2-6-2T's being due off Heaton Mersey shed to work a share of the Manchester Central suburban service. The first of these rings off at 06.10 to work the 07.00 Cheadle Heath - Manchester; the others following at 06.32 and 07.28 for the 07.10 and 08.14 departures respectively.

way. The CLC have a D11 4-4-0 that works a Stockport - Risley passenger and should that fail at the last minute, they would have little compunction in using the engine marked for the 07.00 Cheadle Heath - Manchester. One keeps a very close eye on the 4F 0-6-0 working Target 94. The next time it has to come hurtling up the main to take over a passenger train from a 3P that has failed to materialise from Heaton Mersey will not be the first.

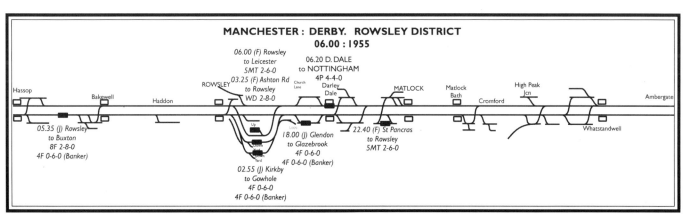

Loco	Class	Aug-55	Sep-55	Oct-55	Nov-55	Dec-55	Jan-56	Feb-56	Mar-56	Apr-56	May-56	Jun-56	Jul-56
48411	8F 2-8-0 (1935)												
48680	8F 2-8-0 (1935)												
48698	8F 2-8-0 (1935)												
48741	8F 2-8-0 (1935)												
45618	5XP 4-6-0 (1934)												
45622	5XP 4-6-0 (1934)												
45628	5XP 4-6-0 (1934)												
45629	5XP 4-6-0 (1934)												
45652	5XP 4-6-0 (1934)												
45655	5XP 4-6-0 (1934)												
44717	5MT 4-6-0 (1934)												
44938	5MT 4-6-0 (1934)												
45006	5MT 4-6-0 (1934)												
45239	5MT 4-6-0 (1934)												
40910	4P 4-4-0 (1924)											W/D	X
41066	4P 4-4-0 (1924)												
41098	4P 4-4-0 (1924)												
41112	4P 4-4-0 (1924)				To Lancaster	X	X	X	X	X	X	X	X
41114	4P 4-4-0 (1924)												
41116	4P 4-4-0 (1924)	X	X	Ex Edge Hill									
41118	4P 4-4-0 (1924)												
41123	4P 4-4-0 (1924)												
41150	4P 4-4-0 (1924)												
41151	4P 4-4-0 (1924)												
41161	4P 4-4-0 (1924)				W/D	X	X	X	X	X	X	X	X
41163	4P 4-4-0 (1924)												
41166	4P 4-4-0 (1924)	X	X	Ex Edge Hill									
41170	4P 4-4-0 (1924)										W/D	X	X
41173	4P 4-4-0 (1924)												
42064	4MT 2-6-4T (1945)												
42065	4MT 2-6-4T (1945)												
42675	4MT 2-6-4T (1945)	X	X	X	Ex Uttoxeter								
42676	4MT 2-6-4T (1945)												
42683	4MT 2-6-4T (1945)												
42452	4MT 2-6-4T (1935)												
42469	4MT 2-6-4T (1935)												
42419	4MT 2-6-4T (1927)	X	X	X	X	X	X	X	X	X	Ex Stoke		
42423	4MT 2-6-4T (1927)												
44080	4F 0-6-0 (1924)	X	X	X	X	X	Ex Heaton M.						
44236	4F 0-6-0 (1924)				To Heaton M.	X	X	X	X	X	X	X	X
44275	4F 0-6-0 (1924)												
44350	4F 0-6-0 (1924)											To S. Oak	X
44361	4F 0-6-0 (1924)						To Heaton M.	X	X	X	X	X	X
44392	4F 0-6-0 (1924)												
40088	3P 2-6-2 (1935)												
40009	3P 2-6-2 (1930)												
40018	3P 2-6-2 (1930)												
40052	3P 2-6-2 (1930)												
40055	3P 2-6-2 (1930)												
62662	3P : D11 4-4-0 (1920)			To Northwich	X	X	X	X	X	X	X	X	X
62668	3P : D11 4-4-0 (1920)												
47672	3F 0-6-0T (1924)	X	X	X	X	X	X	X	X	X	Ex Bidston		
69255	2MT : N5 0-6-2T (1891)											W/D	X
69326	2MT : N5 0-6-2T (1891)												
69343	2MT : N5 0-6-2T (1891)				To Wrexham	X	X	X	X	X	X	X	X
69347	2MT : N5 0-6-2T (1891)												
69358	2MT : N5 0-6-2T (1891)												
69361	2MT : N5 0-6-2T (1891)												
69364	2MT : N5 0-6-2T (1891)	W/D	X	X	X	X	X	X	X	X	X	X	X
69370	2MT : N5 0-6-2T (1891)												
68583	2F : J67 0-6-0T (1890)												
65146	2F : J10 0-6-0 (1892)				To Northgate	X	X	X	X	X	X	X	X
65153	2F : J10 0-6-0 (1892)												
65156	2F : J10 0-6-0 (1892)				To Northgate	X	X	X	X	X	X	X	X
65167	2F : J10 0-6-0 (1892)												
65170	2F : J10 0-6-0 (1892)				To Northgate	X	X	X	X	X	X	X	X
65181	2F : J10 0-6-0 (1892)							To Northgate	X	X	X	X	X
65184	2F : J10 0-6-0 (1892)					To Widnes	X	X	X	X	X	X	X
65186	2F : J10 0-6-0 (1892)	X	X	X	X	Ex Widnes							
65191	2F : J10 0-6-0 (1892)												
65197	2F : J10 0-6-0 (1892)										W/D	X	X
65205	2F : J10 0-6-0 (1892)												W/D
65209	2F : J10 0-6-0 (1892)												

ALLOCATION & MOVEMENTS : TRAFFORD PARK

In addition to working trains on the Rowsley - Buxton - Stockport axis, Buxton shed played a significant role in working trains to and from Sheffield; the majority of workings being goods services which involved the very harsh sections of line from Buxton to Peak Forest and from Chinley to Cowburn East. Passenger work over the route was not neglected and Buxton provided an engine for the 07.09 Chinley - Rotherham Westgate and the 10.50 Sheffield - Chinley. 2P 4-4-0 40433 backs onto the return working at Sheffield Midland.

Loco	Class	Aug-56	Sep-56	Oct-56	Nov-56	Dec-56	Jan-57	Feb-57	Mar-57	Apr-57	May-57	Jun-57	Jul-57
48288	8F 2-8-0 (1935)	X	X	X	Ex Crewe (S)								
48317	8F 2-8-0 (1935)	X	X	X	X	X	X	X	Ex Saltley				
48411	8F 2-8-0 (1935)				To Crewe (S)	X	X	X	X	X	X	X	X
48680	8F 2-8-0 (1935)	To Longsight	X	X	X	X	X	X	X	X	X	X	X
48698	8F 2-8-0 (1935)												
48741	8F 2-8-0 (1935)												
45553	5XP 4-6-0 (1934)	X	Ex Crewe (N)		To Crewe (N)	X	X	X	X	X	X	X	X
45561	5XP 4-6-0 (1934)	X	X	X	X	X	Ex Bristol						
45591	5XP 4-6-0 (1934)	Ex Camden			To Crewe (N)	X	X	X	X	X	X	X	X
45618	5XP 4-6-0 (1934)												
45622	5XP 4-6-0 (1934)		To Longsight	Ex Longsight									
45628	5XP 4-6-0 (1934)		To Longsight	Ex Longsight									
45629	5XP 4-6-0 (1934)				To Longsight	X	X	X	X	X	X	X	X
45652	5XP 4-6-0 (1934)			To Longsight	Ex Longsight								
45655	5XP 4-6-0 (1934)			To Longsight	X	X	X	X	X	X	X	X	X
45712	5XP 4-6-0 (1934)	X	X	X	X	X	X	Ex N. Heath					
44665	5MT 4-6-0 (1934)	X	X	X	X	X	X	X	Ex Millhouses				
44717	5MT 4-6-0 (1934)												
44938	5MT 4-6-0 (1934)		To Longsight	X	X	X	X	X	X	X	X	X	X
45006	5MT 4-6-0 (1934)												
45239	5MT 4-6-0 (1934)												
41066	4P 4-4-0 (1924)												
41098	4P 4-4-0 (1924)		To Lancaster	X	X	X	X	X	X	X	X	X	X
41114	4P 4-4-0 (1924)												
41116	4P 4-4-0 (1924)												
41118	4P 4-4-0 (1924)												
41123	4P 4-4-0 (1924)										To Gloucester	X	X
41150	4P 4-4-0 (1924)												
41151	4P 4-4-0 (1924)		To Lancaster	X	X	X	X	X	X	X	X	X	X
41163	4P 4-4-0 (1924)									X	To Bradford	X	X
41166	4P 4-4-0 (1924)		W/D	X	X	X	X	X	X	X	X	X	X
41173	4P 4-4-0 (1924)												
42064	4MT 2-6-4T (1945)												
42065	4MT 2-6-4T (1945)												
42675	4MT 2-6-4T (1945)												
42676	4MT 2-6-4T (1945)												
42683	4MT 2-6-4T (1945)												
42452	4MT 2-6-4T (1935)												
42469	4MT 2-6-4T (1935)												
42419	4MT 2-6-4T (1927)												
42423	4MT 2-6-4T (1927)		To Patricroft	X	X	X	X	X	X	X	X	X	X
76087	4MT 2-6-0 (1952)	X	X	X	X	X	X	X	X	X	NEW		To Saltley
76088	4MT 2-6-0 (1952)	X	X	X	X	X	X	X	X	X	NEW		
76089	4MT 2-6-0 (1952)	X	X	X	X	X	X	X	X	X	X	NEW	
44080	4F 0-6-0 (1924)												
44275	4F 0-6-0 (1924)												
44392	4F 0-6-0 (1924)												
43846	4F 0-6-0 (1911)	X	X	X	X	X	X	X	Ex Burton				
43921	4F 0-6-0 (1911)	X	X	X	X	X	X	X	X	Ex Rowsley			
40088	3P 2-6-2 (1935)												
40097	3P 2-6-2 (1935)	X	X	X	X	X	X	X	Ex Swansea				
40105	3P 2-6-2 (1935)	X	X	X	X	X	X	X	Ex Swansea				
40141	3P 2-6-2 (1935)	X	X	X	X	X	X	X	Ex A'gavenny				
40208	3P 2-6-2 (1935)	X	X	Ex Willesden									
40009	3P 2-6-2 (1930)												
40012	3P 2-6-2 (1930)	X	X	X	X	X	X	X	X	X	X	Ex Rugby	
40017	3P 2-6-2 (1930)	X	X	X	X	X	X	X	X	X	X	Ex Rugby	
40018	3P 2-6-2 (1930)												
40052	3P 2-6-2 (1930)												
40055	3P 2-6-2 (1930)												
62668	3P : D11 4-4-0 (1920)												
47672	3F 0-6-0T (1924)				To Patricroft	X	X	X	X	X	X	X	X
69326	2MT : N5 0-6-2T (1891)												
69343	2MT : N5 0-6-2T (1891)	X	X	X	Ex Wrexham								
69347	2MT : N5 0-6-2T (1891)												
69358	2MT : N5 0-6-2T (1891)				W/D	X	X	X	X	X	X	X	X
69361	2MT : N5 0-6-2T (1891)												
69370	2MT : N5 0-6-2T (1891)												
68583	2F : J67 0-6-0T (1890)								To Bidston	X	X	X	X
65153	2F : J10 0-6-0 (1892)				To Darlington	X	X	X	X	X	X	X	X
65167	2F : J10 0-6-0 (1892)												
65186	2F : J10 0-6-0 (1892)												
65191	2F : J10 0-6-0 (1892)												
65208	2F : J10 0-6-0 (1892)	X	X	X	X	Ex Northgate							
65209	2F : J10 0-6-0 (1892)												

The complicated nature of LM diagramming resulted in engines regularly working out of course; giving rise to such sights as Aintree 5MT 2-6-0 42715 at Sheffield Midland with a Hope Valley stopping train.

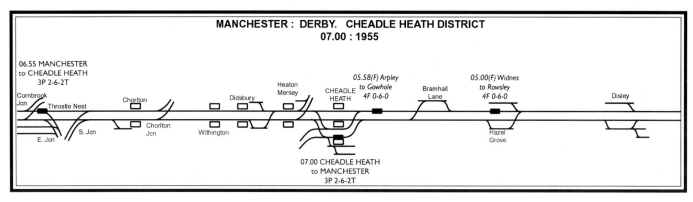

CONTROLLER'S LOG : If one could be outside at this moment, the place of choice would be Monsal Dale. In the last few minutes a Kirkby - Gowhole with a 4F 0-6-0 at each end has slogged its way through the station whilst at the moment a Rowsley - Buxton worked by a Super-D 0-8-0 and a 4F banker is redarkening the sky. Impressive as both trains are, they do no more than pave the way for one that will follow: the 18.00 Glendon (Kettering) - Glazebrook iron ore service which is handled by no less than three 0-6-0's:

comes a continuous exchange of messages and instructions.

Disley: *"Goods down the main, fifty-nine."*

Cheadle North: *"Manchester passenger away right time."*

New Mills S. Jcn: *"Philips Park to Gowhole goods up the slow and Birmingham - Brunswick down the Midland at Oh-one. What's this coming up the Midland to me?"*

Controller: *"Widnes to Runcorn followed by an Arpley - Gowhole. The Runcorn wants to follow the six-five passenger up the main."*

90338 thirty-three equal thirty-six Brewery Sidings."

Controller: *"Well done. Next in to you will be the 03.55 Blackwell, 44162 forty-three L&Y roughs. Then the 03.35 Carlton. 44457 with forty-one Trafford Parks to go forward as the ten-five."*

Chorlton Junction: *Midland passenger up at three."*

Chinley Station N: *Engine 44457 has just been relieved in the down main. Where's it for?"*

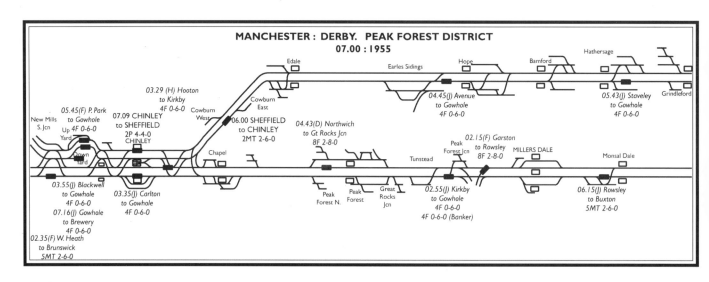

a pair of struggling 4F's at the front and a 3F blasting away in the rear. This is a climax rather than a coda and before the sound of its is allowed to die, its place will have been taken by the 07.05 Rowsley - Gowhole which is about to put away from Rowsley

What an exhibition of sound and fury.

Alas the time for reflecting on the more colourful aspects of outside life is limited, especially as there are signs that the Gowhole/Chinley area is about to become choked with traffic. The control circuit - never quiet - be-

Gowhole Down Yard? Is the Brewery ready to leave yet? Can you get it moving? I've got the Blackwell on the down slow waiting to get in and the Carlton behind it at Chinley."

Peak Forest North: *"Northwich empties up the main at oh-two."*

Chinley North Jn: *"Class H up the main oh-three."*

If Gowhole can get rid of the 07.16 goods a few minutes early, it will ease what is threatening to become a difficult position.

Gowhole Down Yard: *"Leaving now.*

Controller: *"Down the slow for Gowhole."*

Chinley: *"Sheffield passenger in at four."*

Getting the Brewery goods away from Gowhole early has not only allowed the 03.55 ex Blackwell to vacate the down and enter the yard but has permitted the 03.35 Carlton to move down from Chinley. By the time the latter gets to Gowhole the yard will be in a position to accept it and thus the slow lines should be clear for the rest of the trains in the pipeline.

Now to clear a path for the up London....

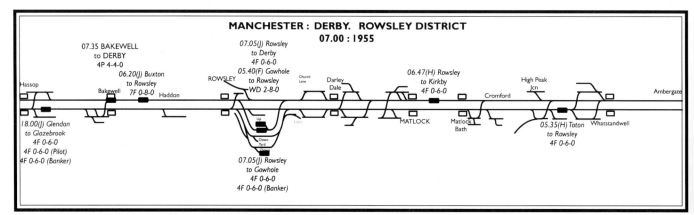

ALLOCATION & MOVEMENTS : TRAFFORD PARK

Loco	Class	Aug-57	Sep-57	Oct-57	Nov-57	Dec-57	Jan-58	Feb-58	Mar-58	Apr-58	May-58	Jun-58	Jul-58
48288	8F 2-8-0 (1935)												
48317	8F 2-8-0 (1935)												
48698	8F 2-8-0 (1935)												
48741	8F 2-8-0 (1935)												
70004	7MT 4-6-2 (1951)	X	X	X	X	X	X	X	X	X	X	X	Ex S. Lane
70014	7MT 4-6-2 (1951)	X	X	X	X	X	X	X	X	X	X	X	Ex S. Lane
70015	7MT 4-6-2 (1951)	X	X	X	X	X	X	X	X	X	X	X	Ex Canton
70017	7MT 4-6-2 (1951)	X	X	X	X	X	X	X	X	X	X	X	Ex Canton
70021	7MT 4-6-2 (1951)	X	X	X	X	X	X	X	X	X	X	X	Ex Canton
70042	7MT 4-6-2 (1951)	X	X	X	X	X	X	X	X	X	X	X	Ex K. Town
45561	5XP 4-6-0 (1934)												To K. Town
45618	5XP 4-6-0 (1934)												To K. Town
45622	5XP 4-6-0 (1934)												To K. Town
45628	5XP 4-6-0 (1934)												To K. Town
45652	5XP 4-6-0 (1934)												To K. Town
45667	5XP 4-6-0 (1934)	X	X	X	Ex Nottingham					To Nottingham	X	X	X
45712	5XP 4-6-0 (1934)												
44665	5MT 4-6-0 (1934)												
44717	5MT 4-6-0 (1934)												
44809	5MT 4-6-0 (1934)	X	X	X	Ex Derby								
45006	5MT 4-6-0 (1934)				To Derby	X	X	X	X	X	X	X	X
45239	5MT 4-6-0 (1934)												
45280	5MT 4-6-0 (1934)	X	X	X	X	X	X	X	X	X	Ex Saltley	To Saltley	X
41066	4P 4-4-0 (1924)		To Saltley	X	X	X	X	X	X	X	X	X	X
41114	4P 4-4-0 (1924)				To K. Town	X	X	X	X	X	X	X	X
41116	4P 4-4-0 (1924)				W/D	X	X	X	X	X	X	X	X
41118	4P 4-4-0 (1924)				To K. Town	X	X	X	X	X	X	X	X
41150	4P 4-4-0 (1924)		W/D	X	X	X	X	X	X	X	X	X	X
41157	4P 4-4-0 (1924)	X	X	X	X	Ex Chester							
41164	4P 4-4-0 (1924)	X	X	X	X	Ex L'dno Jcn							
41173	4P 4-4-0 (1924)												To Lancaster
42064	4MT 2-6-4T (1945)												
42065	4MT 2-6-4T (1945)												
42675	4MT 2-6-4T (1945)												
42676	4MT 2-6-4T (1945)												
42683	4MT 2-6-4T (1945)												
42452	4MT 2-6-4T (1935)												
42466	4MT 2-6-4T (1935)	X	X	X	X	X	Ex Brunswick						
42469	4MT 2-6-4T (1935)												
42479	4MT 2-6-4T (1935)	X	X	X	X	X	Ex Brunswick						
42628	4MT 2-6-4T (1935)	X	X	X	X	X	X	Ex Brunswick					
42326	4MT 2-6-4T (1927)	X	X	X	X	X	X	X	X	X	X	X	Ex Derby
42336	4MT 2-6-4T (1927)	X	X	X	X	X	X	X	X	X	X	Ex Hasland	
42419	4MT 2-6-4T (1927)												
76088	4MT 2-6-0 (1952)												
76089	4MT 2-6-0 (1952)												
44080	4F 0-6-0 (1924)												
44275	4F 0-6-0 (1924)												
44392	4F 0-6-0 (1924)												
44402	4F 0-6-0 (1924)	X	X	X	Ex Derby								
44465	4F 0-6-0 (1924)	X	Ex Kettering		To Derby	X	X	X	X	X	X	X	X
43846	4F 0-6-0 (1911)												
43921	4F 0-6-0 (1911)												
40088	3P 2-6-2 (1935)												
40097	3P 2-6-2 (1935)												
40105	3P 2-6-2 (1935)												
40141	3P 2-6-2 (1935)												
40208	3P 2-6-2 (1935)												
40009	3P 2-6-2 (1930)												
40012	3P 2-6-2 (1930)									To Saltley	X	X	X
40017	3P 2-6-2 (1930)												
40018	3P 2-6-2 (1930)												
40052	3P 2-6-2 (1930)												
40055	3P 2-6-2 (1930)												
62668	3P : D11 4-4-0 (1920)										To Darnall	X	X
69326	2MT : N5 0-6-2T (1891)			W/D	X	X	X	X	X	X	X	X	X
69343	2MT : N5 0-6-2T (1891)										To Darnall	X	X
69347	2MT : N5 0-6-2T (1891)			W/D	X	X	X	X	X	X	X	X	X
69361	2MT : N5 0-6-2T (1891)										To Darnall	X	X
69370	2MT : N5 0-6-2T (1891)										To Darnall	X	X
65166	2F : J10 0-6-0 (1892)	X	X	X	X	X	X	X	X	X	Ex Brunswick		
65167	2F : J10 0-6-0 (1892)												
65186	2F : J10 0-6-0 (1892)	W/D	X	X	X	X	X	X	X	X	X	X	X
65191	2F : J10 0-6-0 (1892)						W/D	X	X	X	X	X	X
65208	2F : J10 0-6-0 (1892)												
65209	2F : J10 0-6-0 (1892)												

Black 5 4-6-0 45495 of Warrington crosses from the CLC to the Midland at Cheadle Heath with the 11.55 Abergele - Sheffield on the 26 July 1952.

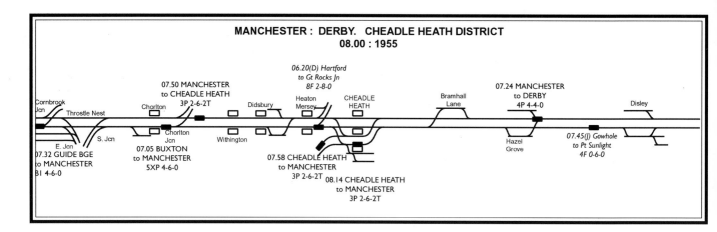

MANCHESTER : DERBY. CHEADLE HEATH DISTRICT
08.00 : 1955

CONTROLLER'S LOG : The focus of attention shifts from Chinley to the Millers Dale area as half a dozen movements which could do with thinning out converge on the station.

The most critical of these is the 07.05 Rowsley - Gowhole which is booked to stand on the slow line at Millers Dale - the fast lines are the outermost tracks - for ten minutes whilst the 06.05 Manchester - Buxton runs round and retraces its steps to Millers Dale Junction. With a 4F at each end, the 07.05 should have no difficulty in knocking ten minutes or so off its

07.15 Manchester - St Pancras; the Jubilee 4-6-0 of the latter currently beating a tattoo over the summit at Peak Forest with nine minutes to go before running into Millers Dale. The presence of a pair of Rowsley-bound light engines a couple of sections ahead of the express seems an uneasy sight but in fact the 4F's - which are returning to base after banking the 02.55 ex Kirkby and 18.00 ex Glazebrook to Peak Forest - will leave the main line at Peak Forest Junction and rejoin it after turning on the angle at Buxton Junction, following the

it actually is. In the down direction, a GC service has joined the line at Chorlton Junction and is being pursued in fairly quick succession by an express from Buxton plus a pair of locals from Cheadle. An 8F-hauled train of ICI hoppers is coming off the Cheshire Lines and will get a run to Chinley in the wake of the 07.24 Manchester - Derby whilst a class J goods for Birkenhead is approaching Hazel Grove and will take the slow line at Cheadle once the 08.14 has cleared the platform. Provided the Hoppers can clear the station before

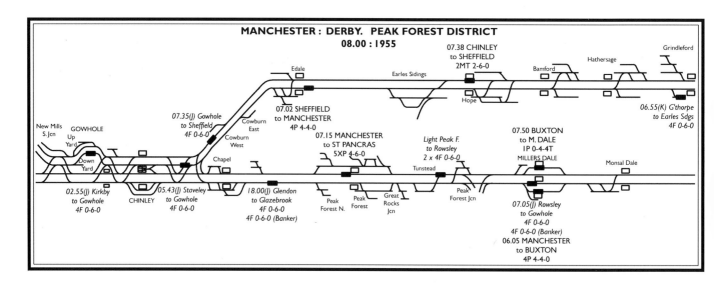

MANCHESTER : DERBY. PEAK FOREST DISTRICT
08.00 : 1955

running time to Millers Dale - goods schedules tend to be compiled on the liberal side - and if it is running true to form, a brief instruction to Millers Dale to pull off will keep it going and avoid blocking the station unnecessarily.

On the opposite side of the station, one of the Buxton motors - two sets operate the morning service - waits to cross over to the down bay to form the Buxton connection out of the

express which will have overtaken in the meantime.

Having given any instructions necessary for the smoother working of Millers Dale, an eye can be cast over the Cheadle Heath section which, for once, has more trains on it than is usual.

The reason for the increase in movements is purely because of the suburban service which is giving the appearance of being busier than

the 08.14 is due away - which it should - then neither of the goods interlopers is likely to do any harm to the passenger service.

At the lower end of the district, an observer might wonder where twenty years of LMS standardisation have gone to. The five trains between Rowsley and Ambergate are largely a mix of designs that were elderly when the grouping took place; the most modern being the Crab 2-6-0 on the Brent goods.

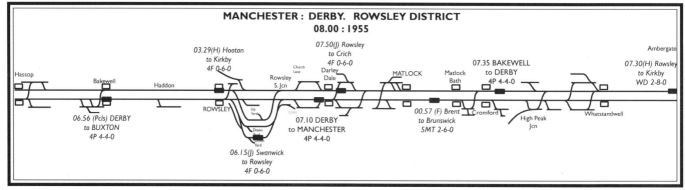

MANCHESTER : DERBY. ROWSLEY DISTRICT
08.00 : 1955

Loco	Class	Aug-58	Sep-58	Oct-58	Nov-58	Dec-58	Jan-59	Feb-59	Mar-59	Apr-59	May-59	Jun-59	Jul-59
	ALLOCATION & MOVEMENTS : TRAFFORD PARK												
48273	8F 2-8-0 (1935)	Ex Toton											
48288	8F 2-8-0 (1935)												
48317	8F 2-8-0 (1935)					To Heaton M.		X	X	X	X	X	X
48344	8F 2-8-0 (1935)	X	X	X	X	X	X	X	X	X	Wx Chester (GW)	X	X
48698	8F 2-8-0 (1935)	To Toton	X	X	X	X	X	X	X	X	X	X	X
48741	8F 2-8-0 (1935)												
45530	7P 4-6-0 (1946)	X	X	X	X	X	X	X	X	X	Ex Longsight	To Longsight	X
46122	7P 4-6-0 (1943)	X	X	X	X	X	X	X	X	X	Ex Longsight	To Upperby	X
70004	7MT 4-6-2 (1951)												
70014	7MT 4-6-2 (1951)												
70015	7MT 4-6-2 (1951)												
70017	7MT 4-6-2 (1951)												
70021	7MT 4-6-2 (1951)												
70042	7MT 4-6-2 (1951)												
45561	5XP 4-6-0 (1934)	X	X	X	X	X	X	X	X	X	X	X	Ex K. Town
45622	5XP 4-6-0 (1934)	X	Ex K. Town			To K. Town	X	X	X	X	X	X	X
45712	5XP 4-6-0 (1934)												
73140	5MT 4-6-0 (1951)	X	Ex Leicester	To Leicester	X	X	X	X	X	X	X	X	X
44665	5MT 4-6-0 (1934)												
44717	5MT 4-6-0 (1934)												
44809	5MT 4-6-0 (1934)												
44839	5MT 4-6-0 (1934)	X	Ex Derby		To Derby	X	X	X	X	X	X	X	X
44842	5MT 4-6-0 (1934)	X	X	X	X	X	X	X	X	X	X	Ex Brunswick	
44964	5MT 4-6-0 (1934)	X	X	X	X	X	X	X	X	X	X	X	Ex Saltley
45239	5MT 4-6-0 (1934)												
41157	4P 4-4-0 (1924)						To Derby	X	X	X	X	X	X
41164	4P 4-4-0 (1924)			W/D	X	X	X	X	X	X	X	X	X
42050	4MT 2-6-4T (1945)	X	X	X	X	Ex Derby				To Brunswick	Ex Brunswick		
42064	4MT 2-6-4T (1945)												
42065	4MT 2-6-4T (1945)												
42111	4MT 2-6-4T (1945)	X	X	X	X	X	X	X	X	X	X	X	Ex Hasland
42161	4MT 2-6-4T (1945)	X	X	X	X	Ex Nottingham	To Nottingham	X	X	X	X	X	X
42174	4MT 2-6-4T (1945)	X	X	X	X	Ex Derby	To Derby	X	X	X	X	X	X
42181	4MT 2-6-4T (1945)	X	X	X	X	Ex Derby		To Derby	X	X	X	X	X
42184	4MT 2-6-4T (1945)	X	X	X	X	Ex Derby	To Derby	X	X	X	X	X	X
42675	4MT 2-6-4T (1945)												
42676	4MT 2-6-4T (1945)												
42683	4MT 2-6-4T (1945)												
42452	4MT 2-6-4T (1935)												
42466	4MT 2-6-4T (1935)												
42469	4MT 2-6-4T (1935)												
42479	4MT 2-6-4T (1935)												
42628	4MT 2-6-4T (1935)												
42326	4MT 2-6-4T (1927)	To Derby	X	X	X	X	X	X	X	X	X	X	X
42336	4MT 2-6-4T (1927)												To Hasland
42419	4MT 2-6-4T (1927)												
76086	4MT 2-6-0 (1952)	X	X	X	X	X	Ex Leicester						
76088	4MT 2-6-0 (1952)												
76089	4MT 2-6-0 (1952)												
44078	4F 0-6-0 (1924)	X	X	X	X	X	X	X	X	X	Ex Gorton		
44080	4F 0-6-0 (1924)												
44138	4F 0-6-0 (1924)	X	X	X	X	X	X	X	X	X	Ex Saltley		
44275	4F 0-6-0 (1924)										To Gorton	X	X
44392	4F 0-6-0 (1924)												
44402	4F 0-6-0 (1924)												
44413	4F 0-6-0 (1924)	X	X	X	X	X	X	X	X	X	Ex Saltley		
43846	4F 0-6-0 (1911)											To St Albans	X
43921	4F 0-6-0 (1911)	To Toton	X	X	X	X	X	X	X	X	X	X	X
43988	4F 0-6-0 (1911)	Ex Toton											
40088	3P 2-6-2 (1935)												
40097	3P 2-6-2 (1935)												
40105	3P 2-6-2 (1935)												
40141	3P 2-6-2 (1935)												
40208	3P 2-6-2 (1935)												
40009	3P 2-6-2 (1930)												
40017	3P 2-6-2 (1930)												
40018	3P 2-6-2 (1930)												
40052	3P 2-6-2 (1930)												
40055	3P 2-6-2 (1930)												
43211	3F 0-6-0 (1896)	X	X	X	X	Ex Hasland							
43400	3F 0-6-0 (1885)	X	X	X	X	X	Ex Rowsley						
43580	3F 0-6-0 (1885)	X	X	X	X	X	Ex W'houses						
43587	3F 0-6-0 (1885)	X	X	X	X	X	Ex Burton						
58213	2F 0-6-0 (1878)	X	X	X	X	X	X	Ex Shrewsbury					W/D
65166	2F : J10 0-6-0 (1892)												
65167	2F : J10 0-6-0 (1892)		W/D	X	X	X	X	X	X	X	X	X	X
65208	2F : J10 0-6-0 (1892)				W/D	X	X	X	X	X	X	X	X
65209	2F : J10 0-6-0 (1892)			W/D	X	X	X	X	X	X	X	X	X

BR Standard 4-6-0's did not play a significant role in the working of the Derby - Manchester route until the very last years of operations. 10 examples arrived at Rowsley in late 1959 as replacements for the shed's Crab 2-6-0's whilst odd representatives of the Derby allocation could be found on former Compound duties. An unidentified BR 5MT 4-6-0 pauses at Heaton Mersey with a Manchester - Derby slow train in 1967.

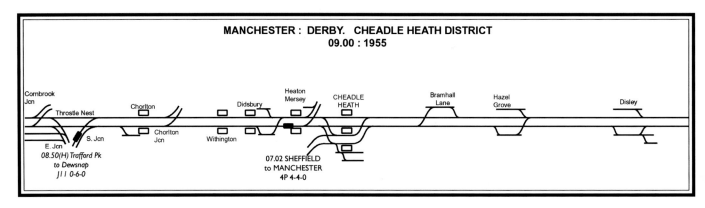

MANCHESTER : DERBY. CHEADLE HEATH DISTRICT
09.00 : 1955

CONTROLLER'S LOG : Although for most people the Manchester rush hour is over, there are still a few passenger trains around and they tend to suggest that the Midland reserves its more interesting motive power for the quieter periods.

The season-ticket trains from Stockport and Cheadle Heath are the preserve of class 3P 2-6-2T's; used on the workings because no other district will have them. The longer distance trains from Sheffield, which are now starting to the Central.

Although it probably means very little to the majority of users, the presence of the Sheffield and Derby trains together in Chinley is one of the last instances of Compounds standing side by side on class A services. The passage of an 8F 2-8-0 on the Hartford - Great Rocks hoppers disturbs the Midland atmosphere a little although nothing like as much as the local Hope - Sheffield passenger which is booked to be worked by a set of Bradford

Manchester - Derby slow, a Derby - Nottingham local and an evening express from Nottingham to St Pancras.

From Peak Forest Junction, the 04.15 will be followed by the 09.15 Buxton - Manchester; the 07.10 ex Derby fitting in between the two from Heaton Mersey after its deviation through Stockport.

As usual, passenger trains exact a high price from the goods service. The multi-engined Glendon - Glazebrook - which is

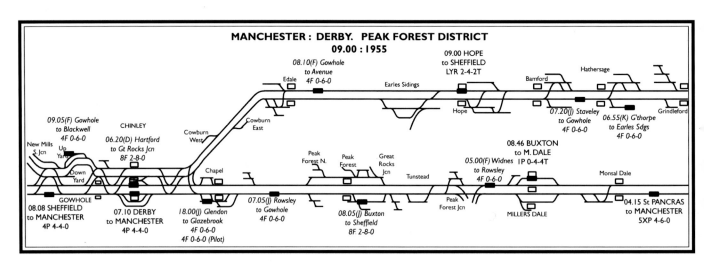

MANCHESTER : DERBY. PEAK FOREST DISTRICT
09.00 : 1955

to make an appearance, are worked by very much more robust machines; the workings being in the hands of 2P and 4P Compound 4-4-0's from Trafford Park, Sheffield and Buxton sheds.

The service is neither frequent not fast and the present time is one of the few occasions when a pair of Sheffield - Manchester trains can be seen only a few miles apart.

The 07.02 ex Sheffield is currently pulling away from Heaton Mersey after running via Stockport whilst the 08.08 Sheffield - Manchester express crosses from slow to main at Chinley, overtaking the 07.10 Derby - Manchester, for a twenty-six minute nonstop trot

(Manningham) men and an L&Y 2-4-2T.

Further back down the main line, the first of the day's London expresses is making an appearance as a 5XP 4-6-0 heads towards Monsal Dale with the eight-coach 04.15 St Pancras - Manchester, a train that derives most of its revenue from newsprint - it detaches BG's of newspapers at Luton (2), Bedford and Leicester - whilst doubling as an express which competes with the GC for the Leicester and Nottingham trade.

Although Manchester produces an appreciable tonnage of newsprint, the 04.15 operates in one direction only and returns to London in a number of stages involving the 19.35

routed via Disley - went inside at Chapel-en-le-Frith three-quarters of an hour ago for the 08.00 Buxton - Manchester and will remain there at least until the 09.15 Buxton has gone by. Several other trains have to be recessed and a beady eye is kept on the 07.05 Rowsley - Gowhole which should just have time to run down to the slow line at Chinley North Junction before the 04.15 catches up with it.

The up line is no more fluid than the down. The 07.24 Manchester - Derby is approaching Bakewell whilst the 09.00 St Pancras is pulling out of the Central and as a result almost every goods train has been - or is about to be - pulled off the main line.

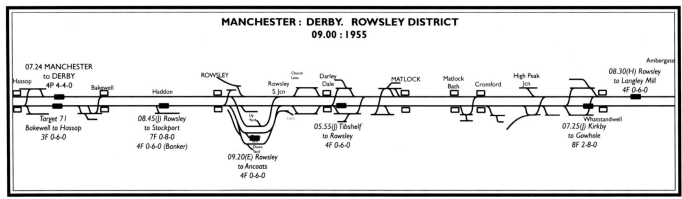

MANCHESTER : DERBY. ROWSLEY DISTRICT
09.00 : 1955

36

Loco	Class	Aug-59	Sep-59	Oct-59	Nov-59	Dec-59	Jan-60	Feb-60	Mar-60	Apr-60	May-60	Jun-60	Jul-60
	ALLOCATION & MOVEMENTS : TRAFFORD PARK												
48273	8F 2-8-0 (1935)												
48288	8F 2-8-0 (1935)												
48344	8F 2-8-0 (1935)												
48741	8F 2-8-0 (1935)												
70004	7MT 4-6-2 (1951)												
70014	7MT 4-6-2 (1951)												
70015	7MT 4-6-2 (1951)												
70017	7MT 4-6-2 (1951)												
70021	7MT 4-6-2 (1951)												
70031	7MT 4-6-2 (1951)	X	X	X	X	X	X	X	X	X	Ex Longsight		
70032	7MT 4-6-2 (1951)	X	X	X	X	X	X	Ex Longsight					
70033	7MT 4-6-2 (1951)	X	X	X	X	X	X	Ex Longsight					
70042	7MT 4-6-2 (1951)												
45561	5XP 4-6-0 (1934)				To K. Town	X	X	X	X	X	X	X	X
45616	5XP 4-6-0 (1934)	X	X	X	X	X	X	Ex Leicester	To Leicester	X	X	X	X
45712	5XP 4-6-0 (1934)		To Neasden	X	X	X	X	X	X	X	X	X	X
44665	5MT 4-6-0 (1934)												
44688	5MT 4-6-0 (1934)	X	X	X	Ex Derby								
44717	5MT 4-6-0 (1934)												
44809	5MT 4-6-0 (1934)												
44842	5MT 4-6-0 (1934)							To Longsight	X	X	X	X	X
44855	5MT 4-6-0 (1934)	X	X	X	X	X	X	X	X	X	Ex Longsight		
44888	5MT 4-6-0 (1934)	Ex Saltley	To Saltley	X	X	X	X	X	X	X	X	X	X
44964	5MT 4-6-0 (1934)												
45239	5MT 4-6-0 (1934)												
45426	5MT 4-6-0 (1934)	X	X	X	X	X	X	X	X	X	Ex Longsight		
42050	4MT 2-6-4T (1945)												
42064	4MT 2-6-4T (1945)												
42065	4MT 2-6-4T (1945)												
42111	4MT 2-6-4T (1945)												
42675	4MT 2-6-4T (1945)												
42676	4MT 2-6-4T (1945)												
42683	4MT 2-6-4T (1945)												
42428	4MT 2-6-4T (1935)	X	X	X	X	X	X	Ex Leicester					
42452	4MT 2-6-4T (1935)												
42466	4MT 2-6-4T (1935)												
42469	4MT 2-6-4T (1935)												
42479	4MT 2-6-4T (1935)												
42560	4MT 2-6-4T (1935)	X	X	X	X	X	Ex Gorton						
42628	4MT 2-6-4T (1935)										To Brunswick	X	X
42300	4MT 2-6-4T (1927)	X	X	X	X	X	X	Ex St Albans					
42328	4MT 2-6-4T (1927)	X	X	X	X	X	Ex Gorton						
42333	4MT 2-6-4T (1927)	X	X	X	X	X	Ex Annesley						
42339	4MT 2-6-4T (1927)	X	X	X	X	X	Ex Annesley						
42361	4MT 2-6-4T (1927)	X	X	X	X	X	Ex Annesley						
42419	4MT 2-6-4T (1927)												
76047	4MT 2-6-0 (1952)	X	X	X	X	X	X	X	X	X	X	X	Ex K. Stephen
76086	4MT 2-6-0 (1952)												
76088	4MT 2-6-0 (1952)												
76089	4MT 2-6-0 (1952)												
44078	4F 0-6-0 (1924)						To Rowsley	X	X	X	X	X	X
44080	4F 0-6-0 (1924)						To Rowsley	X	X	X	X	X	X
44138	4F 0-6-0 (1924)											To K. Town	X
44392	4F 0-6-0 (1924)												
44402	4F 0-6-0 (1924)												
44413	4F 0-6-0 (1924)						To Rowsley	X	X	X	X	X	X
44564	4F 0-6-0 (1924)	X	X	X	X	X	Ex Rowsley						
44565	4F 0-6-0 (1924)	X	X	X	X	X	Ex Rowsley						
44566	4F 0-6-0 (1924)	X	X	X	X	X	Ex Rowsley						
43988	4F 0-6-0 (1911)				To Walton	X	X	X	X	X	X	X	X
40088	3P 2-6-2 (1935)												
40097	3P 2-6-2 (1935)								To Heaton M	X	X	X	X
40105	3P 2-6-2 (1935)								To Heaton M	X	X	X	X
40141	3P 2-6-2 (1935)												
40208	3P 2-6-2 (1935)												
40009	3P 2-6-2 (1930)												
40017	3P 2-6-2 (1930)				W/D	X	X	X	X	X	X	X	X
40018	3P 2-6-2 (1930)												
40052	3P 2-6-2 (1930)		W/D	X	X	X	X	X	X	X	X	X	X
40055	3P 2-6-2 (1930)				W/D	X	X	X	X	X	X	X	X
40056	3P 2-6-2 (1930)	X	Ex Heaton M.		W/D	X	X	X	X	X	X	X	X
43211	3F 0-6-0 (1896)												
43400	3F 0-6-0 (1885)									To Gorton	X	X	X
43572	3F 0-6-0 (1885)	X	X	X	Ex Heaton M.								
43580	3F 0-6-0 (1885)												
43587	3F 0-6-0 (1885)			W/D	X	X	X	X	X	X	X	X	X
43650	3F 0-6-0 (1885)	X	X	X	Ex Toton								
65166	2F : J10 0-6-0 (1892)				W/D	X	X	X	X	X	X	X	X
D3847	0F : Diesel 0-6-0	NEW		To Camden	X	X	X	X	X	X	X	X	X
D3848	0F : Diesel 0-6-0	NEW		To Camden	X	X	X	X	X	X	X	X	X

THE MIDLAND RAILWAY CENTRE
Butterley Station, Ripley, Derbyshire DE5 3QZ
(Nr. Junction 28 - M1, signposted from A38)
Telephone: (01773) 570140

The MIDLAND RAILWAY CENTRE is quite different from most heritage railways. It has a fine 3.5-mile railway with magnificently restored locomotives and rolling stock. It also boasts a huge museum site incorporating a large Railway Museum with a wide range of exhibits, a country park, a farm park, a narrow gauge railway, a miniature railway, a demonstration signalbox and a railwayman's Victorian Church. Exhibits range from an 1865 passenger coach to 1960's diesel locomotives and from tiny saddle tank shunting engines to mighty express passenger Pacific locomotives.

You don't know your railways until you know the Midland Railway Centre.

The passenger timetable suggested that the Chinley - Sheffield line was little more than a branch line whereas in fact it carried a very heavy service of goods trains from the Manchester area to the North Nottingham coalfields and the Sheffield steel producing area. Traffic joining the line from the Buxton area was sufficient to warrant a through connection allowing trains to run from Chapel-en-le-Frith to Hathersage without having to reverse at Chinley. In the upper view an up goods train passes Chinley East Junction; the point of convergence with the angle - Chinley East Curve - from the south. In the lower view 8F 2-8-0 48709 of Buxton proceeds cautiously over the East Curve viaduct with the 13.50 Buxton - Wincobank (Sheffield) goods.

By the mid-1950's with most Midland passenger services worked by post-Stanier locomotives, the number of routes that could guarantee a 4-4-0 were far from numerous. Occupying a rather low rung on the ladder of relative importance, the Hope Valley trains were never embraced by LMS standardisation and 4-4-0's operated most of the services until the arrival of diesels during the 1960's. En route to Chinley and Manchester, Compound 41116 of Trafford Park heads a typical Hope Valley passenger train at Hathersage in 1956. Below 3F 0-6-0 43254 of Sheffield runs through Bamford with one of the many freight services that used the route

During the final days of steam the Sheffield district was transferred to the Great Central and although this made very little difference to the main line, it did result in B1 4-6-0's making regular appearances over the Hope Valley. 61372 of Darnall brings the 16.31 Sheffield (M) - Chinley into Grindleford on 26th April 1965. Strange as the B1's were to regulars on the line, they came almost as a revelation to the crew working the above service who were based at Buxton - almost as far as it was possible to get from the Eastern Region - and went out with the 14.50 Chinley - Sheffield

The Hope Valley from the 5MT 4-6-0 working the 15.10 Chinley - Sheffield passenger; a service that was added to the timetable during the late 1950's.

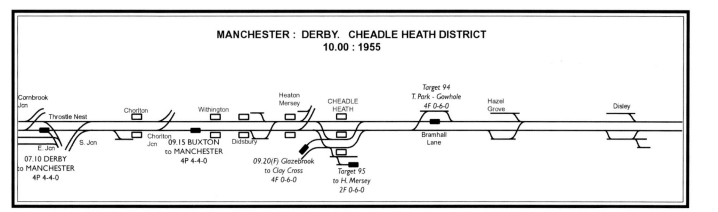

MANCHESTER : DERBY. CHEADLE HEATH DISTRICT
10.00 : 1955

CONTROLLER'S LOG : One of the absurdities of the Midland Railway - still perpetuated - was their almost paranoid aversion to facing points; one result being that to shunt a goods train, it has to reverse into a refuge - with all the fuss and additional time involved - as opposed to running straight from the main line into a loop as is the practice everywhere else in the country.

A product of this obsession is to place a very serious limit on the freedom with which northbound trains can be despatched from

ted express goods) from Rowsley to Ancoats ought to get to New Mills South without causing trouble but the 4F 0-6-0 on the forty-eight wagon train is unassisted and the class are not the best of steamers. A careful watch is kept on its progress, ready to put it inside at Peak Forest or Chapel should it show any signs of weakening.

Similar precautions have to be taken with the 07.25 Kirkby - Gowhole which is one of the few trains to be honoured with a Rowsley 8F 2-8-0. Following it as it picks its way

where goods trains have the luxury of their own set of metals.

It is amusing to note how goods trains appear like maggots in an apple as the 09.00 Manchester - London makes its way up towards Derby. Apart from Target 70 which is about to shunt the yard at Matlock Bath, the line is clear all the way ahead whilst in its wake to the south, goods trains are popping out all over the place.

Concern at running margins over Peak Forest must not be used as an excuse to over-

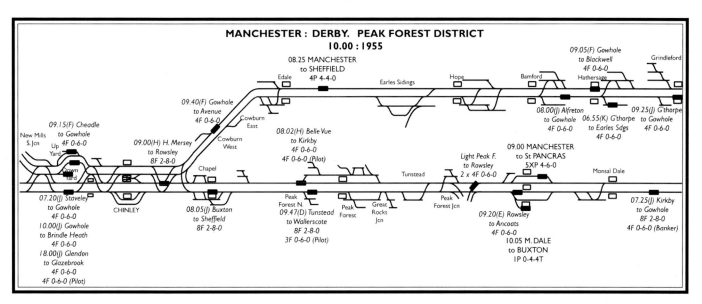

MANCHESTER : DERBY. PEAK FOREST DISTRICT
10.00 : 1955

Rowsley marshalling yard; fifty-three minutes being needed for a J-class goods to leave the yard, attach a banker and run for the safety of the slow line at Millers Dale.

The 09.06 Nottingham - Liverpool express is on the point of entering the district at Ambergate and, apart from a local goods from Derby which is very close to Rowsley, the line has been cleared for a distance of almost twenty miles.

Having left Rowsley an hour before the express is due to pass, the 09.20 class E (unfit-

through Bakewell and Monsal is like watching water boil but with a load only four wagons greater than that of a 4F, the 2-8-0 should get to Peak Forest - where it loses its banker - on time and, if it can make up a few minutes, may be given a run as far as the slow line at Chinley. How much more simple life would be if the Midland spent a few pounds on its pointwork and created a few goods loops of the conventional type. The hand to mouth operating of the Peak District contrasts strongly with the extravagance shown south of Trent

look the Hope Valley which is often as busy as the main line. Most of the trains via Hope are through services without problems of relief or engine-changing whilst the passenger service is infrequent enough to allow goods to operate far more freely than is the case via Peak Forest. The exceptions to the free-running rule are the three daily workings between Buxton and Sheffield which are timed to meet at either Earles Sidings or Hathersage to allow the crews to change footplates: a piece of planning which is rather more of a hope than a promise.

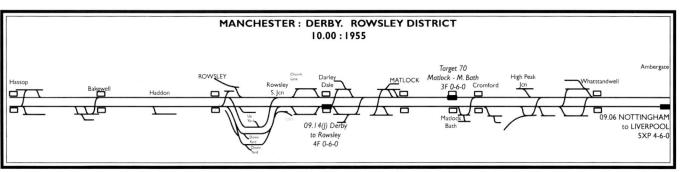

MANCHESTER : DERBY. ROWSLEY DISTRICT
10.00 : 1955

WORKING TIMETABLE 1954 : PASSENGER & GOODS

Station	H	J	C 20.37 Bolton	H 23.35 H.M	Light Banker	H	A 00.00	H	Light Banker	F	E 21.05 H'son	H 22.40 Ancoats	H	Light HM Loco	F 18.50 Latchford	F	Light	2 light Banker
MANCHESTER (CENT)							00.00											
Trafford Park						23.20												
Throstle Nest S.						23/29	00/05											
Chorlton																		
Chorlton Jcn						23/34	00/08											
Withington																		
Didsbury																		
Heaton Mersey						23/43												
CHEADLE HEATH							00.15 (Via				23w52							
Bramhall Moor Lane							GC)											
Disley																		
New Mills S. Jcn			00/07	00/15		00/28	00/32				00/23				01/05			
GOWHOLE				00.20		00.33						00.44		00.55	01.08			
Buxworth Jcn												00/49						
CHINLEY			00/14				00/38				00/42	00/59		01/10				
Chinley N. Jcn											00/52	01/03		01/16				
Chinley S. Jcn														(To				
Chapel														W'bank)				
Dove Holes T. North											01/02	01/12						
Peak Forest N					00.32													
Peak Forest			00/27				00/50				01/12	01/23						
Gt Rocks Jcn																		
Tunstead																	01.50	
Peak Forest Jcn					00/42						01/18	01/30					01/57	
Millers Dale Jcn									01/04							01/44		02/07
MILLERS DALE			00/35				00/56		01/07		01/23	01/35				01/50	02/02	02/12
Monsal Dale																		
Hassop																		
Bakewell																		
Haddon																		
Rowsley			00/48				01/09											02/37
ROWSLEY YARD	00.10	00.20						01.30	01.32	01.50	01.50	02.04			02.20	02.30		02.43
Rowsley S. Jcn	00/14	00/25						01/34		01/54					02/34			
Church Lane																		
Darley Dale																		
MATLOCK																		
Matlock Bath																		
Cromford																		
High Peak Jcn																		
Whatstandwell	00/35	00/44							01/52	02/13					02/52	03/01		
Johnson's Sdgs																		
Ambergate	00/40	00/49	01/03				01/24		02/00	02/18					03/00	03/08		
Destination	Lawley St	Kirkby	Leic				St.P		Burton	Leic					St.P	Derby		

Station	H 22.14 Stockport	H 21.00 Dundas	H 23.38 Moston	F 22.55 Walton	J 00.45 Glaze	F	F 21.16 Garston	F	H 20.35 Heysham	H 23.38 Moston	Light Target 91	F	H 23.55 Brunswick	F 01.24 Partington	F	H 23.38 Moston	H 22.55 Walton	F
MANCHESTER (CENT)																		
Trafford Park																01.30		
Throstle Nest S.				00/43	01/15								01/27			01/39		
Chorlton																		
Chorlton Jcn				00/48	01/21								01/30			01/44		
Withington					(To													
Didsbury					Wath)													
Heaton Mersey				00/57									01/39			01/54		
CHEADLE HEATH		00/55		01.09									01/57	02.10		(Via		
Bramhall Moor Lane							(Via									GC)		
Disley							GC)											
New Mills S. Jcn		01/28	01/30	01/40			01/54		02/13	02/26			02/31	02/40		02/48		
GOWHOLE			01.35	01.45		01.45			02.15	02.30	02.30					02.53		03.00
Buxworth Jcn			(Fwd	(Fwd														
CHINLEY		01/40	at	at		02.00	02/04		02/25	02/27			02/40	02L55		02/44		03/12
Chinley N. Jcn			02.15)	03.00)		02/08	02/10		02/31	02/38			03/02			02/52		03/18
Chinley S. Jcn						(To							(To	(To				(To
Chapel						Leeds)	02w19			02.45			Avenue)	Avenue)		02.58		Sheffield)
Dove Holes T. North							02/25		02/37	02/52	(Fwd							
Peak Forest N											at							
Peak Forest			02/13				02/35			02.58)	02.52		03.03			03.15		
Gt Rocks Jcn											02.58							
Tunstead																(Fwd		
Peak Forest Jcn			02/25				02/41						03/09			(Fwd		
Millers Dale Jcn	02/18															03.45)		
MILLERS DALE	02/23	02/32					02/46						03/14					
Monsal Dale																		
Hassop																		
Bakewell																		
Haddon																		
Rowsley														03.45				
ROWSLEY YARD	02.52	03.05					03.14		03.25				03.35					
Rowsley S. Jcn									03/29				03/39	03/50				
Church Lane																		
Darley Dale																		
MATLOCK																		
Matlock Bath																		
Cromford																		
High Peak Jcn																		
Whatstandwell									03/45				03/55	04/07				
Johnson's Sdgs																		
Ambergate									03/50				04/00	04/13				
Destination									Notts				Derby	Spondon				

WORKING TIMETABLE 1954 : PASSENGER & GOODS

Class	C	H	F	J	F	H	J	J	F	H	J	J	E	H	J	H	E	E
Train	23.55	23.45	22.50	21.10	23.25			00.20	22.35	23.45	22.18	20.30	22.20	22.35		00.55		20.55
From	G. Bge	Ashton Rd	G'thorpe	Avenue	C'field			Mottram	Notts	G'thorpe	Notts	Kirkby	B'ham	Notts		G'thorpe		P'boro
AMBERGATE									23/49	00/00			00/27					01/12
Johnson's Sdgs																		
Whatstandwell									23/59	00/10			00/34					01/17
High Peak Jcn																		
Cromford																		
Matlock Bath																		
MATLOCK																		
Darley Dale																		
Church Lane																		
Rowsley S. Jcn									00/26	00/41			00/55					01/33
ROWSLEY YARD					00.25				00.30	00.45			00.58			01.10	01.35	01.36
Rowsley					00B34											01/14		01/39
Haddon																		
Bakewell																		
Hassop																		
Monsal Dale																		
MILLERS DALE					01/15											01/48		02/12
Millers Dale Jcn					01/20													
Peak Forest Jcn					(To											01/54		02/18
Tunstead					Buxton)													
Great Rocks Jcn																		
Peak Forest																		
P. Forest North																02/06		02.28
Chapel																		
Chinley S. Jcn																		
Chinley N. Jcn			00/22	00/38	00/55					01/27						02/17	02/35	02/38
CHINLEY			00/30	00/44	01/00					01/30						02/20	02/40	02/41
Buxworth																		
GOWHOLE			00.42	01.00	01.10	01.25						01.45		02.30			02.50	
New Mills S. Jcn						01/31				01/37		01/50	02/27	02/36				02/47
Disley						(To				(To		(To						(To
Bramhall Moor Lane						Heaton				Edge		Ashton						Ancoats)
CHEADLE HEATH						Mersey)				Hill)		Rd)	02/50	03/05				
Heaton Mersey													(To	(To				
Didsbury													Bruns-	Walton)				
Withington													wick)					
Chorlton Jcn	00/11	00/22					01/34											
Chorlton																		
Throstle Nest S.	00/17	00/27					01/39											
Trafford Park	(To	00.33					01.46											
MANCHESTER (CENT)	L'pool)																	

Class	E	J	J	Pcls	H	J	H	T.91	J	E	J	H	J	C	J	E	H	J
Train	02.10	23.55	00.01	10.40	02.30		03.50		01.10				03.30	21.35	03.30	01.00	01.50	01.40
From	Mottram	C. Park	Kirkby	St. P	Mottram		Park		Avenue				Buxton	Somers T.	Buxton	York	S'gate	Kirkby
AMBERGATE		01/19	01/34	02/14												02/52		03/01
Johnson's Sdgs																		
Whatstandwell		01/26	01/44													02/59		03/07
High Peak Jcn																		
Cromford																		
Matlock Bath																		
MATLOCK																		
Darley Dale																		
Church Lane																		
Rowsley S. Jcn		01/50	02/09													03/21		03/27
ROWSLEY YARD		01.53	02.12						02.32				03.00			03.25		
Rowsley				02/31					02/36				03/04					03.38
Haddon																		
Bakewell																		
Hassop																		
Monsal Dale																		
MILLERS DALE				02/48					03/10				03/38					
Millers Dale Jcn																		
Peak Forest Jcn									03/16				03/44		03/52			
Tunstead																		
Great Rocks Jcn																		
Peak Forest															04.08	04.18		
P. Forest North									03/26				03/56			04/23		
Chapel															(Det Pilot)			
Chinley S. Jcn																04/36		
Chinley N. Jcn				03/03					03/24	03/40		04/07		04/23		(To		
CHINLEY				03/05					03/30	03/43		04/10		04/26		Shef		
Buxworth										03L50		04L20				field)		
GOWHOLE					03.20		03.30		03.42		03.55							
New Mills S. Jcn				03/08	03/26		03/35		03/53		04/00	04/25		04/32				
Disley				(Via			(To		(To		(To	(To		(To				
Bramhall Moor Lane				GC)			Ancoats)		Brewery)		Heaton	Heaton		Ancoats)				
CHEADLE HEATH							04/00				Mersey)	Mersey)						
Heaton Mersey				03/41			04/04											
Didsbury																		
Withington																		
Chorlton Jcn	03/20			03/45	03/47		04/15	04/20									04/43	
Chorlton																		
Throstle Nest S.	03/27			03/48	03/56		04/21	04/25									04/48	
Trafford Park	(To				04.05		04.30	(To								(To		
MANCHESTER (CENT)	Walton)			03.54				Lowton)								B'wick)		

WORKING TIMETABLE 1954 : PASSENGER & GOODS

Class	F	E	H	D	H	F	H	J	H	F	E	Light	F	H	F	H	Light
Train	21.25		03.15	00.50	23.38	23.25					00.45		00.05	01.30	02.45	01.15	
From	Garston		Buxton	Hartford	Moston	Brunswick					Walton		Garston	Garston	Glazeb'k	B'wick	
MANCHESTER (CENT)												02.50					
Trafford Park											02.40						
Throstle Nest S.						02/09				02/40	02/49	02/55				03/24	
Chorlton																	
Chorlton Jcn						02/14				02/47	02/54	02/59				03/39	
Withington										(To	(To	(To				(To	
Didsbury										York)	Col-	Godley)				Dews-	
Heaton Mersey						02/27					wick)					nap)	
CHEADLE HEATH				02.32		(To								03w15	03w32		
Bramhall Moor Lane						White-											
Disley						moor)											
New Mills S. Jcn				03/06										03/47	04/03		
GOWHOLE							03.45										
Buxworth Jcn																	
CHINLEY				03L17			03/57							04/00	04/17		
Chinley N. Jcn				03/20			04/02								04/20		
Chinley S. Jcn							(To								(To		
Chapel							Chest-								Clay		
Dove Holes T. North				03/27			erfield)							04/17	Cross)		
Peak Forest N																	
Peak Forest			03.50		03.45									04/30			
Gt Rocks Jcn			03.55														
Tunstead																	
Peak Forest Jcn					03/54									04/46			
Millers Dale Jcn	03/20		03/36										04/40				
MILLERS DALE	03/25		03/42		04/01								04/45	04/54			
Monsal Dale																	
Hassop																	
Bakewell																	
Haddon																	
Rowsley																	05.42
ROWSLEY YARD	03.55	04.00	04.15		04.28			04.38	04.50	05.10			05.15	05.30			05.44
Rowsley S. Jcn		04.04						04/42	04/54	05/14							
Church Lane																	
Darley Dale																	05.50
MATLOCK																	
Matlock Bath																	
Cromford																	
High Peak Jcn																	
Whatstandwell		04/18						04/59	05/20	05/42							
Johnson's Sdgs																	
Ambergate		04/22						05/03	05/28	05/54							
Destination		B'ham						Kirkby	Ilkeston	Kirkby			Kirkby				

Class	F	F	Light	B	T.70	F	Light	Light	F	H	F	F	F	F	J	J	J	J
Train		03.25	ex		01.50					03.15			02.50				06.20	03.25
From		Ashton Rd	B. Vue		Elles Pt					H'wood			Garston				Buxton	G'thorpe
MANCHESTER (CENT)																		
Trafford Park													05.20					
Throstle Nest S.													05/31					
Chorlton																		
Chorlton Jcn													05/38					
Withington													(To					
Didsbury													Work-					
Heaton Mersey													sop)					
CHEADLE HEATH						04w33							05w12					
Bramhall Moor Lane																		
Disley																		
New Mills S. Jcn		04/26	04/50			05/07				05/12			05/48					
GOWHOLE			04.54						05.10	05.17	05.30	05.40						
Buxworth Jcn																		
CHINLEY		04/40				05/20			05/22		05/41	05/53	06/03					
Chinley N. Jcn		04/45				05/25			05/30		05/45	06/07						
Chinley S. Jcn									(To		(To	(To						06/02
Chapel		05w03							Avenue)		Winco-	Stav-						06w12
Dove Holes T. North		05/10				05/36					bank)	eley)	06/04					06/20
Peak Forest N					05.53													
Peak Forest		05/21				05/47							06/14					06.33
Gt Rocks Jcn																		
Tunstead																		
Peak Forest Jcn		05/27				05/53	06/02						06/20					
Millers Dale Jcn									06/10									06/40
MILLERS DALE		05/32				05/59			06/13				06/25					06/45
Monsal Dale																		
Hassop																		
Bakewell																		
Haddon																		
Rowsley																		
ROWSLEY YARD	06.00	06.00				06.20	06.30	06.40	06.47				06.51				07.05	07.15
Rowsley S. Jcn	06/04					06/24											07/09	
Church Lane																		
Darley Dale				06.20														
MATLOCK				06.27	06.35													
Matlock Bath				06.31														
Cromford				06.34														
High Peak Jcn																		
Whatstandwell	06/21			06.40						07/10							07/32	
Johnson's Sdgs																		
Ambergate	06/26			06.45						07/16							07/39	
Destination	Leic			Notts						Kirkby							Derby	

44

Upper table

	F	J	Light	D	J	H	F	H	E	J	J	F	T.94	J	B	J	2 Light
Class (Train)		02.20		04.45	03.05	04.55		04.45		03.10	01.40	00.20				01.40	ex
From		W'bank		G. Bge	Avenue	Park		Mottram		Derby	Kirkby	Leic				Kirkby	Buxton
AMBERGATE										03/38		04/03					
Johnson's Sdgs																	
Whatstandwell										03/50		04/09					
High Peak Jcn																	
Cromford																	
Matlock Bath																	
MATLOCK																	
Darley Dale																	
Church Lane																	
Rowsley S. Jcn										04/20		04/31					
ROWSLEY YARD	03.40					03.50		04.05	04.15	04.24		04/35					
Rowsley	03.44					03.54		04.09	04.19	04B28							
Haddon																	
Bakewell																	
Hassop																	
Monsal Dale																	
MILLERS DALE	04/17					04/35		04/44	04/55		05/08						
Millers Dale Jcn					04/40												
Peak Forest Jcn					(To			04/50	05/01		05/14						05/45
Tunstead					Buxton)									05.23			
Great Rocks Jcn				04.40													
Peak Forest											05.30					05.40	05.55
P. Forest North	04.33			04.46				05/01	05/11					05D42		05D48	
Chapel																	
Chinley S. Jcn																	
Chinley N. Jcn	04/40	04/50	05/00	05/08				05/11	05/22					06/01		06/12	
CHINLEY	04.46	04.54	05.03	05.12				05.14	05.25					06.04		06.17	
Buxworth																	
GOWHOLE		05.05		05.22													06.28
New Mills S. Jcn	04/52	05/11						05/21	05/32					06/14			
Disley	(To		(To				(To										
Bramhall Moor Lane	Ancoats)		B. Vue)				Brindle										
CHEADLE HEATH							Heath)		05/57				06.20	06/43	07.00		
Heaton Mersey								(To					06/27	(To	07.04		
Didsbury								Walton)						North-	07.07		
Withington														wich)	07.10		
Chorlton Jcn					05/05	05/26			05/55				06/38		07/13		
Chorlton															07/15		
Throstle Nest S.					05/11	05/33			06/02				06/43		07/18		
Trafford Park						05.41			06.10				06.51				
MANCHESTER (CENT)					05.20										07.23		

Lower table

	Light	B	J	J	J	J	J	F	J	J	J	J	B	B	B	B	B	B
Class (Train)			03.43	03.10	03.43	03.18	03.55	02.35		03.20		03.35	06.00	07.32	07.05			08.21
From			Derby	Derby	Derby	Staveley	B'well	W.Heath		Kirkby		Carlton	Sheff	G. Bge	Buxton			T. Dale
AMBERGATE			04/10			04/30	04/50			04/58								
Johnson's Sdgs																		
Whatstandwell			04/17			04/39	04/58			05/05								
High Peak Jcn																		
Cromford																		
Matlock Bath																		
MATLOCK			04.30			04.42												
Darley Dale																		
Church Lane																		
Rowsley S. Jcn					04/59	05/09	05/20			05/31								
ROWSLEY YARD				04.55	05.03	05.13		05.35		05.35								
Rowsley					05B04			05W30		05B43								
Haddon																		
Bakewell																		
Hassop																		
Monsal Dale																		
MILLERS DALE					05/50			06/12	06/26									
Millers Dale Jcn									06/33									
Peak Forest Jcn					05/56			06/19	(To						07/12			
Tunstead									Buxton)									
Great Rocks Jcn																		
Peak Forest	06.00														07.19			
P. Forest North					06D16			06/32										
Chapel															07.28			
Chinley S. Jcn																		
Chinley N. Jcn	06/28				06/34		06/37	06/49				06/54	07/04					
CHINLEY	06.30				06.38		06/43	06/53				07L05	07/06		07.34			
Buxworth																		
GOWHOLE	(For				06/50		06/55			07.16		07/20						
New Mills S. Jcn	07.04							07/10		07/22					07/40			
Disley	Pass)									(To	(Fwd							
Bramhall Moor Lane										Brew	at							
CHEADLE HEATH		07.30						07/46		-ery)	10.05)				07.52	07.58	08.14	
Heaton Mersey		07.34						(To								08.02	08.18	08/27
Didsbury		07.37						Bruns-								08.05	08.21	08.30
Withington		07.40						wick)								08.08	08.24	08.34
Chorlton Jcn		07/48												07/54	07/59	08.11	08.27	08.37
Chorlton		07.45												07.56		08.13	08.29	08.39
Throstle Nest S.		07/47												07/58	08/02	08.16	08.31	08.41
Trafford Park																		
MANCHESTER (CENT)		07.53												08.04	08.08	08.22	08.37	08.47

Station	J 03.25 G'thorpe	2 Light ex B. Vue	H	F 02.15 Garston	D 04.43 Northwich	B	T73	H 03.29 Hooton	F 05.45 P. Park	B	B	B	F 05.00 Widnes	Motor 07.50 Buxton	Light	F 05.58 Arpley	B	B
MANCHESTER (CENT)										06.05							06.55	
Trafford Park																		
Throstle Nest S.										06/11							07/00	
Chorlton										06/13							07/03	
Chorlton Jcn										06/15							07/04	
Withington										06/19							07/07	
Didsbury										06/22							07/10	
Heaton Mersey										06/26							07/14	
CHEADLE HEATH				06w01				06w12		(Via			06L42			06w58	07.17	
Bramhall Moor Lane										GC)								
Disley																		
New Mills S. Jcn			06/11		06/32			06/46	06/54	07/08			07/15			07/29		
GOWHOLE		06.14							07.00							07.33		
Buxworth Jcn										07.14								
CHINLEY					06/42			06/58	07.09	07.18	07.23		07/27					07.38
Chinley N. Jcn					06/45				07/12		07/26		07/32					07/41
Chinley S. Jcn										(To Sheff)								(To Sheffield)
Chapel											07.32		07.42					
Dove Holes T. North					06/53			07/10										
Peak Forest N																		
Peak Forest	06.43				07/03			07/21			07.43					07.54		
Gt Rocks Jcn					07/10													
Tunstead																		
Peak Forest Jcn	06/53							07/27					07/47			08.02		
Millers Dale Jcn	(To			07/00										07/57				
MILLERS DALE	Buxton)			07/05				07/32					07.50	07.59				
Monsal Dale																		
Hassop																		
Bakewell						07.35												
Haddon																		
Rowsley						07.42	08w04											
ROWSLEY YARD			07.30	07.34			07.50											
Rowsley S. Jcn			07/34				07/54	08/08										
Church Lane																		
Darley Dale						07.47												
MATLOCK						07.52												
Matlock Bath						07.56												
Cromford						07.59												
High Peak Jcn																		
Whatstandwell			07/53			08.05	08/16	08/27										
Johnson's Sdgs																		
Ambergate			07/59			08.10	08/22	08/32										
Destination			Kirkby			Derby	Crich	Kirkby										

Station	J 06.00 Moston	H	A	H	Light	Motor 08.16 Buxton	T.95 H. Mersey	B	F	Motor 08.46 Buxton	T.70	F 05.00 Widnes	B	2 Light	H 08.02 B. Vue	B	D 06.20 Hartford	B
MANCHESTER (CENT)			07.15					07.24					07.35			07.50		08.15
Trafford Park																		
Throstle Nest S.			07/20					07/30					07/40			07/55		08/20
Chorlton								07/33					07/43			07/58		08/23
Chorlton Jcn			07/23					07/34					07/44			07/59		08/24
Withington								07/38					(To			08/02		08/27
Didsbury			07.27					07.41					G. Bge)			08.05		08.30
Heaton Mersey								07.45								08.09		08.34
CHEADLE HEATH			07/31				07/33	07.49								08.12	08w13	08.37
New Mills S. Jcn		07/34	07/45					08/06								08/38	08/48	
GOWHOLE	07.35	07/38							08.10							08.43		
Buxworth Jcn								08.12								(Fwd		
CHINLEY	07/48		07/50					08.19	08/23							09.30)	09/00	
Chinley N. Jcn	07/53								08/30								09/03	
Chinley S. Jcn	(To Sheffield)								(To Avenue)									
Chapel								08.27				08.32						
Dove Holes T. North												08/40					09/11	
Peak Forest N																		
Peak Forest			08.01					08.37				08/51					09/20	
Gt Rocks Jcn																	09.26	
Tunstead																		
Peak Forest Jcn												08/58						
Millers Dale Jcn					08/16	08/23				08/53					09/14			
MILLERS DALE			08.10		08/19	08.25		08.47		08/55		09.03			09.17			
Monsal Dale								08.53										
Hassop								08.57										
Bakewell								09.03										
Haddon																		
Rowsley			08/23					09.10										
ROWSLEY YARD				08.30	08.44									09.35	09.44			
Rowsley S. Jcn				08/34														
Church Lane																		
Darley Dale								09.15										
MATLOCK			08.32					09.22				09.35						
Matlock Bath								09.26				09.42						
Cromford								09.29										
High Peak Jcn																		
Whatstandwell				08.56				09.35										
Johnson's Sdgs																		
Ambergate			08.42	09.05				09.40										
Destination			St. P	L. Mill				Derby										

	J	J	J	B	Light	J	B	J	B	B	B		Light	T.92	F	J	F
Train	04.45	02.55	02.55			05.43	07.02		07.02	08.00	08.43				22.40	18.00	22.40
From	Avenue	Kirkby	Kirkby			Staveley	Sheff		Sheff	Buxton	G. Bge				St. P	Glendon	St. P
AMBERGATE		05/10													05/37	05/21	
Johnson's Sdgs																	
Whatstandwell		05/19													05/43	05/30	
High Peak Jcn																	
Cromford																	
Matlock Bath																	
MATLOCK															05.55		06.20
Darley Dale																	
Church Lane																	
Rowsley S. Jcn		05B50														06B25	06/32
ROWSLEY YARD								06.15									06.35
Rowsley		06W08						06B28					06.20			06W40	
Haddon																	
Bakewell													06.30				
Hassop																	
Monsal Dale																	
MILLERS DALE		06/50						07/11								07/23	
Millers Dale Jcn								07/17									
Peak Forest Jcn		06/58						(To		08/08						07/34	
Tunstead								Buxton)									
Great Rocks Jcn																	
Peak Forest		07.15	07.23							08.14							
P. Forest North			07D30													07D55	
Chapel										08.21						08.10	
Chinley S. Jcn																	
Chinley N. Jcn		07/35	07/46			08/00	08/11			08/23							
CHINLEY		07L42	07/50			08/05	08.13		08.18	08.28							
Buxworth									08.21								
GOWHOLE	07.45	07.55	08.00		08.03	08.20								08.29			
New Mills S. Jcn	07/51				08/08				08/24	08/32				08/35			
Disley									(Via		(Via			(To			
Bramhall Moor Lane									GC)		GC)			Strines)			
CHEADLE HEATH	08/20			08.31	08.34					08.44							
Heaton Mersey	(To			08.35	(To								08.59				
Didsbury	Port			08.38	H.M.								09.03				
Withington	Sun			08.41	loco)								09.06				
Chorlton Jcn	-light)			08/44						08/51		09/04	09/09				
Chorlton				08.46								09.07	09.11				
Throstle Nest S.				08/48						08/54		09/09	09/13				
Trafford Park																	
MANCHESTER (CENT)				08.54						09.00		09.15	09.19				

	J	Buxton)	T.71	H	T.71	J	Motor	Pcls	Pcls	J	B	A	B	Motor	F	A	Motor	J
Train	06.05		05.35			07.05		06.56	06.56	06.15	07.10	08.08	07.10		00.57	04.18		
From	M'ter		Toton			Rowsley		Derby	Derby	Swanwick	Derby	Sheff	Derby		Brent	St. P		
AMBERGATE			06/47					07/08		07/20	07.32				07/40	08.26		
Johnson's Sdgs																		
Whatstandwell			06/54							07/27	07.37				07/46			
High Peak Jcn																		
Cromford								07.18			07.44							
Matlock Bath								07.23			07.48							
MATLOCK								07.26	07.36		07.53					08.39		
Darley Dale									07.44		07.59							
Church Lane															08.12			
Rowsley S. Jcn				07/16					07/48	07.56								
ROWSLEY YARD	07.05		07.20	07.20						08.00								
Rowsley	07B13		07/24						07.52		08.05					08.48		
Haddon			07.37	07.40														
Bakewell				07.45					08.03		08.13							
Hassop											08.19							
Monsal Dale											08.24							
MILLERS DALE	07.55	08.00				08.05	08.13		08.19		08.32			08.38	09.07	09.13		
Millers Dale Jcn		08/02				08/11	08/15		08/21					08/40		09/15		
Peak Forest Jcn		(To				08/15	(To		(To		08/38			(To			(To	
Tunstead		Buxton)					Buxton)		Buxton)					Buxton)			Buxton)	
Great Rocks Jcn																		
Peak Forest						08.32					08.44					09.17		
P. Forest North																		
Chapel											08.50							
Chinley S. Jcn																		
Chinley N. Jcn											08/52	08/54				09/24		
CHINLEY											08.54	08.58	09.05			09/26		
Buxworth													09.08					
GOWHOLE																		09.30
New Mills S. Jcn											09/01		09/11			09/29		09/36
Disley													(Via					(To
Bramhall Moor Lane													GC)					Colly
CHEADLE HEATH											09/11					09/39		-hurst
Heaton Mersey																		St)
Didsbury																		
Withington																		
Chorlton Jcn											09/16					09/44		
Chorlton																		
Throstle Nest S.											09/19					09/47		
Trafford Park																		
MANCHESTER (CENT)											09.24					09.52		

WORKING TIMETABLE 1954 : PASSENGER & GOODS

	F	B	2 light	Motor	A	H	F	J	2 light	F	H	H	B	F	H	Motor	H
Train				09.40				09.05			08.02	08.02	08.25		09.00	10.25	09.00
From				Buxton				C'brook			B. Vue	B. Vue	MTR		H. Mersey	Buxton	H. Mersey
MANCHESTER (CENT)		08.25			09.00												
Trafford Park						08.50											
Throstle Nest S.		08/30			09/05	09/07	09/10										
Chorlton		08.33															
Chorlton Jcn		08/34			09/08	09/12	09/14										
Withington		08.38				(To	(To										
Didsbury		08.41			09.12	Dews-	Wath)										
Heaton Mersey		08.45				nap)											
CHEADLE HEATH		(Via			09/16												
Bramhall Moor Lane		GC)															
Disley																	
New Mills S. Jcn		09/21			09/30												09/43
GOWHOLE	09.05										09.30				09.40		
Buxworth Jcn																	
CHINLEY	09/18	09.27			09.38						09/42		09.43		09/51		09/55
Chinley N. Jcn	09/25										09/45		09/46		09/55		09/58
Chinley S. Jcn	(To												(To			(To	
Chapel	Black-												Sheff)			Avenue)	
Dove Holes T. North	well)										09/54				10/07		
Peak Forest N				09.40													
Peak Forest					09/50						10.05				10.20		10.40
Gt Rocks Jcn																	
Tunstead																	
Peak Forest Jcn				09/47							10/11						10/49
Millers Dale Jcn			09/47						10/00							10/32	
MILLERS DALE			09/49		09.59				10/06		10/16					10/34	10/54
Monsal Dale																	
Hassop																	
Bakewell																	
Haddon																	
Rowsley					10/12												
ROWSLEY YARD								10.22	10.30	10.35	10.42			10W49			11.25
Rowsley S. Jcn								10/26	10/39	10/46							
Church Lane											10.55	11.10					
Darley Dale																	
MATLOCK					10.21												
Matlock Bath																	
Cromford																	
High Peak Jcn																	
Whatstandwell								10/42		10/59	11/08			11/25			
Johnson's Sdgs																	
Ambergate					10/31			10/47		11/04	11/14			11/31			
Destination					St. P			Brands	B'well	Wigston	Kirkby						

	F	T.94	F	F	T.78	H	T.87	F	2 Light	T.71	T.71	T.71	T.45	F	Motor	T.70	T.71	T.45
Train	09.15			09.25		08.18								09.20	11.30			
From	Cheadle			C. St		Moston								Glaze	Buxton			
MANCHESTER (CENT)																		
Trafford Park		09.15																
Throstle Nest S.		09/24																
Chorlton																		
Chorlton Jcn		09/29																
Withington																		
Didsbury																		
Heaton Mersey		09/38																
CHEADLE HEATH	09/22	09/42												10w15				
Bramhall Moor Lane																		
Disley																		
New Mills S. Jcn	09/50	10/15		10/22		10/32	10/43							10/46				
GOWHOLE	09.55	10.20	10.25	10.27		10.38	10.48											
Buxworth Jcn														10L58				
CHINLEY		10/37												11/03				
Chinley N. Jcn		10/42												11/07				
Chinley S. Jcn		(To												(To				
Chapel		Stav-												Clay				
Dove Holes T. North		eley)												Cross)				
Peak Forest N																		
Peak Forest					10.32													
Gt Rocks Jcn																		
Tunstead																		
Peak Forest Jcn					10.40													
Millers Dale Jcn										11/10					11/37			
MILLERS DALE										11/13					11/39			
Monsal Dale																		
Hassop										11.14								
Bakewell										11.20	11.33							
Haddon										11.40	11.43							
Rowsley																		
ROWSLEY YARD					11.30		11.40				11.56					12.13	12.23	
Rowsley S. Jcn					11.34											12.17	12.27	
Church Lane																		
Darley Dale																	12.33	
MATLOCK																12.28		
Matlock Bath																		
Cromford																		
High Peak Jcn												12.00						
Whatstandwell						11/51						12.08						12.18
Johnson's Sdgs																		
Ambergate						11/56												12/23
Destination						Kirkby												A'gate

WORKING TIMETABLE 1954 : PASSENGER & GOODS

Class	J	J	B	A	A	T95	J		J	T.71	J	J	J	J	J	T95	D	E
Train	07.05	08.05	07.10	09.15	06.45			05.55			07.20	18.00		08.05	03.35			
From	Rowsley	Buxton	Derby	Buxton	Leic (GC)			Tibshelf			Staveley	Glendon		Buxton	Carlton			
AMBERGATE								08/31										
Johnson's Sdgs																		
Whatstandwell								08/39										
High Peak Jcn																		
Cromford																		
Matlock Bath																		
MATLOCK																		
Darley Dale																		
Church Lane																		
Rowsley S. Jcn								09/05										
ROWSLEY YARD							08.45	09.08										09.20
Rowsley							08B54											09/24
Haddon																		
Bakewell										08.57								
Hassop										09.05								
Monsal Dale																		
MILLERS DALE							09/35											09/59
Millers Dale Jcn							09/40											
Peak Forest Jcn		08/42		09/20			(To											10/05
Tunstead							Stock									09.47		
Great Rocks Jcn							-port)											
Peak Forest	08.45	09.00		09.27										09.41				
P. Forest North	08D53													09.48		10D06	10/16	
Chapel				09.33								09.38						
Chinley S. Jcn														10/04				
Chinley N. Jcn	09/10			09/35						09/46	09/48		(To			10/20	10/27	
CHINLEY	09/27			09.39						09/50	09/52		Sheff			10/23	10/30	
Buxworth													-ield)					
GOWHOLE	09.40							09.50		10.00		10.00		10.05				
New Mills S. Jcn				09/43				09/56			10/02	10/06		10/11		10/30	10/38	
Disley								(To				(To						(To
Bramhall Moor Lane			(Via					Stock				Brindle						Ancoats)
CHEADLE HEATH			GC)	09.55		10.05		-port)			10/30	Heath)		10/37		10/57		
Heaton Mersey			09.47			10.10					(To			10/43	10.50	(To		
Didsbury			09.50								Glaze				10.56	Wallers-		
Withington			09.53								-brook)					cote)		
Chorlton Jcn			09.55	10.01	10.06									10.53				
Chorlton			09.57															
Throstle Nest S.			10.00	10.04	10.09									10.58				
Trafford Park														11.07				
MANCHESTER (CENT)			10.06	10.09	10.14													

Class	H	J	Motor	H	J	J	A	Motor	J	T.70	T.45	T.45	H	J	J	D	F	B
Train		10.40		09.50	07.25	09.14	09.06		10.15		08.33	08.33		09.25	07.25		00.57	10.55
From		Avenue		Mottram	Kirkby	Derby	Notts		Mottram		Duffield	Duffield		G'thorpe	Kirkby		Brent	Sheff
AMBERGATE					08/50	09/35	10/02				10/15							
Johnson's Sdgs											10.20	10.27						
Whatstandwell					08/58	09/42						10.35						
High Peak Jcn																		
Cromford																		
Matlock Bath										10.15								
MATLOCK							10.13			10.22								
Darley Dale																		
Church Lane																	10.22	
Rowsley S. Jcn					09B31	10/05											10/24	
ROWSLEY YARD					09/34	10/09												
Rowsley					09/36		10/22										10/27	
Haddon																		
Bakewell							10.28											
Hassop																		
Monsal Dale																		
MILLERS DALE				10.05	10/14		10.43	10.48									10/58	
Millers Dale Jcn				10/07			10/50											
Peak Forest Jcn			(To		10/20		10/48	(To										
Tunstead			Buxton)					Buxton)							11.04	11/12		
Great Rocks Jcn																		
Peak Forest					10.40		10/53							10.55				
P. Forest North														11D04	11D23	11/33		
Chapel																		
Chinley S. Jcn																		
Chinley N. Jcn		10/50					11/01							11/17	11/26	11/37	11/47	11/58
CHINLEY		10/55					11/05							11/22	11/32	11/40	11/50	12.00
Buxworth																		
GOWHOLE	10.40	11.08												11.10	11.35	11.45		
New Mills S. Jcn	10/46						11/09							11/16		11/47	12/00	
Disley	(To																	
Bramhall Moor Lane	Heaton													11/39				
CHEADLE HEATH	Mersey)						11/19									12/10	12/30	
Heaton Mersey														(To		(To	(To	
Didsbury														Hale-		Hart-	Bruns-	
Withington														wood)		ford)	wick)	
Chorlton Jcn					11/07		11/24		11/34									
Chorlton																		
Throstle Nest S.					11/12		11/27		11/41									
Trafford Park					11.20				(To									
MANCHESTER (CENT)							11.32		Glaze)									

Class	H	K	H	D	F	A	Motor	Light	Light	F	B	H	K	A	B	J	J	Light
Train			11.35	08.45		09.30	12.05			09.00		08.52	12.35		10.50	09.45	08.00	
From			Buxton	W'cote		L'pool	Buxton			Port S.		B'wick	Rowsley		MTR	Walton	Garston	
MANCHESTER (CENT)						10.35					10.50				11.35			
Trafford Park																		
Throstle Nest S.						10/39					10/56	11/08			11/40		11/44	
Chorlton											10.59							
Chorlton Jcn						10/43					11/00	11/14			11/43		11/51	
Withington						(To					11.04	(To					(To	
Didsbury						Hull)					11.07	Dews-					Sheff)	
Heaton Mersey											11.11	nap)						
CHEADLE HEATH				10w51							11w17	(Via GC)			11/48			
Bramhall Moor Lane																		
Disley																		
New Mills S. Jcn				11/20							11.48	11/51			12/02			
GOWHOLE	10.50				11.25						11.53							
Buxworth Jcn											11.57							
CHINLEY	11/08			11/28	11/36						12.01				12.10	12.18			12.25
Chinley N. Jcn	11/14			11/31	11/40											12/21			12/28
Chinley S. Jcn					(To Stav-										12.18	(To Sheffield)		
Chapel					eley)													
Dove Holes T. North	11/25			11/40	eley)													
Peak Forest N								12.03										
Peak Forest	11/36			11/52											12.28				12/45
Gt Rocks Jcn				12.00														
Tunstead																		
Peak Forest Jcn	11/44							12/14										12/55
Millers Dale Jcn				11/56			**12/12**		12/26						12.37			12/40
MILLERS DALE	11/49			12/01			**12.14**		12/29						12.43			12/45	(to Buxton)
Monsal Dale															12.47			
Hassop																		
Bakewell															12.54			
Haddon																		
Rowsley															13.01			
ROWSLEY YARD	12.25	12.35	12.36					12.50										13.15
Rowsley S. Jcn				12/39														
Church Lane																		
Darley Dale															13.06			
MATLOCK															13.11			
Matlock Bath															13.15			
Cromford															13.18			
High Peak Jcn				12.55									13.10					
Whatstandwell													13.15		13.24			
Johnson's Sdgs																		
Ambergate															13.29			
Destination															**Derby**			

Class	F	T. 86	Light	H	Motor	F	H	T.70	H	T.94	T.92	T. 93	H	F	Light	B	T.95	J
Train				12.55	**13.20**	11.48	12.35						14.05	10.55	Ex			11.18
From				Buxton	**Buxton**	Cheadle	Rowsley						Rowsley	Northwich	B. Vue			G'thorpe
MANCHESTER (CENT)																12.06		
Trafford Park																		
Throstle Nest S.																12/11		
Chorlton																12.14		
Chorlton Jcn																12/15		
Withington																12.18		
Didsbury																12.21	12.27	
Heaton Mersey																12.25	12/32	
CHEADLE HEATH						11/55					12.03			12w18		(To S'port)	12.39	
Bramhall Moor Lane											12.13							
Disley																		
New Mills S. Jcn		12/15				12/25						12/34		12/49	12/54			
GOWHOLE	12.15	12.20									12.30	12.38			12.57			
Buxworth Jcn																		
CHINLEY	12/27					12/38				12.45				12/59				
Chinley N. Jcn	12/33					12/43								13/04				
Chinley S. Jcn		(To Black-				(To Round												13/18
Chapel		well)				-wood)												13/22
Dove Holes T. North														13/15				
Peak Forest N																		
Peak Forest														13.27				
Gt Rocks Jcn														13.37				
Tunstead																		
Peak Forest Jcn																		
Millers Dale Jcn				13/08	13/17	**13/27**												
MILLERS DALE				13/12	13/22	**13.29**												
ROWSLEY YARD				13.43	13.55								14.05					
Rowsley S. Jcn													14/09					
Church Lane																		
Darley Dale																		
MATLOCK								14.05										
Matlock Bath								14.13										
Cromford																		
High Peak Jcn									14.28				14.44					
Whatstandwell							14.02						14/48					
Johnson's Sdgs																		
Ambergate							14/10						14/54					
Destination							Derby						Staveley					

Class	J	T.93	J	A	J	B	T.78	J	T.87	J	T.73	K	T.70	H	A	Motor	J	B
Train				09.27	07.40	10.24		09.55			10.45			08.48	08.15		10.05	
From				Hull	Staveley	Derby		G'thorpe			A'gate			B'ham	St.P		Staveley	
AMBERGATE					10/36	10.46					10/54			11/20	11/40			
Johnson's Sdgs																		
Whatstandwell					10/42	10.51					11/00			11/26				
High Peak Jcn																		
Cromford						10.58												
Matlock Bath						11.02												
MATLOCK						11.07							11.21		11.52			
Darley Dale						11.13												
Church Lane																		
Rowsley S. Jcn						11/05					11/24		11/31	11/47				
ROWSLEY YARD			10.28			11.09				11.15	11.28	11.33	11.35	11.51				
Rowsley			10B36			11.21				11B26	11/38				12/01			
Haddon																		
Bakewell						11.29						11.51						
Hassop						11.35												
Monsal Dale						11.40												
MILLERS DALE			11/17			11.48					12/07				12.19		12.25	
Millers Dale Jcn			11/22								12/12						12/27	
Peak Forest Jcn			(To					12.01			(To						(To	
Tunstead			Long-								Buxton)						Buxton)	
Great Rocks Jcn			sight)															
Peak Forest						12.01		12.15							12/29			
P. Forest North						12.08												
Chapel																		
Chinley S. Jcn																		
Chinley N. Jcn						12/10		12/13							12/37		12/48	
CHINLEY						12.12		12/19							12.41		12/53	
Buxworth																		
GOWHOLE	12.10							12/30	12.35								13.05	
New Mills S. Jcn	12/16								12/41						12/45			
Disley									(To									
Bramhall Moor Lane		13.07							Ashton									
CHEADLE HEATH		13.36							Rd)						12/55			13.02
Heaton Mersey	(To																	13.06
Didsbury	Brindle																	13.09
Withington	Heath)																	13.12
Chorlton Jcn				12/37											13/00			13.15
Chorlton																		13.17
Throstle Nest S.				12/40											13/03			13.19
Trafford Park																		
MANCHESTER (CENT)				12.45											13.08			13.25

Class	B	B	Motor	Light	H	B	J	T.45	J	J	J	J	B	J	J	J	J	A	Motor
Train	10.24	13.37					10.23	08.33		10.02	10.23		12.35	10.30		11.40	10.40	10.15	
From	Derby	T. Dale					Codnor Pk	Duffield		Carlton	Codnor Pk		Sheff	Kirkby		Derby	Avenue	St.P	
AMBERGATE							11/08							11/49		12/15	12/23	13/05	
Johnson's Sdgs																			
Whatstandwell							11/14	11.17						11/56		12/22	12/30		
High Peak Jcn								11.20											
Cromford																			
Matlock Bath																			
MATLOCK																		13.17	
Darley Dale																			
Church Lane							11.44				12.01								
Rowsley S. Jcn											12B11			12B25		12/45	12/53		
ROWSLEY YARD				12.02							12/14			12/28	12.40	12.48	12.57		
Rowsley				12/07							12W20			12W34	12B50			13/26	
Haddon																			
Bakewell																			
Hassop																			
Monsal Dale																			
MILLERS DALE			12.40		12/44						13/01			13/15	13/31			13.41	13.50
Millers Dale Jcn			12/42											13/35					13.52
Peak Forest Jcn			(To		12/50						13/07			13/21					(To
Tunstead			Buxton)											Long-					Buxton)
Great Rocks Jcn														sight)					
Peak Forest												13B36						13/54	
P. Forest North					13/02						13D26								
Chapel											13.38								
Chinley S. Jcn																			
Chinley N. Jcn					13/14						13/30		13/39					14/02	
CHINLEY	12.50				13L20						13/35		13.41					14.06	
Buxworth	12.53																		
GOWHOLE			13.25							13.45	13.48								
New Mills S. Jcn	12/57		13/28	13/30						13/50								14/10	
Disley	(Via			(To						(To									
Bramhall Moor Lane	GC)			HM						Brew-									
CHEADLE HEATH				loco)	13/53	13.55				ery)								14/20	
Heaton Mersey	13.30	13.43			(To	13.59													
Didsbury	13.34	13.46			Walton)	14.03													
Withington	13.37	13.49				14.06													
Chorlton Jcn	13/40	13/52				14/09												14/25	
Chorlton	13.42	13.54				14.11													
Throstle Nest S.	13/45	13/56				14/13												14/28	
Trafford Park																			
MANCHESTER (CENT)	13.50	14.02				14.19												14.33	

Class	H	J	H	H	J	B		J	Light	F	H	T.94	H	B	F	Motor	T.92	A	A	B
Train		13.25	09.15				11.18			11.38			10.40		10.25	14.22			12.50	13.04
From		Buxton	Walton				G'thorpe			P'ton Jn			Walton		Walton	Buxton			L'pool	MTR
MANCHESTER (CENT)						12.30									13.04					13.45		13.50
Trafford Park						12.15			12.25												
Throstle Nest S.					12/26	12/35			12/44				12/50	13/09					13/50		13/55
Chorlton						12.38								13.12							
Chorlton Jcn					12/31	12/39			12/50				12/56	13/13					13/55		14/00
Withington					(To	12.42							(To	13.17						(To	
Didsbury					Sheff)	12.45							Dews-	13.20						PQ)	
Heaton Mersey						12.49			13.04				nap)	13.24							
CHEADLE HEATH			12w46			12.52			13w05							13w25			13/58		
Bramhall Moor Lane														(Via							
Disley									(To H.M. Loco)					GC)							
New Mills S. Jcn			13/20							13/40				14/04	13/53				14/12		
GOWHOLE	13.08			13.28						13.45					13.58		14.10				
Buxworth Jcn	13/13																14.18				
CHINLEY	13.20		13.32	13.40						14.10					14.11				14.20		14.23
Chinley N. Jcn	13/24			13/45																	14.28
Chinley S. Jcn				(To																	(To
Chapel				Sheffield)			13.46			14/18											Sheff)
Dove Holes T. North	13/32		13/45				13/57														
Peak Forest N																					
Peak Forest	13/43		13/56				14/09												14/32		
Gt Rocks Jcn																					
Tunstead																					
Peak Forest Jcn	13/50		14/06				14/17														
Millers Dale Jcn		13/58	14/10				(To Buxton)									14/29					
MILLERS DALE	13.55	14.03	14.14													14.31			14.41		
Monsal Dale																					
Hassop																					
Bakewell																					
Haddon																					
Rowsley																			14/54		
ROWSLEY YARD	14.30		14.42																		
Rowsley S. Jcn																					
Church Lane																					
Darley Dale																					
MATLOCK																			15.03		
Matlock Bath																					
Cromford																					
High Peak Jcn																					
Whatstandwell																					
Johnson's Sdgs																					
Ambergate																			15/13		
Destination																			St. P		

Class	J	H	J	F	Light	F	J	Light	T.93	3 light	3 light	J	H	J	D	H	Engine & Brake	T.94
Train		15.00	13.20			11.05	11.05					09.35	13.50	14.08	12.40	13.50		
From		Rowsley	P. Park			Garston	E. Port					Flint	P. Park	Glaze	Hartford	P. Park	Brake	
MANCHESTER (CENT)																		
Trafford Park																		
Throstle Nest S.														14/32				
Chorlton																		
Chorlton Jcn														14/38				
Withington														(To				
Didsbury														Wath)				
Heaton Mersey																		
CHEADLE HEATH						14w08			14.22							14w40		
Bramhall Moor Lane																		
Disley																		
New Mills S. Jcn				14/19		14/39	14/43		14/56				15/00		15/06			
GOWHOLE				14L28			14/47		14.55			15.00	15.05			15L10		
Buxworth Jcn																		
CHINLEY				14/42		14/54			15/07						15/14	15/22		
Chinley N. Jcn				14/50		14/58			15/12						15/18	15/26		
Chinley S. Jcn									(To									
Chapel									Royston)									15.36
Dove Holes T. North				15/00		15/10									15/23	15/34		15.44
Peak Forest N												15.27						
Peak Forest				15/12		15/22						15/30			15/31	15/46		15.56
Gt Rocks Jcn															15/40			
Tunstead																		
Peak Forest Jcn				15/22		15/30						15/38				15/57		
Millers Dale Jcn												15/44	15/50					
MILLERS DALE				15/28		15/37						15/47	15/55			16/04		
Monsal Dale																		
Hassop																		
Bakewell																		
Haddon																		
Rowsley				15w59														
ROWSLEY YARD	15.00	15.15		16.05			16.08					16.16	16.30			16.38	16.40	
Rowsley S. Jcn	15/04	15/19		16/10													16/44	
Church Lane																		
Darley Dale																		
MATLOCK																		
Matlock Bath																		
Cromford																		
High Peak Jcn	15.30		15.50															
Whatstandwell		15/40	15/55	16/21		16/33											17/06	
Johnson's Sdgs																		
Ambergate		15/48	16/01	16/28		16/40											17/13	
Destination		B'ham	Avenue	Kirkby		Derby											Toton	

Class	A	J	J	H	J	D	J	J	J	T.92	B	F	B	Motor	T.71	K	K	J
Train	08.00		10.23	14.40	10.30			13.50		T.92	13.05	12.08	13.05	Motor	T.71	11.33	11.33	
From	PQ		Codnor Pk	Park	Kirkby			Buxton			Derby	Avenue	Derby			Rowsley	Rowsley	
AMBERGATE											13.28							
Johnson's Sdgs																		
Whatstandwell											13.33							
High Peak Jcn																		
Cromford											13.40							
Matlock Bath											13.44							
MATLOCK											13.48							
Darley Dale											13.54				14.00			
Church Lane																		
Rowsley S. Jcn															14/09			
ROWSLEY YARD						13.24									14.13			
Rowsley						13B33					14.01							
Haddon																		
Bakewell											14.09					14.15		
Hassop											14.15							
Monsal Dale											14.19							
MILLERS DALE							14/14				14.25		14.38	14.45		14.48	15.00	
Millers Dale Jcn														14/47				
Peak Forest Jcn							14/20	14/28						(To			15.10	
Tunstead						14.06								Buxton)				
Great Rocks Jcn																		
Peak Forest					14.00		14B37	14.43					14.51					
P. Forest North					14/05	14D25												
Chapel			14.08										14.58					
Chinley S. Jcn																		
Chinley N. Jcn			14/16		14/24	14/39						14/55	15/00					
CHINLEY			14/20		14/29	14/42						15/00	15.06					
Buxworth											14.50		15.09					
GOWHOLE		14.20			14.38				14.50	14.57		15.15						15.12
New Mills S. Jcn		14/26	14/36			14/49			14/56				15/12					15/18
Disley		(To	(To										(Via					(To
Bramhall Moor Lane		Colly-	Age-										GC)					Heaton
CHEADLE HEATH		hurst	croft)			15/12			15/24									Mersey)
Heaton Mersey		St)				(To			15/28				15.47					
Didsbury						North-							15.51					
Withington						wich)							15.54					
Chorlton Jcn	14/28			15/11					15/38				15.57					
Chorlton													15.59					
Throstle Nest S.	14/31			15/16					15/43				16.01					
Trafford Park				(To					15.52									
MANCHESTER (CENT)	14.37			Widnes)									16.07					

Class	J	J	J	J	K	J	ECS	H	J	B	H	T.92	J	K	D	T.93	J	H
Train	13.10	13.24	10.30	13.50	11.33	13.05		11.10			14.30	T.92	14.10			T.93		15.50
From	Avenue	Rowsley	Kirkby	Buxton	Rowsley	B'well		S. Gate			Rowsley		W'bank					Mottram
AMBERGATE								13/45										
Johnson's Sdgs																		
Whatstandwell								13/58										
High Peak Jcn																		
Cromford																		
Matlock Bath																		
MATLOCK																		
Darley Dale																		
Church Lane																		
Rowsley S. Jcn									14/26									
ROWSLEY YARD								14.30	14.30									14.45
Rowsley								14/34										14B53
Haddon																		
Bakewell																		
Hassop																		
Monsal Dale																		
MILLERS DALE								15/12					15.20					15/34
Millers Dale Jcn													15/25					
Peak Forest Jcn					15.30			15/20					(To					15/40
Tunstead													Buxton)		15.43			
Great Rocks Jcn					15.40													
Peak Forest		14.54		15.23														
P. Forest North		14/59		15/26					15/36						16D02			
Chapel																		
Chinley S. Jcn				15.42														
Chinley N. Jcn	15/13	15/15		(To		15/37		15/52					16/11		16/15			
CHINLEY	15/18	15/19		Winco-		15/42	15.45	15/55					16/15		16/19			
Buxworth				bank)														
GOWHOLE	15.30		15.27			15.52						16.20	16.27			16.35		
New Mills S. Jcn		15/29	15/32				15/50	16/02					16/26		16/30	16/41		
Disley		(To											(To			16.48		
Bramhall Moor Lane		Ashton											Heaton					
CHEADLE HEATH		15/57	Rd)					16w27		16.32	16w40	Mersey)			17/00			
Heaton Mersey		(To						(To		16.36	16/47				(To			
Didsbury		Gars-						New		16.40					Wallers-			
Withington		ton)						Mills)		16.43					cote)			
Chorlton Jcn										16/46	16/57							17/06
Chorlton										16/48								
Throstle Nest S.										16/50	17/02							17/11
Trafford Park											17.11							17/24
MANCHESTER (CENT)										16.56								

WORKING TIMETABLE 1954 : PASSENGER & GOODS

Class	Motor	F	F	J	B	B	F	F	Light	Motor	B	F	B	A	B	Light	J	Light
Train	16.03			12.30		14.50	13.40	14.18		16.33	16.10	13.17			14.50		12.30	
From	Buxton			Walton		MTR	B. Heath	Hartford		Buxton	N. Mills	Garston			MTR		Walton	
MANCHESTER (CENT)					14.50									15.35	16.00			
Trafford Park																		
Throstle Nest S.					14/55									15/40	16/05			
Chorlton					14.59									15.43				
Chorlton Jcn					15.00									15.44	16/08			
Withington					15.04									15.47				
Didsbury					15.07									15.50				
Heaton Mersey					15.11									15.54				
CHEADLE HEATH				15w00	(Via						15L45			15.57	16/13			
Bramhall Moor Lane					GC)													
Disley																		
New Mills S. Jcn				15.34	15/48		16/01	16/09		16/13	16/18				16/27			
GOWHOLE	15.15	15.25					16.05	16.14										
Buxworth Jcn					15.54					16.19								
CHINLEY	15.29	15.37	15.46	15.58	16.03					16.25					16/32			
Chinley N. Jcn	15.35	15.42	15.50	16/05						16.28	16/35							
Chinley S. Jcn	(To	(To								(To	(To							
Chapel	Stav-	W'bank)			16.11					H'sage)	Danes-							
Dove Holes T. North	eley)		15.58								moor)							
Peak Forest N									16.25									16.52
Peak Forest			16/09		16.21				16/28						16/43			16/55
Gt Rocks Jcn																		
Tunstead																		
Peak Forest Jcn			16/15						16/31									17/00
Millers Dale Jcn	16.10									16/40						16/56		
MILLERS DALE	16.12			16.22	16.30					16.42					16.52	16/59	17.03	
Monsal Dale					16.36													
Hassop					16.40													
Bakewell					16.46													
Haddon																		
Rowsley					16.53										17/05		17w35	
ROWSLEY YARD																17.25		
Rowsley S. Jcn																		
Church Lane					16.58										17.21			
Darley Dale															17.25			
MATLOCK														17.15	17.35			
Matlock Bath															17.39			
Cromford															17.44			
High Peak Jcn																		
Whatstandwell															17.50		17/58	
Johnson's Sdgs																		
Ambergate														17/25	17.55		18/04	
Destination														St.P	Derby		Kirkby	

Class	J	Light	F	B	H	B	B	F	Motor	A	B	Light	H	H	B	B	Light	Light
Train			16.10		15.03	16.03			17.20		17.46			15.03		17.24		
From			Cheadle		G'thorpe	MTR			Buxton		Buxton			G'thorpe		N. Mills		
MANCHESTER (CENT)						16.03	16.15			16.32					16.36			
Trafford Park																		
Throstle Nest S.						16/08	16/19			16/37					16/41			
Chorlton						16.11	16.23								16.44			
Chorlton Jcn						16/12	16/24			16/40					16/45			
Withington						16.16	(To								16.48			
Didsbury						16.19	G. Bge)								16.51			
Heaton Mersey						16.23				16/44					16.55			
CHEADLE HEATH			16/17			(Via				(Via					(To			
Bramhall Moor Lane						GC)				GC)					S'port)			
Disley																		
New Mills S. Jcn					16/45	17/01				17/14						17/27		
GOWHOLE					16.50			17.10										
Buxworth Jcn						17.07				17.22						17.33		
CHINLEY						17.11		17.21		17.22						17.37		
Chinley N. Jcn						17/18		17/25		17/25								
Chinley S. Jcn					17/15	(To		(To										
Chapel					17w10	Cheff)		Avenue)		17.31				17w37				
Dove Holes T. North														17/44				
Peak Forest N											17.42							
Peak Forest	17.00									17.39	17.45			17.55				
Gt Rocks Jcn																		
Tunstead																		
Peak Forest Jcn	17/10										17/58							
Millers Dale Jcn	17/15								17.27		17.53							18/07
MILLERS DALE	17.15	17.22							17.29	17.48	17.56							18/12
Monsal Dale											18.02							
Hassop											18.06							
Bakewell										17.59	18.11					18.27		
Haddon																		
Rowsley										18.05	18.18					18.39		
ROWSLEY YARD													18.25			18.50		
Rowsley S. Jcn													18.29					
Church Lane																		
Darley Dale											18.23							
MATLOCK										18.13	18.30							
Matlock Bath											18.34							
Cromford											18.38							
High Peak Jcn																		
Whatstandwell											18.44			18/50				
Johnson's Sdgs																		
Ambergate										18/23	18.50			18/56				
Destination										Notts	Derby			Beeston				

WORKING TIMETABLE 1954 : PASSENGER & GOODS

Class	K	J	J	B	T.93	B	J	B	B	J	T.70	Motor	J	Motor	J	J	J	B
Train	11.33	14.45	14.15			17.42	03.35	16.25	16.25	13.17						03.35	14.45	16.30
From	Rowsley	Rowsley	Avenue			T. Dale	Glendon	Buxton	Buxton	Kirkby						Glendon	B'well	Sheff
AMBERGATE							14/16			14/44								
Johnson's Sdgs																		
Whatstandwell							14/23			14/51								
High Peak Jcn																		
Cromford																		
Matlock Bath										15.10								
MATLOCK										15.17								
Darley Dale																		
Church Lane																		
Rowsley S. Jcn							14B54			15B19								
ROWSLEY YARD							14/57			15/22		15.40				16.20		
Rowsley							15w07			15w31		15B50				16B26		
Haddon																		
Bakewell																		
Hassop																		
Monsal Dale																		
MILLERS DALE							15/54			16/12		16.18	16/31	16.56		17/09		
Millers Dale Jcn												16/20		16/58		17/14		
Peak Forest Jcn		15.49					16/00	16/32		16/18		(To Buxton)	16/38	(To Buxton)		(To Stockport)		
Tunstead																		
Great Rocks Jcn	16.07																	
Peak Forest	16.15							16.39		16D44								
P. Forest North		16D10					16B20			16/50			17D01					
Chapel								16.48					17.16					
Chinley S. Jcn																		
Chinley N. Jcn		16/28	16/28				16/39	16/50		17/08							17/24	17/33
CHINLEY		16/32	16/37				16L48	16.52	17.03	17/12							17/28	17/35
Buxworth									17.06									
GOWHOLE		16.43	16.50				17.03			17.25							17.35	17.47
New Mills S. Jcn									17/09								17/40	
Disley					17.18				(To New Mills)									
Bramhall Moor Lane					17.33													
CHEADLE HEATH				17.31													18/10	
Heaton Mersey				17.35		17.48											(To Glaze-brook)	
Didsbury				17.38		17.51												
Withington				17.41		17.54												
Chorlton Jcn				17.44		17.57												
Chorlton				17.46		17.59												
Throstle Nest S.				17.48		18.01												
Trafford Park																		
MANCHESTER (CENT)				17.54		18.07												

Class	ECS	J	J	B	B	A	B	Motor	B	T.93	J	J	H	J	B	B	D	J
Train	17.15	14.45	15.00	18.04	16.10	14.15	16.10					13.58		15.40	17.05	17.05		16.45
From	H'sage	C. Park	Kirkby	G. Bge	Derby	St.P	Derby					Codnor Pk		Rowsley	R'ham	R'ham		Buxton
AMBERGATE		15/50	16.20		16.32	17/12												
Johnson's Sdgs																		
Whatstandwell		15/58	16/27		16.37													
High Peak Jcn																		
Cromford					16.44													
Matlock Bath					16.48													
MATLOCK					16.53													
Darley Dale					16.59													
Church Lane																		
Rowsley S. Jcn		16/26	16/51															
ROWSLEY YARD		16.30	16.55															
Rowsley					17.05	17/28												
Haddon																		
Bakewell					17.13													
Hassop					17.19													
Monsal Dale					17.24													
MILLERS DALE					17.32	17.48	17.53											
Millers Dale Jcn							17/55											
Peak Forest Jcn							(To Buxton)											18/30
Tunstead																		
Great Rocks Jcn																		
Peak Forest					17.45	17.58												18.46
P. Forest North																18D29		
Chapel					17.52									18.10				
Chinley S. Jcn																		
Chinley N. Jcn	17.48				17.54	18.06						18.09			18.39			18.50
CHINLEY	17.50				17.59	18.10						18L17		18.28	18.41	18.47		18.54
Buxworth					18.02											18.50		19L02
GOWHOLE												18.30	18.30	18.45				
New Mills S. Jcn					18/05	18/14						18/36		18/51		18/53		19/07
Disley					(Via GC)		(Via GC)					(To Brewery)				(Via GC)		
Bramhall Moor Lane												18.33						
CHEADLE HEATH						18.27						19.00		19.00	18.45	19/14		19/37
Heaton Mersey							18.39						(To Halewood)		18.49	19.25		(To Hartford)
Didsbury							18.43								18.53	19.29		
Withington							18.46								18.56	19.32		
Chorlton Jcn				18/24	18/33		18/49								18/59	19/35		
Chorlton				18.26			18.51								19.01	19.37		
Throstle Nest S.				18.28	18/36		18/53								19.03	19/39		
Trafford Park																		
MANCHESTER (CENT)				18.34	18.41		18.59								19.09	19.45		

WORKING TIMETABLE 1954 : PASSENGER & GOODS

	B	Light	B	B	A	B	Motor	B	A	B	A	B	F	B	F	B	F	J
Class																		
Train	17.24						18.25		16.30									18.35
From	N. Mills						Buxton		L'pool									Buxton
MANCHESTER (CENT)			17.00	17.10	17.22			17.30	17.35	17.43	17.50			17.55		18.05		
Trafford Park		16.38																
Throstle Nest S.		16/45	17/05	17/15	17/27			17/35	17/39	17/48	17/55			18/00		18/10		
Chorlton			17.08	17.18				17.38						18.03		18.13		
Chorlton Jcn		16/52	17/09	17/19	17/30			17/39	17/43	17.51	17/58			18/04		18/14		
Withington			17.12	17.22				17.43	(To Hull)	17/53				18.08		18.18		
Didsbury			17.16	17.25				17.46		(To G. Bge)				18.11		18.21		
Heaton Mersey		17/05	17.20	17.29				17.50						18.15		18.25		
CHEADLE HEATH		(To H.M. loco)	17.23	(To S'port)	17.38			17.53			18/03			18.18		18.28		
Bramhall Moor Lane																		
Disley																		
New Mills S. Jcn					17/54						18/17							
GOWHOLE															18.20			
Buxworth Jcn																		
CHINLEY	17.45				18.02	18.05					18.26	18.31			18/36			
Chinley N. Jcn	17/48					18/08						18/34			18/40			
Chinley S. Jcn						(To Sheff)					(To Sheff)				(To Avenue)			
Chapel	17.54				18.10													
Dove Holes T. North																		
Peak Forest N																		
Peak Forest	18.06				18.21						18/38							
Gt Rocks Jcn																		
Tunstead																		
Peak Forest Jcn	18.11				18/26													
Millers Dale Jcn	(To Buxton)				(To Buxton)		18/32											18/55
MILLERS DALE							18.34				18.47							19.00
Monsal Dale																		
Hassop																		
Bakewell																		
Haddon																		
Rowsley											19/00							
ROWSLEY YARD														19.05		19.42		
Rowsley S. Jcn														19/09		19/46		
Church Lane																		
Darley Dale																		
MATLOCK											19.11							
Matlock Bath																		
Cromford																		
High Peak Jcn																		
Whatstandwell														19/26		20/05		
Johnson's Sdgs																		
Ambergate											19/24			19/31		20/10		
Destination											St P.			L. Mill		B'well		

	J	F	Light	Light	T.45	J	Motor	Light	Light	Light	B	Motor	D	F	J	B	E	H
Class																		
Train	18.35	ex	ex		16.35	19.40						20.24	17.00				17.15	
From	Buxton	Buxton	Buxton		G'thorpe	Buxton						Buxton	Hartford				Wigan	
MANCHESTER (CENT)											18.30					18.45		
Trafford Park																		19.00
Throstle Nest S.											18.35					18.50	19/03	19/09
Chorlton											18.39					18.54		
Chorlton Jcn											18.40					18/55	19/08	19/15
Withington											18.43					18.59	(To Dews-nap)	
Didsbury											18.46					19.02		
Heaton Mersey											18.50					19.06		19/24
CHEADLE HEATH											18.53		18w58			(Via GC)		19.30
Bramhall Moor Lane																		
Disley																		
New Mills S. Jcn													19/24			19/49		
GOWHOLE		18.42											19.30					
Buxworth Jcn																19.55		
CHINLEY		18/54											19/32	19/43		19.59		
Chinley N. Jcn		19/00											19/36	19/48				
Chinley S. Jcn		(To W'bank)				19/06							(To					
Chapel						19|14							Black-					
Dove Holes T. North						19/21							well) 19/41					
Peak Forest N								19.40										
Peak Forest						19/35		19/43					19.49					
Gt Rocks Jcn													19.58					
Tunstead																		
Peak Forest Jcn						19/42		19/48										
Millers Dale Jcn			19/25	19/37		(To Buxton)	19/47		20/06			20/31						
MILLERS DALE	19.18		19.30	19.40			19.49		20.10			20.33						
Monsal Dale																		
Hassop																		
Bakewell																		
Haddon																		
Rowsley																		
ROWSLEY YARD	19.51		20.00	20.10	20.15						20.35	20.37				20.50		
Rowsley S. Jcn				20/19								20/40				20/54		
Church Lane																		
Darley Dale																		
MATLOCK												20.53						
Matlock Bath																		
Cromford																		
High Peak Jcn																		
Whatstandwell					20/42											21/17		
Johnson's Sdgs																		
Ambergate					20/49											21/21		
Destination					Derby											Kirkby		

	J	H	B	B	A	J	J	J	J	Motor	J	J	F	B	J	T.70	J	B
Train	15.40		17.05	18.00	16.13			18.55			13.17	16.30	15.50	18.45	16.35		15.45	17.50
From	Rowsley		Derby	Sheff	Hull			Peak F.			Kirkby	Avenue	Toton	Sheff	Corby		Tibshelf	Derby
AMBERGATE			17/23												17/28		17/58	18/17
Johnson's Sdgs																		
Whatstandwell			17.27												17/40		18/04	18.22
High Peak Jcn																		
Cromford			17.34															18.29
Matlock Bath			17.38															18.33
MATLOCK			17.42													18.13		18.37
Darley Dale			17.48															18.42
Church Lane																		
Rowsley S. Jcn															18B10	18/28	18/36	
ROWSLEY YARD		17.20													18/14	18.33	18.40	
Rowsley		17B32		17.54											18w24			
Haddon																		
Bakewell				18.01														
Hassop																		
Monsal Dale																		
MILLERS DALE		18/25						18.55							19/11			
Millers Dale Jcn		18/32						18/57										
Peak Forest Jcn		(To						(To							19/18			
Tunstead		Garston)						Buxton)										
Great Rocks Jcn																		
Peak Forest						18.55												
P. Forest North						19/02									19B43			
Chapel						19.12	19L20											
Chinley S. Jcn							19/25											
Chinley N. Jcn				19/11			(To					19/30	19/38	19/55	20/07			
CHINLEY	19.02			19.13			Winco					19/35	19/43	19.57	20L15			
Buxworth							-bank)											
GOWHOLE	19.15					19.20			19.30		19.40	19.47						
New Mills S. Jcn						19/26			19/38		19/46	19/51						
Disley						(To			(To		(To							
Bramhall Moor Lane						Heaton			Stuart		Ashton							
CHEADLE HEATH						Mersey)			St)		Rd)	20/12						
Heaton Mersey												20/16						
Didsbury																		
Withington																		
Chorlton Jcn					19/53							20/26						
Chorlton																		
Throstle Nest S.					19/56							20/35						
Trafford Park												20.44						
MANCHESTER (CENT)					20.01													

	T.45	Light	T.45	A	B	Motor	J	J	T.94	H	H	K	J	B	B	Motor	H	T94
Train	18.02		18.02	16.15	18.45		16.35	15.40		11.55	20.20	18.50	18.35	19.16	19.16		21.35	Light
From	A'gate		A'gate	St.P	Sheff		Corby	Rowsley		C'field	Mottram	Buxton	Derby	Derby	Derby		Park	
AMBERGATE	18/24			19/21									19/30	19.40				
Johnson's Sdgs																		
Whatstandwell	18/33												19/37	19.45				
High Peak Jcn																		
Cromford														19.52				
Matlock Bath														19.56				
MATLOCK	18.49		19.01	19.33										20.01				
Darley Dale		18.50												20.06				
Church Lane																		
Rowsley S. Jcn			19/16										20/00					
ROWSLEY YARD			19.20										20.04					
Rowsley		18.56		19/42										20.11				
Haddon																		
Bakewell														20.19				
Hassop																		
Monsal Dale																		
MILLERS DALE				20.01	20.07									20.35	20.39	20.55		
Millers Dale Jcn					20/09											20/57		
Peak Forest Jcn					(To							20/16				(To		
Tunstead					Buxton)											Buxton)		
Great Rocks Jcn																		
Peak Forest				20/11					20.14			20.35			20.52			
P. Forest North									20/21									
Chapel															21.00			
Chinley S. Jcn																		
Chinley N. Jcn				20/19						20/35	20/40				21/02			
CHINLEY				20.23	20.26		20L17			20/40	20/48				21.07			
Buxworth															21.10			
GOWHOLE								20.40		20.52	21.00							21.30
New Mills S. Jcn				20/27	20/31		20/34	20/45							21/13			21/33
Disley					(Via										(Via			(To
Bramhall Moor Lane					GC)										GC)			H.M.
CHEADLE HEATH				20/37			21/02		21/13									loco)
Heaton Mersey					21.01		(To		21/17						21.47			
Didsbury				20.41	21.05		Glaze								21.51			
Withington					21.08		-brook)								21.54			
Chorlton Jcn				20/45	21/11			21/27			21/38				21/57		22/05	
Chorlton					21.13										21.59			
Throstle Nest S.				20/48	21/15			21/32			21/43				22/01		22/10	
Trafford Park								21.41			21.51						(To Wigan)	
MANCHESTER (CENT)				20.53	21.21										22.07			

WORKING TIMETABLE 1954 : PASSENGER & GOODS

Class	H	A	A	J	T.87	B	E	J	T.78	H	2 light	E	H	C	T.88	H	F	Motor
Train			19.35		19.42	18.45	19.30	19.30	Light	19.00	ex		19.35	ECS	17.55		18.10	22.00
From			MTR		Bredbury	MTR	Ancoats	H. Mersey		T. Park	Buxton		P. Park		Ashton Rd		Husk'son	Buxton
MANCHESTER (CENT)			19.35															
Trafford Park	19.15																19.55	
Throstle Nest S.	19/24	19/40															20/04	
Chorlton																		
Chorlton Jcn	19/29	19/43															20/08	
Withington	(To																(To	
Didsbury	Dews-																Ashton	
Heaton Mersey	nap)																Rd)	
CHEADLE HEATH		19.50								19.55							20w42	
Bramhall Moor Lane																		
Disley																		
New Mills S. Jcn		20/06			20/09		20/16	20/30		20/32			20/40		21/06		21/15	
GOWHOLE						20.14		20.35					20.45		21.11			
Buxworth Jcn																		
CHINLEY		20.12	20.19			20.27	20.30			20.44				21.02			21.25	
Chinley N. Jcn			20/22			20/30	20/33			20/47								
Chinley S. Jcn						(To												
Chapel			20.28			Sheff)												
Dove Holes T. North							20/41			20/56							21/36	
Peak Forest N																		
Peak Forest			20.38				20/51		20.58	21/07				21/18			21/46	
Gt Rocks Jcn																		
Tunstead																		
Peak Forest Jcn							20/57		21/06	21/13				21/25			21/52	
Millers Dale Jcn									(To Buxton)		21/30			(To Buxton)				22/07
MILLERS DALE			20.49				21/02			21/18	21/33						21/57	22.09
Monsal Dale																		
Hassop			20.56															
Bakewell			21.02															
Haddon																		
Rowsley			21.09															
ROWSLEY YARD							21.28			21.50	22.00		22.05				22.23	
Rowsley S. Jcn													22/09					
Church Lane																		
Darley Dale			21.14															
MATLOCK			21.20	21.27														
Matlock Bath			21.24															
Cromford			21.27															
High Peak Jcn																		
Whatstandwell			21.33	21.44									22/25					
Johnson's Sdgs																		
Ambergate			21.28	21/54									22/30					
Destination			Derby	Derby									Brent					

Class	F	H	H	J	F	Light	H	F	F	T.79	E	E	B	D	B	2 light	2 light
Train	18.05	19.35			18.50	ex		20.25		Light	21.20	21.20	21.30	19.25	21.30		
From	B'wick	P. Park			Halew'd	B. Vue		Moston			Ancoats	Ancoats		Husk'son	MTR		
MANCHESTER (CENT)													21.30				
Trafford Park		20/20									21.17						
Throstle Nest S.											21/25		21.35	21.40			
Chorlton		20/26											21.38				
Chorlton Jcn		(To									21/30		21.39	21.45			
Withington		Dews-									(To						
Didsbury		nap)									York)		21.44				
Heaton Mersey													21.48	21.55			
CHEADLE HEATH					21w00								(Via	(To			
Bramhall Moor Lane													GC)	York)			
Disley																	
New Mills S. Jcn					21/32	21/37		21/53				22/10	22/25				
GOWHOLE			21.25					21.55									
Buxworth Jcn			21/33										22.31				
CHINLEY			21/39		21/46	21/52		22/03	22/08			22/20	22.35		22.46		
Chinley N. Jcn			21/43		21/50	21/57		22/07	22/12			22/25			22/49		
Chinley S. Jcn					(To				(To			22/28			(To		
Chapel					Avenue)				Avenue)	22w33		22w38			Sheff)		
Dove Holes T. North			21/51			22/04		22/14				22/46					
Peak Forest N																23.07	
Peak Forest			22/02	22.06		22/12		22/24		22.43		22/57				23.10	
Gt Rocks Jcn						22.15											
Tunstead																	
Peak Forest Jcn			22/08	22/16				22/30		22/50		23/06				23/14	
Millers Dale Jcn			22/15	(To						(To						23/25	
MILLERS DALE			22/20	Buxton)				22/35		Buxton)		23/11				23/27	
Monsal Dale																	
Hassop																	
Bakewell																	
Haddon																	
Rowsley																	
ROWSLEY YARD	22.30				22.48			22.55	23.01			23.37				23.52	
Rowsley S. Jcn	22/36							22/59									
Church Lane																	
Darley Dale																	
MATLOCK																	
Matlock Bath																	
Cromford																	
High Peak Jcn																	
Whatstandwell	22/53							23/20									
Johnson's Sdgs																	
Ambergate	22/58							23/26									
Destination	Derby							Staveley									

Class	H	J	J	J	Light	T.87	J	J	J	H	H	J	B	A	B	Motor	D
Train	11.55	18.50		19.05	ex			18.08		21.25			21.24	18.40	21.24		
From	C'field	B'well		Staveley	G. Bge			G'thorpe		Mottram			Sheff	St. P	Sheff		
AMBERGATE															21/43		
Johnson's Sdgs																	
Whatstandwell																	
High Peak Jcn																	
Cromford																	
Matlock Bath																	
MATLOCK															21.54		
Darley Dale																	
Church Lane																	
Rowsley S. Jcn																	
ROWSLEY YARD			20.10					20.20	20.35		20.45	21.00					
Rowsley			20B18					20B28	20B43		20B53	21B08			22/03		
Haddon																	
Bakewell																	
Hassop																	
Monsal Dale																	
MILLERS DALE			20/59					21/09	21/22		21/34	21.52			22.20	22.25	
Millers Dale Jcn									21/29							22/27	
Peak Forest Jcn			21/05					21/15	(To		21/40					(To	22.00
Tunstead									Stock							Buxton)	
Great Rocks Jcn									-port)			(Fwd					
Peak Forest												at					
P. Forest North			21D26					21D37			21B59	22.32)			22/30		22D38
Chapel											22.15						
Chinley S. Jcn																	
Chinley N. Jcn		21/36	21/45	21/50				21/54		22/10	(Fwd		22/24	22/38			22/50
CHINLEY		21/41	21/50	21/55				22w03		22/17	at 22.53)		22/26	22/41	22/46		22/54
Buxworth																	
GOWHOLE	21.35	21.55		22.05		22.10		22.30									
New Mills S. Jcn	21/41		22/00			22/15	22/20						22/45	22/50			23/01
Disley	(To		(To			(To	(To								(Via		
Bramhall Moor Lane	Cheadle)		Brindle			Brindle	Heaton								GC)		
CHEADLE HEATH	22/10		Heath)			Heath)	Mersey)						22/55				23/24
Heaton Mersey	(To													23/21			(To
Didsbury	Cheadle)												22.59	23.24			Hartford)
Withington																	
Chorlton Jcn				22/29						22/45			23/03	23/27			
Chorlton																	
Throstle Nest S.				22/33						22/52			23/06	23/30			
Trafford Park				22.40						(To							
MANCHESTER (CENT)										Glaze)			23.11	23.36			

Class	J	H	E	T.88	J	J	J	E	F	J	J	J	F	E	J	E
Train		20.45	19.35		21.00	21.00		20.25	22.18			20.30	21.50	21.10		21.30
From		Rowsley	Derby		Rowsley	Rowsley		Burton	G'thorpe			Kirkby	Derby	Leic		B'ham
AMBERGATE								21/53				22/14	22/38	23/23		23/32
Johnson's Sdgs																
Whatstandwell								21/58				22/23	22/44	23/28		23/37
High Peak Jcn																
Cromford																
Matlock Bath																
MATLOCK																
Darley Dale																
Church Lane																
Rowsley S. Jcn								22/14				22B52	23/10	23/44		23/54
ROWSLEY YARD					21.58			22.18	22.40			22/55	23/13	23.48	23.55	23.58
Rowsley					22B12				22B49			23w02	23w20		00B04	
Haddon																
Bakewell																
Hassop																
Monsal Dale																
MILLERS DALE					22.32	22.53			23.31			23.43	00/00			00/46
Millers Dale Jcn						22.57			23.40							00/51
Peak Forest Jcn					22/41			(To	(To			23/50	00/10			(To
Tunstead								Edge	Ash				00.20			Long-
Great Rocks Jcn								Hill)	Bridge)			23.35				sight)
Peak Forest																
P. Forest North					23D01							23D50	00D10			
Chapel		22.53														
Chinley S. Jcn																
Chinley N. Jcn		22/57	23/05		23/18			23/55				00/08	00/31			
CHINLEY		23/01	23/10		23.23			00w06				00/15	00/36			
Buxworth																
GOWHOLE	23.00				23/20	23.35	23.55									00.51
New Mills S. Jcn	23/06	23/08			23/20	23/26	00/01					00/15	00/35			
Disley	(To		(To		(To	(To		(To				(To				
Bramhall Moor Lane	Heaton		Garston)		B.Vue)	Ashton		St				Heysham)				
CHEADLE HEATH	Mersey)	23/35		23L55	Rd)			Helens)								
Heaton Mersey		(To		00/02												
Didsbury		Garston)														
Withington																
Chorlton Jcn				00/12												
Chorlton																
Throstle Nest S.				00.16												
Trafford Park				(To												
MANCHESTER (CENT)				Warr'ton)												

	C	C	F	B	Light	F	A	H	F	F
WORKING TIMETABLE 1954 : PASSENGER & GOODS										
Class	C	C	F	**B**	Light	F	**A**	H	F	F
Train	22.00	22.00							22.35	22.40
From	Ancoats	Ancoats							H.M.	Ancoats
MANCHESTER (CENT)				**22.10**			**22.35**			
Trafford Park		21.40			22.17			22.36		
Throstle Nest S.		21/49		**22/15**	22/22		**22/40**	22/47		
Chorlton				**22.18**						
Chorlton Jcn		21/54		**22/19**	22/27		**22/44**	22/52		
Withington				**22.22**			**(To M'bone)**	(To Dews		
Didsbury				**22.25**				-nap)		
Heaton Mersey		22/04		**22/29**	22/36					
CHEADLE HEATH		22.14		**22.32**	22/39					
Bramhall Moor Lane										
Disley										
New Mills S. Jcn	22/42			22/53	23/07				23/25	23/40
GOWHOLE						23.20			23/45	23.55
Buxworth Jcn								23/30	(Fwd	
CHINLEY	22/56			23/07	23/17	23/32		23/38	at	00/07
Chinley N. Jcn	22/59			23/10	23/20	23/37		23/42	00.44)	00/12
Chinley S. Jcn					(To	(To				(To
Chapel	23w06	23w11			Sheffield)	Black-				Stav-
Dove Holes T. North		23/15		23/25	well)			23/52		eley)
Peak Forest N										
Peak Forest		23/22		23/35				00/03		
Gt Rocks Jcn										
Tunstead										
Peak Forest Jcn		23/32		23/42				00/09		
Millers Dale Jcn										
MILLERS DALE		23/37		23/47				00/14		
Monsal Dale										
Hassop										
Bakewell										
Haddon										
Rowsley		23/58								
ROWSLEY YARD				00.15				00.42		
Rowsley S. Jcn										
Church Lane										
Darley Dale										
MATLOCK										
Matlock Bath										
Cromford										
High Peak Jcn										
Whatstandwell		00/13								
Johnson's Sdgs										
Ambergate		00/18								
Destination				St. P						

Black 5 4-6-0 44694 of Low Moor, Bradford, finds itself filling-in with the 16.31 Sheffield - Chinley on a summer day in 1963 and enters its fireman's viewfinder during the stop at Edale. 44694's driver, B. Emmerson, was something of a celebrity locally, being the grandson of the first man to drive a train into Buxton. His grandfather originated in the North East, where he had been one of George Stephenson's drivers, before moving initially to Rowsley and latterly to Buxton where he retired as a locomotive Inspector. His son and two grandsons were all footplatemen at Buxton.

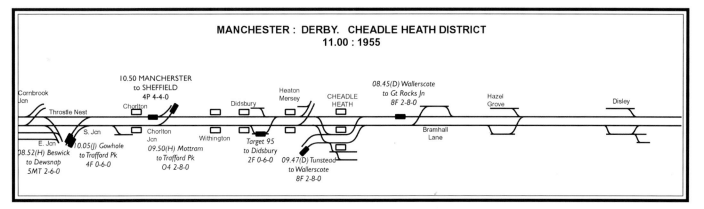

MANCHESTER : DERBY. CHEADLE HEATH DISTRICT
11.00 : 1955

CONTROLLER'S LOG : The problem with crew changeovers is the obvious one of getting two trains to meet in the right place at (more or less) the right time.   Such arrangements are usually an invitation for one of the trains concerned to run at least an hour late so that the crew of the other throws in the towel by returning home passenger, leaving their train nicely blocking the main line.

The risks are all the greater when changeovers are arranged near a boundary and it is therefore essential that a close liaison is maintained with one's opposite number so that

Although all the eastbound Hope Valley passenger trains terminate at Sheffield (apart from one service which runs through to Rotherham Westgate), freight traffic runs to and from a much wider series of destinations making the goods map a very different animal from the familiar passenger one.

In the eastbound direction there is a booked service of thirty-eight trains - one every thirty-eight minutes - which run to eleven destinations: three in the Sheffield area and six in or just to the north of the Erewash Valley.   There is also one long distance service to Hunslet

unusual business of running in reverse for four miles, trains having to propel themselves between Tapton Junction and Barrow Hill.

The general rule for train routing is that traffic for points on the Midland main line north of Westhouses (Alfreton) is worked via the Hope Valley whilst workings to Erewash Valley locations south of Pye Bridge Junction generally run via Peak Forest, Ambergate and the Butterley branch.   The last mentioned is usually written off by enthusiasts as it lost its passenger service in 1947 yet it sustains as many as thirty goods trains in each direction - which

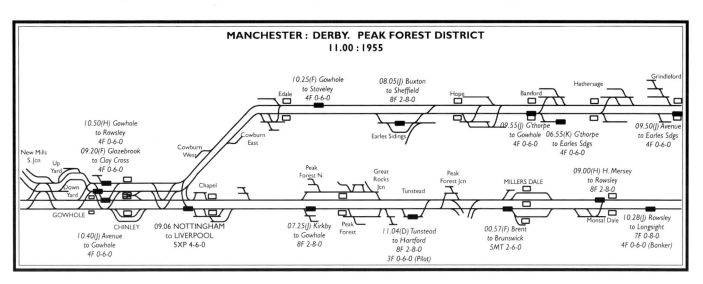

MANCHESTER : DERBY. PEAK FOREST DISTRICT
11.00 : 1955

an accurate assessment of running came be obtained.

The chances of the two trains meeting as booked is not great and to guard against the possibility of one service blocking the line for an hour whilst it waits for its counterpart, the 08.05 Buxton - Queens Road (Sheffield) is given half an hour's shunting inside Earles Cement Sidings before being allowed to go forward to Hathersage for its rendezvous with the 11.18 Grimesthorpe - Buxton. Two other such changeovers take place on the Hope Valley at five in the morning and five at night.

Lane, Leeds.

Most of the Sheffield services, fourteen workings, are concerned with either ordinary goods traffic or steel empties whilst the twenty-four trains that turn south at Dore West Junction convey mineral empties to collieries in the Alfreton and Chesterfield mining areas.   The principal destination is Avenue marshalling yard, a short distance south of Chesterfield, where empties are sorted before being tripped out for loading.   Others run to yards in the Westhouses complex whilst five services operate to Staveley which involves the highly

is double the number of goods trains that arrive in the district via Derby.

Reverting for a moment to what is actually taking place outside, the progress of the Nottingham - Liverpool, fast approaching Chinley, visibly reinforces what has already been said about the effect of passenger trains on the working of the district.   North of Chinley everything has been cleared from its path almost all the way to Manchester.   To the south trains are crawling out of the woodwork all over the place, hoping to get a run before the 10.24 Derby - Manchester closes them in again.

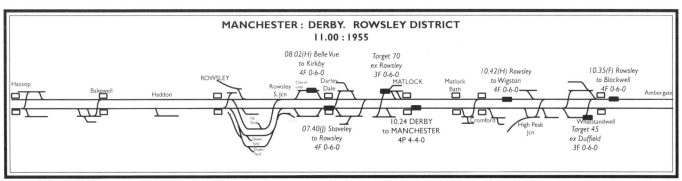

MANCHESTER : DERBY. ROWSLEY DISTRICT
11.00 : 1955

The weakest point in the system was Dove Holes Tunnel between Peak Forest and Chapel-en-le-Frith which continuously presented problems of one sort or another. In normal times the atmosphere through the bore required breathing to be rationed whilst during winter icicles hanging from the tunnel roof had been known to cause injuries to footplatemen. An alarm wire, severed to stop approaching trains, ran through the bore as a safety aid - and presumed that the tunnel was sufficiently free of smoke for a fireman to locate it. In 1956 the decision was taken to reline the bore, the line being closed during the night shift for almost six months. In the interim trains were diverted over the already crowded Hope Valley route. In the view above, trouble has clearly struck since single-line working has been introduced; Austin 7 0-8-0 49638 of Wigan approaching the tunnel 'bang road' with a Rowsley - Brewery goods on 23rd January 1955.

It is astonishing to realise that at the time of the photograph, 7th July 1930, construction of the Midland Compounds has been under way for twenty-eight years and examples would continue to be produced for a further two years. An unidentified member of the class hauls the 12.30 Manchester - St Pancras out of Dove Holes Tunnel and up the hill to Peak Forest.

After twenty miles of climbing during the very hot summer of 1959, the fireman of 45614 'Leeward Islands' puts his shovel down and takes a breath of fresh air. The Manchester - St Pancras trains were not the easiest of services to fire. The 5XP 4-6-0's were only just large enough to cope with the weight of the trains whilst one's working routine had to be interrupted by the long tunnels at Disley and Dove Holes where firing was frowned upon. One was by no means unhappy to get to the summit at Peak Forest and the downhill run to Rowsley and Derby.

Although Buxton was off the beaten track as far as through trains were concerned, the depot played a significant role in the running of main line trains, several of the Manchester - London workings being manned by Buxton crews between Manchester and Derby. In addition the engine for the 17.22 Manchester - Buxton was a London engine which powered the 12.25 St Pancras - Manchester, working out from Buxton with the next morning's 07.05 to Manchester. As a disposal fireman at Buxton, the author remembers the engines on this working for the amount of clearing their smokeboxes required. Black Five 44696 working in lieu of the usual 5XP pulls away from Peak Forest with the 17.22 ex Manchester.

8F 2-8-0 48062 of Buxton barks its way up to Peak Forest summit, past Great Rocks Junction with a Buxton - Sheffield service in August 1964. On the right of the picture is one of the 'Planet' chain-driven locomotives with which ICI did much of its internal shunting.

The 17.00 Vacuum empties arrive in the ICI sidings at Great Rocks Junction, the train slowing to a stand prior to picking up the ICI shunter who had to accompany all BR movements. After positioning the vehicles for loading, the engine will turn and prepare to work the train back to Hartford as the 22.00 ex Tunstead.

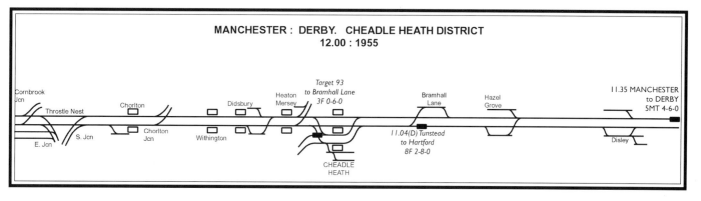

MANCHESTER : DERBY. CHEADLE HEATH DISTRICT
12.00 : 1955

CONTROLLER'S LOG : As the individuality of passenger trains makes each distinct in the eyes of the enthusiast - the stops and formation of the 08.15 St Pancras - Manchester, for example, give it a unique character - so freight services make themselves similarly recognisable; most having some particular characteristic which sets them apart from the rest. One such is the 10.23 Codnor Park - Agecroft, a service that runs from the Erewash Valley to the Lancashire & Yorkshire via the Butterley branch, Ambergate and New Mills South.

The defining characteristic of the 10.23 is the type of engine it turns up behind. The

required' to be taken light the following morning to Codnor Park in order to work the 10.23.

Apart from the rather wasteful practice of diagramming an engine to be idle for nearly 23 hours, the idea that an engine can somehow be spirited from Rowsley to Toton by the magic words 'as required' is the ultimate in wishful thinking - especially as the move is planned without an engine crew.

In reality the engine is regarded as spare on arrival at Rowsley. If a special to Toton happens to be required - and a set of men can be found to work it - then the 2-8-0 is usually the engine of first choice but even when it does get as far as Toton, the chances of it remaining

whilst Toton, who have to send an engine to Codnor Park for the 10.23, can be relied upon to select the largest unbalanced engine that happens to be on shed at the time. Requests - more a matter of routine than expectation - are made by the Nottingham district for a Heaton Mersey engine to be worked into Rowsley so as to be in position to re-engine the 10.23 but by the time these are made the booked engine is probably several counties away.

Whatever the engine, the train is recessed in Church Lane loop to let the 08.15 St Pancras go by and then drawn down to the South Junction where a 4F 0-6-0 banker comes onto the rear for the climb up to Peak Forest. With a

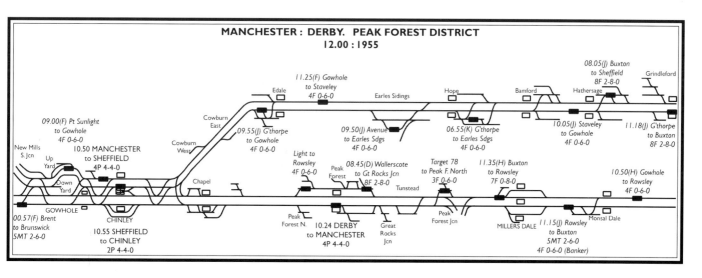

MANCHESTER : DERBY. PEAK FOREST DISTRICT
12.00 : 1955

booked working is for a Heaton Mersey 8F 2-8-0 but thanks to some wildly optimistic diagramming it is almost certain to leave Codnor Park with anything but the correct engine at its head.

For both engine and men the 10.23 is the return working of the 09.00 Heaton Mersey to Rowsley but where the crew work both trains in the same shift, the engine is always a day behind since it is booked to run to Toton 'as

untouched to be run light to Codnor Park the following day are not great.

To erode further the chances of the diagram working, the engine that works in to Rowsley with the 11.10 from Stantongate is booked back to Toton with its brakevan and this return working naturally absorbs the first trainload of any surplus Toton traffic.

Thus nine mornings out of ten, the Heaton Mersey 8F is anywhere but where it should be

full load of coal for Agecroft power station, progress is slow and it is a considerable relief to see it creep into Chapel-en-le-Frith loop a few minutes ahead of the 10.15 St Pancras - Manchester. Progress is not helped by the equally heavy 12.02 Rowsley - Walton which is rarely more than a block section in advance.

From the lineside one goods train may look very much like another but from the inside almost all of them have their particular hallmark.

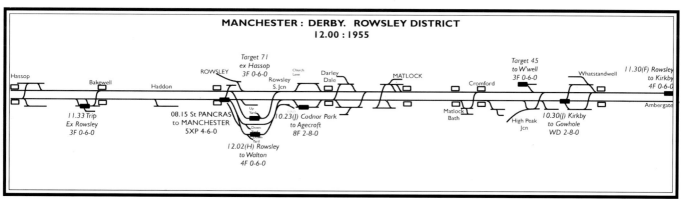

MANCHESTER : DERBY. ROWSLEY DISTRICT
12.00 : 1955

ALLOCATION & MOVEMENTS : BELLE VUE

Loco	Class	Aug-50	Sep-50	Oct-50	Nov-50	Dec-50	Jan-51	Feb-51	Mar-51	Apr-51	May-51	Jun-51	Jul-51
48110	8F 2-8-0 (1935)			To Willesden	X	Ex N. Heath							
48330	8F 2-8-0 (1935)												
48348	8F 2-8-0 (1935)												
48349	8F 2-8-0 (1935)												
48531	8F 2-8-0 (1935)												
48714	8F 2-8-0 (1935)	X	X	Ex N. Heath									
48715	8F 2-8-0 (1935)	X	X	Ex N. Heath									
44803	5MT 4-6-0 (1934)												
44845	5MT 4-6-0 (1934)	X	X	Ex Sheffield									
44921	5MT 4-6-0 (1934)				To Accrington	X	X	X	X	X	X	X	X
45031	5MT 4-6-0 (1934)												
45226	5MT 4-6-0 (1934)	X	Ex Bank Hall										
45284	5MT 4-6-0 (1934)												
45450	5MT 4-6-0 (1934)												
42765	5MT 2-6-0 (1926)		To Rose Grove	X	X	X	X	X	X	X	X	X	X
42898	5MT 2-6-0 (1926)		To Rose Grove	X	X	X	X	X	X	X	X	X	X
42675	4MT 2-6-4T (1945)												
44040	4F 0-6-0 (1924)												
44114	4F 0-6-0 (1924)												
44119	4F 0-6-0 (1924)												
44486	4F 0-6-0 (1924)	X	X	Ex Accrington									
43927	4F 0-6-0 (1911)												
43952	4F 0-6-0 (1911)									To L. Darwen	X	X	X
44019	4F 0-6-0 (1911)												
44022	4F 0-6-0 (1911)												
44025	4F 0-6-0 (1911)												
47336	3F 0-6-0T (1924)												
47440	3F 0-6-0T (1924)												
43612	3F 0-6-0 (1885)												
43630	3F 0-6-0 (1885)												
43638	3F 0-6-0 (1885)												
43756	3F 0-6-0 (1885)												
41690	1F 0-6-0T (1878)										W/D	X	X
41702	1F 0-6-0T (1878)												
41814	1F 0-6-0T (1878)												

Loco	Class	Aug-51	Sep-51	Oct-51	Nov-51	Dec-51	Jan-52	Feb-52	Mar-52	Apr-52	May-52	Jun-52	Jul-52
48188	8F 2-8-0 (1935)						To Warrington	X	X	X	X	X	X
48330	8F 2-8-0 (1935)												
48348	8F 2-8-0 (1935)						To Warrington	X	X	X	X	X	X
48349	8F 2-8-0 (1935)						To Warrington	X	X	X	X	X	X
48531	8F 2-8-0 (1935)						To Warrington	X	X	X	X	X	X
48714	8F 2-8-0 (1935)						To Warrington	X	X	X	X	X	X
48715	8F 2-8-0 (1935)						To Warrington	X	X	X	X	X	X
90122	8F : WD 2-8-0 (1943)	X	X	X	X	X	Ex Warrington						
90126	8F : WD 2-8-0 (1943)	X	X	X	X	X	Ex Warrington						
90140	8F : WD 2-8-0 (1943)	X	X	X	X	X	Ex Warrington						
90163	8F : WD 2-8-0 (1943)	X	X	X	X	X	Ex Warrington						
90197	8F : WD 2-8-0 (1943)	X	X	X	X	X	Ex Warrington						
90204	8F : WD 2-8-0 (1943)	X	X	X	X	X	Ex Warrington						
90552	8F : WD 2-8-0 (1943)	X	X	X	X	X	X	Ex N. Heath					
44803	5MT 4-6-0 (1934)												
44845	5MT 4-6-0 (1934)												
45031	5MT 4-6-0 (1934)												
45226	5MT 4-6-0 (1934)				To Accrington	X	X	X	X	X	X	X	X
45284	5MT 4-6-0 (1934)												
45450	5MT 4-6-0 (1934)				To Blackpool	X	X	X	X	X	X	X	X
42675	4MT 2-6-4T (1945)												
44040	4F 0-6-0 (1924)												
44114	4F 0-6-0 (1924)												
44119	4F 0-6-0 (1924)												
44486	4F 0-6-0 (1924)												
43927	4F 0-6-0 (1911)												
44019	4F 0-6-0 (1911)											To Wakefield	X
44022	4F 0-6-0 (1911)												
44025	4F 0-6-0 (1911)												
47336	3F 0-6-0T (1924)												
47440	3F 0-6-0T (1924)												
43612	3F 0-6-0 (1885)												
43630	3F 0-6-0 (1885)												
43638	3F 0-6-0 (1885)												
43756	3F 0-6-0 (1885)												
51510	2F 0-6-0ST (1877/1901)	Ex N. Heath											
41702	1F 0-6-0T (1878)												
41814	1F 0-6-0T (1878)												

Loco	Class	Aug-52	Sep-52	Oct-52	Nov-52	Dec-52	Jan-53	Feb-53	Mar-53	Apr-53	May-53	Jun-53	Jul-53
48330	8F 2-8-0 (1935)												
90122	8F : WD 2-8-0 (1943)												
90126	8F : WD 2-8-0 (1943)												
90140	8F : WD 2-8-0 (1943)												
90163	8F : WD 2-8-0 (1943)												
90197	8F : WD 2-8-0 (1943)												
90204	8F : WD 2-8-0 (1943)												
90552	8F : WD 2-8-0 (1943)												
44803	5MT 4-6-0 (1934)												
44845	5MT 4-6-0 (1934)												
45031	5MT 4-6-0 (1934)												
45284	5MT 4-6-0 (1934)												
42675	4MT 2-6-4T (1945)												
44040	4F 0-6-0 (1924)												
44114	4F 0-6-0 (1924)												
44119	4F 0-6-0 (1924)												
44486	4F 0-6-0 (1924)												
43927	4F 0-6-0 (1911)												
44022	4F 0-6-0 (1911)												
44025	4F 0-6-0 (1911)												
47336	3F 0-6-0T (1924)												
47440	3F 0-6-0T (1924)												
43612	3F 0-6-0 (1885)												
43630	3F 0-6-0 (1885)												
43638	3F 0-6-0 (1885)												
43756	3F 0-6-0 (1885)												
51510	2F 0-6-0ST (1877/1901)												
41702	1F 0-6-0T (1878)												
41814	1F 0-6-0T (1878)												

LOCOMOTIVE MOVEMENTS : Belle Vue shed not only worked Midland services south of Midland Junction, Ancoats - where an end-on junction was made with the L&Y - but also over the Settle & Carlisle as though the Midland was a continuous system from London to Carlisle via Manchester. Locally many of the shed's duties were concerned with trip working around Ancoats, Ashton Road and local connections to and from

An unidentified rebuilt Royal Scot works the up Palatine towards Hassop on a pleasant June day in 1960. Extramural efforts by the p. way staff are in evidence.

B1 4-6-0's did not appear on the Midland until the late 1950's when the Eastern Region drafted the type into the Sheffield area and stating using them on Hope Valley trains. Prior to that the only sightings of the class could be had between Chorlton Junction and Manchester Central. 61181 of Darnall has its fire cleaned at Central before returning to Sheffield. Its driver picks his way through the debris.

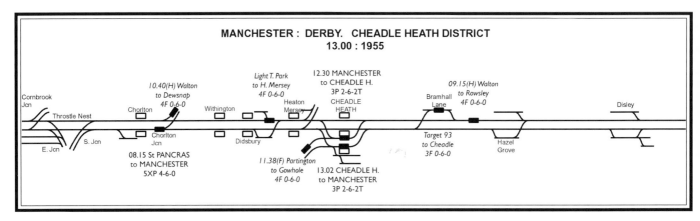

MANCHESTER : DERBY. CHEADLE HEATH DISTRICT
13.00 : 1955

CONTROLLER'S LOG : For not the first time during the shift one reflects on the fireworks being expended over Peak Forest and wishes one could see it at first hand. One after another, a splendid procession of trains is squeezed into the gap between the 10.24 Derby - Manchester and the 10.15 ex St Pancras. The 12.02 Rowsley - Liverpool (Walton), the 10.23 Codnor Park - Manchester (Agecroft), the 10.30 Kirkby - Gowhole, the 11.33 Rowsley - Great Rocks local goods and the 12.40 Rowsley - Manchester (Longsight) all follow each other; the last-mentioned being very much an

LNWR in Manchester are nonexistent for practical purposes (transferring traffic via Cornbrook, the MSJ&A and London Road would bring the city to a halt) and traffic therefore has to be extracted at Rowsley and worked via Buxton.

With gradients like the side of a house, the Buxton route is, if anything, more difficult to operate than the Midland over Peak Forest and recognition of the fact is given by the LNWR in the form of seven G2a 0-8-0 locomotives which, with fourteen Standard 2-8-0's, work most of the Buxton-line trains.

to assist well beyond Buxton itself, coming off at either Bibbington or Dove Holes (depending upon the signalling arrangements at the time), and whilst a pair of engines can take 52 wagons of minerals as far as Buxton and 50 beyond, the curve between the Midland and LNW at Buxton is restricted to no more than 40 wagons which, as a result, becomes the standard load for all Rowsley - Stockport trains.

Not only are the eight coupled engines of Buxton a wasted asset so far as Rowsley is concerned but the mathematics of operations are something that should have been engi-

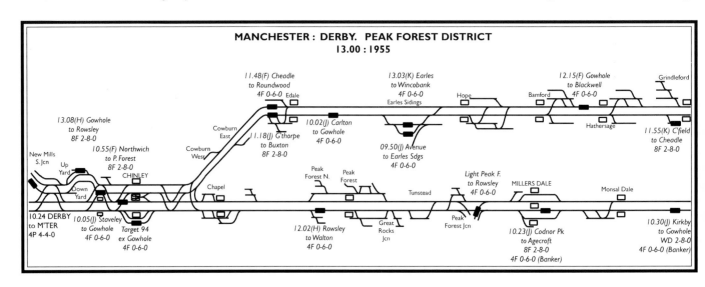

MANCHESTER : DERBY. PEAK FOREST DISTRICT
13.00 : 1955

LNW service, travelling via Buxton and worked by a Super-D 0-8-0.

The 12.40 is a reminder of the importance of Buxton in goods matters and whilst the town may something of a passenger backwater, it is the principal conduit through which goods traffic is exchanged with the LNW.

Extracting Buxton-line LNW traffic from the tonnage that arrives from the south is one of the reasons for Rowsley's existence. Connections between the Midland/CLC and the

The provision of so much eight-coupled power at Buxton seems at first to exemplify the large engine policy of the North Western as opposed to that of the Midland until, that is, one realises that the maximum load allowed on the route is 26 wagons - a load that can be handled by an unassisted 4F 0-6-0. One wagon more and a second - banking - engine has to be provided.

But that is far from being the worst of it. For through services the banking engine has

neered away years ago.

Rowsley despatches fourteen daily services towards Buxton; nine working through to the LNW to terminate in Stockport (4), Manchester (3) and Liverpool (2). All except the 03.50 Rowsley - Buxton have to be given 0-6-0 bankers and many are worked by Buxton 0-8-0's. In spite of the fact that a 7F and a 4F have the tractive capability to work 60 loaded vehicles, only two-third of this can be conveyed because of the absurd restriction at Buxton.

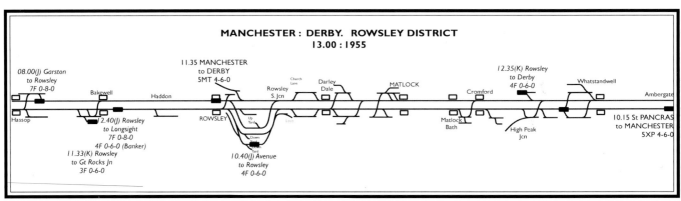

MANCHESTER : DERBY. ROWSLEY DISTRICT
13.00 : 1955

ALLOCATION & MOVEMENTS : BELLE VUE

Loco	Class	Aug-53	Sep-53	Oct-53	Nov-53	Dec-53	Jan-54	Feb-54	Mar-54	Apr-54	May-54	Jun-54	Jul-54
48330	8F 2-8-0 (1935)												
90122	8F : WD 2-8-0 (1943)												
90126	8F : WD 2-8-0 (1943)												
90140	8F : WD 2-8-0 (1943)												
90163	8F : WD 2-8-0 (1943)												
90197	8F : WD 2-8-0 (1943)												
90204	8F : WD 2-8-0 (1943)												
90552	8F : WD 2-8-0 (1943)												
44803	5MT 4-6-0 (1934)												
44845	5MT 4-6-0 (1934)												
45031	5MT 4-6-0 (1934)												
45284	5MT 4-6-0 (1934)												To N. Heath
42675	4MT 2-6-4T (1945)	To Uttoxeter	X	X	X	X	X	X	X	X	X	X	X
44040	4F 0-6-0 (1924)												
44042	4F 0-6-0 (1924)	X	X	Ex Mirfield									
44114	4F 0-6-0 (1924)												
44119	4F 0-6-0 (1924)												
44291	4F 0-6-0 (1924)	X	X	X	X	X	Ex Wigan (L&Y)						
44486	4F 0-6-0 (1924)												
43927	4F 0-6-0 (1911)												
44022	4F 0-6-0 (1911)												
44025	4F 0-6-0 (1911)												
47336	3F 0-6-0T (1924)												
47440	3F 0-6-0T (1924)												
43612	3F 0-6-0 (1885)												
43630	3F 0-6-0 (1885)												
43638	3F 0-6-0 (1885)												
43756	3F 0-6-0 (1885)												
51510	2F 0-6-0ST (1877/1901)												
41702	1F 0-6-0T (1878)												
41814	1F 0-6-0T (1878)												

Loco	Class	Aug-54	Sep-54	Oct-54	Nov-54	Dec-54	Jan-55	Feb-55	Mar-55	Apr-55	May-55	Jun-55	Jul-55
48330	8F 2-8-0 (1935)												
90122	8F : WD 2-8-0 (1943)												
90126	8F : WD 2-8-0 (1943)												
90140	8F : WD 2-8-0 (1943)												
90142	8F : WD 2-8-0 (1943)	X	X	X	X	X	X	Ex Aintree					
90163	8F : WD 2-8-0 (1943)												
90197	8F : WD 2-8-0 (1943)												
90204	8F : WD 2-8-0 (1943)				To Aintree	X	X	X	X	X	X	X	X
90552	8F : WD 2-8-0 (1943)												
44803	5MT 4-6-0 (1934)												
44845	5MT 4-6-0 (1934)												
45031	5MT 4-6-0 (1934)												
44040	4F 0-6-0 (1924)												
44042	4F 0-6-0 (1924)												
44114	4F 0-6-0 (1924)												
44119	4F 0-6-0 (1924)												
44291	4F 0-6-0 (1924)												
44486	4F 0-6-0 (1924)												
43927	4F 0-6-0 (1911)												
44022	4F 0-6-0 (1911)												
44025	4F 0-6-0 (1911)												
47336	3F 0-6-0T (1924)												
47440	3F 0-6-0T (1924)												
43612	3F 0-6-0 (1885)												
43630	3F 0-6-0 (1885)												
43638	3F 0-6-0 (1885)												
43756	3F 0-6-0 (1885)												
51510	2F 0-6-0ST (1877/1901)												
41702	1F 0-6-0T (1878)												
41814	1F 0-6-0T (1878)												

Loco	Class	Aug-55	Sep-55	Oct-55	Nov-55	Dec-55	Jan-56	Feb-56	Mar-56	Apr-56	May-56	Jun-56	Jul-56
48330	8F 2-8-0 (1935)								To Swansea	X	X	X	X
90122	8F : WD 2-8-0 (1943)								To N. Heath	X	X	X	X
90126	8F : WD 2-8-0 (1943)								To N. Heath	X	X	X	X
90140	8F : WD 2-8-0 (1943)								To N. Heath	X	X	X	X
90142	8F : WD 2-8-0 (1943)								To N. Heath	X	X	X	X
90163	8F : WD 2-8-0 (1943)								To N. Heath	X	X	X	X
90197	8F : WD 2-8-0 (1943)								To N. Heath	X	X	X	X
90316	8F : WD 2-8-0 (1943)	X	X	Ex Bolton					To N. Heath	X	X	X	X
90552	8F : WD 2-8-0 (1943)								To N. Heath	X	X	X	X
44803	5MT 4-6-0 (1934)								To N. Heath	X	X	X	X
44845	5MT 4-6-0 (1934)								To N. Heath	X	X	X	X
45031	5MT 4-6-0 (1934)								To N. Heath	X	X	X	X
44040	4F 0-6-0 (1924)			To N. Heath	X	X	X	X	X	X	X	X	X
44042	4F 0-6-0 (1924)								To Derby	X	X	X	X
44114	4F 0-6-0 (1924)								To Gorton	X	X	X	X
44119	4F 0-6-0 (1924)								To N. Heath	X	X	X	X
44291	4F 0-6-0 (1924)			To N. Heath	X	X	X	X	X	X	X	X	X
44486	4F 0-6-0 (1924)								To N. Heath	X	X	X	X
43927	4F 0-6-0 (1911)								To Gorton	X	X	X	X
44022	4F 0-6-0 (1911)								To N. Heath	X	X	X	X
44025	4F 0-6-0 (1911)								To Gorton	X	X	X	X
47336	3F 0-6-0T (1924)								To Gorton	X	X	X	X
47440	3F 0-6-0T (1924)								To N. Heath	X	X	X	X
43612	3F 0-6-0 (1885)								To Gorton	X	X	X	X
43630	3F 0-6-0 (1885)								To Gorton	X	X	X	X
43638	3F 0-6-0 (1885)								To Gorton	X	X	X	X
43756	3F 0-6-0 (1885)								To N. Heath	X	X	X	X
51504	2F 0-6-0ST (1891)	X	X	X	Ex Bury				To Gorton	X	X	X	X
51510	2F 0-6-0ST (1891)			W/D	X	X	X	X	X	X	X	X	X
41702	1F 0-6-0T (1878)								To Gorton	X	X	X	X
41814	1F 0-6-0T (1878)								W/D	X	X	X	X

the L&Y although there were several diagrams involving work to Rowsley and beyond.   The 1950's were not the happiest of times for the shed and there were few celebrations when most of its standard LMS 8F 2-8-0 were exchanged for Austerity 2-8-0's in early 1952.   Very much on a Midland limb and geographically closer to the Lancashire & Yorkshire than its parent system, the shed was a very early casualty of rationalisation and closed in March 1956, its engines being divided between Newton Heath and Gorton.

Not even the 9F 2-10-0's of 1954 could tame Peak Forest and any Northbound mineral train from Rowsley that exceeded twenty-six vehicles had to be assisted in the rear by an 0-6-0. Thus it was that most of the class spent their early years working between Wellingborough and Brent where they were allowed to take up to 74 wagons of coal - without assistance. In Derbyshire the class were better utilised on the few fast goods services that existed; 92161 is seen passing Great Rocks with a fifty-wagon fully fitted Ancoats - Cricklewood relief train. In the background an 8F 2-8-0 waits for the road before running light to pick up the 22.00 Tunstead - Hartford.

After coaxing 4F 0-6-0 44339 uphill from Tunstead to Peak Forest, the fireman of Target 79 exchanges his shovel for a camera to record 5XP 4-6-0 45641 'Sandwich' as it overtakes with the 07.10 Derby - Manchester stopping train in 1962. This was something of a last post for the 4-6-0 as 2500hp Sulzer diesels had pretty well taken over the Midland passenger services.

The gradient from Rowsley to Peak Forest rose at an average of 1 in 120 for over fourteen miles and provided a rigorous testing ground for new and novel forms of traction as they appeared from Derby works. On June 30th 1950 800hp diesel 10800 made its maiden voyage and ran from Derby to Manchester on the test train that in later years was not only to become a regular feature of operation but provided the two Peak Forest trip engines which hours of unplanned work.
with

In an attempt to avoid the expense and complication of electric transmission, the Fell diesel-mechanical 10100 completed several years of relatively successful work between Manchester and St Pancras before catching fire in Manchester Central. Remarkable for its bright red coupling rods, 10100 is seen passing Great Rocks Junction on March 11th 1954.

Loco	Class	Aug-50	Sep-50	Oct-50	Nov-50	Dec-50	Jan-51	Feb-51	Mar-51	Apr-51	May-51	Jun-51	Jul-51
48089	8F 2-8-0 (1935)												
48099	8F 2-8-0 (1935)												
48127	8F 2-8-0 (1935)												
48134	8F 2-8-0 (1935)												
48154	8F 2-8-0 (1935)												
48155	8F 2-8-0 (1935)												
48190	8F 2-8-0 (1935)												
48208	8F 2-8-0 (1935)												
48220	8F 2-8-0 (1935)												
48275	8F 2-8-0 (1935)												
48315	8F 2-8-0 (1935)												
48316	8F 2-8-0 (1935)												
48329	8F 2-8-0 (1935)												
48406	8F 2-8-0 (1935)												
48503	8F 2-8-0 (1935)												
48527	8F 2-8-0 (1935)												
48557	8F 2-8-0 (1935)	X	X	X	Ex Willesden								
48676	8F 2-8-0 (1935)												
48682	8F 2-8-0 (1935)												
48683	8F 2-8-0 (1935)												
48751	8F 2-8-0 (1935)	X	X	X	X	X	Ex Crewe (S)						
42775	5MT 2-6-0 (1926)	X	X	X	X	X	Ex Longsight						
42788	5MT 2-6-0 (1926)	X	X	X	X	X	Ex Longsight						
64727	5F : J39 0-6-0 (1926)						To Carlisle ©	X	X	X	X	X	X
64733	5F : J39 0-6-0 (1926)						To Carlisle ©	X	X	X	X	X	X
44080	4F 0-6-0 (1924)												
44090	4F 0-6-0 (1924)												
44144	4F 0-6-0 (1924)												
44178	4F 0-6-0 (1924)												
44286	4F 0-6-0 (1924)												
44407	4F 0-6-0 (1924)												
44421	4F 0-6-0 (1924)					To Brunswick	X	X	X	X	X	X	X
44593	4F 0-6-0 (1924)	X	Ex Warrington										
43836	4F 0-6-0 (1911)												
43945	4F 0-6-0 (1911)												
40089	3P 2-6-2 (1935)												
40094	3P 2-6-2 (1935)	X	X	X	X	X	Ex T. Park						
40095	3P 2-6-2 (1935)			To L'dno Jn	X	X	X	X	X	X	X	X	X
40113	3P 2-6-2 (1935)												
40118	3P 2-6-2 (1935)	X	Ex T. Park				To T. Park	X	X	X	X	X	X
40124	3P 2-6-2 (1935)	X	X	Ex L.dno Jcn									
62663	3P : D11 4-4-0 (1920)												
62665	3P : D11 4-4-0 (1920)												
43811	3F 0-6-0 (1906)							W/D	X	X	X	X	X
40430	2P 4-4-0 (1891/1912)	X	X	X	X	X	X	X	X	X	X	X	Ex Chester
46428	2MT 2-6-0 (1946)		To Preston	X	X	X	X	X	X	X	X	X	X
46434	2MT 2-6-0 (1946)		To Widnes	X	X	X	X	X	X	X	X	X	X
69276	2MT : N5 0-6-2T (1891)												
69317	2MT : N5 0-6-2T (1891)												
69328	2MT : N5 0-6-2T (1891)												
69331	2MT : N5 0-6-2T (1891)												
69332	2MT : N5 0-6-2T (1891)												
69359	2MT : N5 0-6-2T (1891)												
58303	2F 0-6-0 (1878)	X	Ex Willesden										
58128	2F 0-6-0 (1875)												
65132	2F : J10 0-6-0 (1892)												
65135	2F : J10 0-6-0 (1892)					To Wigan	X	X	X	X	X	X	X
65135	2F : J10 0-6-0 (1892)	X	X	X	X	X	X	X	X	Ex Wigan	X	X	X
65144	2F : J10 0-6-0 (1892)		To T. Park	Ex T. Park				To T. Park	Ex T. Park	To Wigan	X	X	X
65145	2F : J10 0-6-0 (1892)		To T. Park	Ex T. Park				To T. Park	Ex T. Park				
65146	2F : J10 0-6-0 (1892)		To T. Park	Ex T. Park				To T. Park	Ex T. Park				
65148	2F : J10 0-6-0 (1892)		To T. Park	Ex T. Park				To T. Park	Ex T. Park				
65157	2F : J10 0-6-0 (1892)												
65160	2F : J10 0-6-0 (1892)												
65178	2F : J10 0-6-0 (1892)												
65181	2F : J10 0-6-0 (1892)												
65185	2F : J10 0-6-0 (1892)												
65188	2F : J10 0-6-0 (1892)												
65193	2F : J10 0-6-0 (1892)												
65194	2F : J10 0-6-0 (1892)												
65197	2F : J10 0-6-0 (1892)												
65198	2F : J10 0-6-0 (1892)												
65200	2F : J10 0-6-0 (1892)												
65209	2F : J10 0-6-0 (1892)												

LOCO MOVEMENTS : As with Trafford Park, Heaton Mersey loco was a joint depot with the responsibility for providing engines for services over the Cheshire Lines system and the Midland.

The former concerned services between Heaton Mersey Yard (Stockport) and the various yards the CLC operated in Liverpool; much of the traffic coming into Heaton Mersey from the Midland via Chinley.

The Midland services worked by the shed varied from trains based on Heaton Mersey Yard, Gowhole and the exchange sidings at Cheadle Heath where traffic was handed over by the Cheshire Lines. Most of the shed's workings revolved around goods traffic but six of the forty-two duties were passenger diagrams; four for the Manchester Central suburban service which was shared with Trafford Park and two 4-4-0's for the small amount of CLC passenger work that was not covered by either Brunswick or Trafford Park. Whilst the amount of passenger work was not great, it did not lack interest. The shed's sole Crab 2-6-0 turn worked down to Merseyside with the Liverpool Central portion of the 22.00 overnight train from Marylebone whilst the 2P 4-4-0 which rang off for the 05.35 Tiviot Dale - Liverpool later worked the 12.30 Manchester Central - Liverpool express.

The allocation of engines did not change greatly during the decade. The mainstay of the shed was its 25-odd Standard 8F 2-8-0's and both these and the dozen or so 4F 0-6-0 remained in strength until the shed's closure. As Midland influence pervaded the CLC system so the number of GC locomotives declined. At the beginning of the decade just under a third of the allocation consisted of D11, N5 and J10 locomotives yet by 1955 the D11's had disappeared completely whilst the number of J10's had dropped from eighteen to seven. The last N5 left the shed in 1957 and a solitary J10 all but survived into 1960.

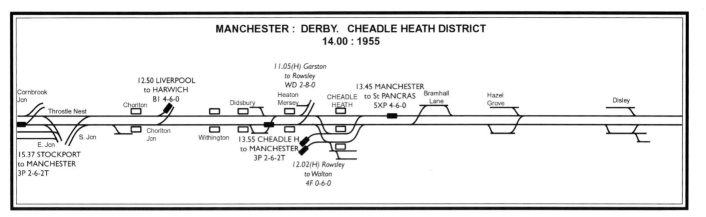

MANCHESTER : DERBY. CHEADLE HEATH DISTRICT
14.00 : 1955

CONTROLLER'S LOG : At 14.00 a fresh shift takes over and as the early turn disappears for an hour on the Worthington shunt, the late takes over. A quick scan of the train board and train cards - each train has a card showing its engine, crew, load and schedule - gives an instant picture of the state of play on the running lines and generally acclimatises one to the job very quickly.

Having established that all is well (or otherwise), a quick perusal is made of the yard stock reports - every couple of hours the major

the discussion rather one sided with Barrow Hill dictating the loads the trains will bring - usually Gowhole roughs (ie assorted traffic to be remarshalled upon arrival) - and specifying the type of empties they want each train to return with.

The control of empty wagons is a complex business but it is based upon individual colliery output, aggregated for each division; the final figure being thrown at the receiving districts as the number of empties that have to be returned to the coal producing districts within

One can achieve a certain amount with booked resources. The 17.25 Gowhole to Avenue, for example, is booked to be double headed by an unbalanced Westhouses 4F whilst the 19.00 to Wincobank has a Grimesthorpe 0-6-0 as pilot and - if guards can be found - the surplus engines can be used to move another fifty-wagon train each. Generally, however, the ball is thrown back into the Barrow Hill court: *"If you want three hundred extra empties - come and get them."*

The regional office at Derby which sup-

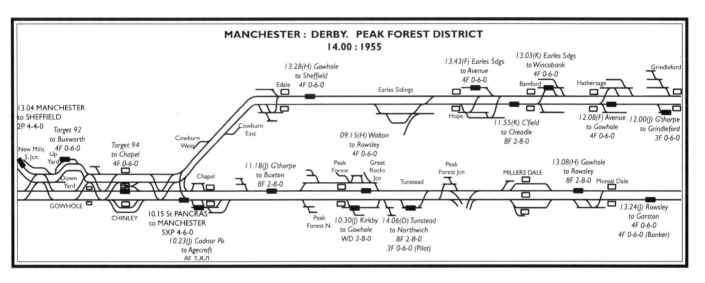

MANCHESTER : DERBY. PEAK FOREST DISTRICT
14.00 : 1955

yards give a traffic report which consists of the number of wagons and type of traffic on hand for each destination. Reading this in conjunction with the details on the train cards - which show the volume en route - the traffic is divided into train loads and allocated to booked services which is then 'agreed' together with the return workings with the receiving districts.

In the case of Gowhole, which has no motive power facilities and therefore no starting trains, the discussion on train loadings tends to be a rather one-way process since the Rotherham district provides power and men (from Hasland shed) for almost all Hope Valley workings. Possession of the engines and men makes

the coming twenty-four hours.

The numbers involved are huge with mineral empties being reckoned in units of hundreds. The capacity of Hope Valley services to Avenue Sidings alone is - assuming trains will work under class H conditions with a 4F 0-6-0 - 450 wagons and the actual demand for a given day can often be well in excess of what the booked service can take. When this happens there will be a certain amount of pressure from Barrow Hill for special trains to be arranged from Gowhole even though the nearest motive power depots belong to the CLC who are not known for putting themselves out to meet foreign interests.

posedly coordinates the work of the District Controllers will usually take the side of the Barrow Hill camp and demand (!) that three specials be worked out of Gowhole to Avenue - a proposal to which there is a stock response: *"Certainly...if you can find me some engines and men."*

A little later Barrow Hill comes back on the line. *"47980, 44054 and 48407 coming light to Gowhole for specials of empty pools (mineral wagons) for Avenue Yard. Two trips each : Hasland crews all."*

They must be desperate: one of the engines is a Garratt, no less.

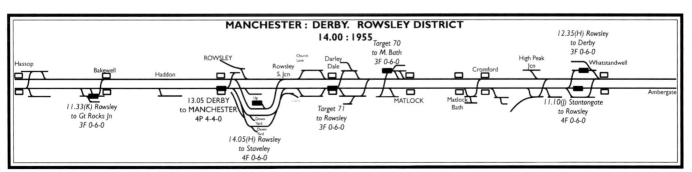

MANCHESTER : DERBY. ROWSLEY DISTRICT
14.00 : 1955

Loco	Class	Aug-51	Sep-51	Oct-51	Nov-51	Dec-51	Jan-52	Feb-52	Mar-52	Apr-52	May-52	Jun-52	Jul-52
48089	8F 2-8-0 (1935)												
48099	8F 2-8-0 (1935)												
48127	8F 2-8-0 (1935)												
48134	8F 2-8-0 (1935)												
48135	8F 2-8-0 (1935)	X	Ex Northwich										
48148	8F 2-8-0 (1935)	X	X	X	X	X	X	X	Ex Lancaster				
48154	8F 2-8-0 (1935)												
48155	8F 2-8-0 (1935)												
48161	8F 2-8-0 (1935)	X	X	X	X	X	X	X	Ex Lancaster				
48190	8F 2-8-0 (1935)												
48208	8F 2-8-0 (1935)												
48220	8F 2-8-0 (1935)												
48275	8F 2-8-0 (1935)												
48315	8F 2-8-0 (1935)												
48316	8F 2-8-0 (1935)												
48329	8F 2-8-0 (1935)												
48406	8F 2-8-0 (1935)												
48429	8F 2-8-0 (1935)	X	X	X	X	X	X	Ex Longsight					
48503	8F 2-8-0 (1935)												
48527	8F 2-8-0 (1935)												
48557	8F 2-8-0 (1935)												
48667	8F 2-8-0 (1935)	X	X	X	X	X	X	X	Ex Northwich				
48676	8F 2-8-0 (1935)												
48682	8F 2-8-0 (1935)												
48683	8F 2-8-0 (1935)												
48731	8F 2-8-0 (1935)	X	X	X	X	X	Ex Buxton	To Longsight	X	X	X	X	X
48751	8F 2-8-0 (1935)												
42772	5MT 2-6-0 (1926)	X	X	X	X	X	X	X	X	X	X	X	Ex Longsight
42775	5MT 2-6-0 (1926)												
42788	5MT 2-6-0 (1926)												
42925	5MT 2-6-0 (1926)	X	X	X	X	X	X	X	X	X	X	X	Ex Longsight
64723	5F : J39 0-6-0 (1926)	Ex Colwick											
44080	4F 0-6-0 (1924)												
44090	4F 0-6-0 (1924)												To Longsight
44144	4F 0-6-0 (1924)												
44178	4F 0-6-0 (1924)												
44286	4F 0-6-0 (1924)												
44407	4F 0-6-0 (1924)												
44593	4F 0-6-0 (1924)	To Bletchley	X	X	X	X	X	X	X	X	X	X	X
43836	4F 0-6-0 (1911)												
43945	4F 0-6-0 (1911)												To Longsight
40089	3P 2-6-2 (1935)												
40094	3P 2-6-2 (1935)												
40113	3P 2-6-2 (1935)												
40124	3P 2-6-2 (1935)												
62663	3P : D11 4-4-0 (1920)												
62665	3P : D11 4-4-0 (1920)												
40405	2P 4-4-0 (1891/1912)	X	X	X	X	X	X	X	X	X	Ex Stafford		
40430	2P 4-4-0 (1891/1912)									W/D	X	X	X
69276	2MT : N5 0-6-2T (1891)												
69317	2MT : N5 0-6-2T (1891)												
69328	2MT : N5 0-6-2T (1891)												
69331	2MT : N5 0-6-2T (1891)												
69332	2MT : N5 0-6-2T (1891)												
69359	2MT : N5 0-6-2T (1891)												
58303	2F 0-6-0 (1878)										To Barrow	X	X
58128	2F 0-6-0 (1875)												
65132	2F : J10 0-6-0 (1892)												
65135	2F : J10 0-6-0 (1892)												
65145	2F : J10 0-6-0 (1892)						To T. Park	Ex T. Park					
65146	2F : J10 0-6-0 (1892)						To T. Park	Ex T. Park					
65148	2F : J10 0-6-0 (1892)						To T. Park	Ex T. Park					
65157	2F : J10 0-6-0 (1892)												
65160	2F : J10 0-6-0 (1892)												
65178	2F : J10 0-6-0 (1892)												
65181	2F : J10 0-6-0 (1892)												
65185	2F : J10 0-6-0 (1892)												
65188	2F : J10 0-6-0 (1892)												
65193	2F : J10 0-6-0 (1892)												
65194	2F : J10 0-6-0 (1892)												
65197	2F : J10 0-6-0 (1892)												
65198	2F : J10 0-6-0 (1892)												
65200	2F : J10 0-6-0 (1892)												
65209	2F : J10 0-6-0 (1892)												

HEATON MERSEY MPD : ENGINE ARRANGEMENTS 1952

Inward working	On Shed	Engine	Off Shed	Train
10.23 Codnor Park	15.05	8F 2-8-0	00.30	01.00 H. Mersey - Hellifield
18.10 Tunstead - Cheadle	07.52	8F 2-8-0	01.20	01.50 Cheadle - Hartford
07.10 Gowhole - H. Mersey	08.07	8F 2-8-0	01.20	02.45 Glazebrook - Clay Cross
08.52 Halewood - Dewsnap	12.30	5MT 2-6-0	03.20	04.10 Godley Jcn - Liverpool Central
09.25 Baguley - H. Mersey	09.50	J10 0-6-0	04.00	05.15 Godley - Baguley
16.35 Cheadle - H. Mersey	17.03	2F 0-6-0	04.05	04.35 H. Mersey - Cheadle
20.15 Tunstead - Cheadle	22.03	8F 2-8-0	04.15	07.25 Tunstead - Cheadle
20.55 Tunstead - Cheadle	22.40	8F 2-8-0	04.20	04.50 Cheadle - Hartford
08.17 Macclesfield - H. Mersey	10.30	J10 0-6-0	04.30	05.00 H. Mersey - Macclesfield
16.20 Gowhole - H. Mersey	17.20	4F 0-6-0	04.35	05.20 Cheadle - Gowhole
17.05 Warrington - Tiviot Dale	18.09	2P 4-4-0	05.00	05.35 Stockport - Liverpool Central
17.12 Gowhole - Cheadle	20.10	8F 2-8-0	05.40	06.10 H. Mersey - Hartford
20.14 Peak Forest - Gowhole	22.09	4F 0-6-0	05.50	06.20 Cheadle - Trafford Park
16.40 Liverpool Central - Tiviot Dale	18.51	D11 4-4-0	06.00	06.35 Tiviot Dale - Risley
18.30 Manchester - Cheadle Heath	19.08	3P 2-6-2T	06.10	06.45 Tiviot Dale - Manchester
H. Mersey local trips	20.40	N5 0-6-2T	06.10	H. Mersey local trips
23.20 16.20 Derby (SM) - Glazebrook	23.55	8F 2-8-0	06.15	06.45 H. Mersey - Glazebrook
17.10 Manchester - Tiviot Dale	17.49	3P 2-6-2T	06.19	07.10 Cheadle Heath - Manchester
04.55 Northwich - Cheadle	06.20	8F 2-8-0	06.26	06.56 Cheadle - Northwich
18.05 Manchester - Cheadle Heath	18.43	3P 2-6-2T	07.28	08.14 Cheadle Heath - Manchester
22.00 Gowhole - Cheadle	22.50	8F 2-8-0	07.30	08.28 Godley Jcn - Macclesfield
18.05 Hartford - H. Mersey	19.45	8F 2-8-0	07.50	08.20 H. Mersey - Guide Bridge
Portwood pilot	04.15	4F 0-6-0	07.50	Portwood pilot
23.30 Godley Jcn - Northwich	02.00	8F 2-8-0	08.30	09.00 H. Mersey - Rowsley
01.05 Glazebrook - H. Mersey	01.45	4F 0-6-0	08.30	09.20 Glazebrook - Clay Cross
23.45 Partington Jcn - H. Mersey	02.30	4F 0-6-0	09.15	09.45 H. Mersey - Northwich
Trips as required	23.30		09.45	10.10 Cheadle - Didsbury (T. 93)
22.40 Hellifield - H. Mersey	04.05	8F 2-8-0	11.10	11.45 H. Mersey - Glazebrook
08.15 Manchester - Cheadle Heath	08.52	3P 2-6-2T	11.20	13.02 Cheadle Heath - Manchester
Godley Jcn pilot	00.35	N5 0-6-2T	11.30	Godley Jcn pilot
Godley pilot	00.35	N5 0-6-2T	11.30	Godley pilot
00.30 Gowhole - Cheadle	01.25	3F 0-6-0	13.35	14.05 H. Mersey - Widnes
10.47 Macclesfield - H. Mersey	12.43	8F 2-8-0	15.15	15.45 Cheadle - Bamford
05.23 Tunstead - Cheadle	06.56	8F 2-8-0	19.09	19.39 Cheadle - Hartford
14.35 Northwich - H. Mersey	15.55	4F 0-6-0	19.50	20.48 Godley - Partington Jcn
12.20 Gowhole - Portwood	14.00	8F 2-8-0	20.10	23.00 Gowhole - H. Mersey
04.38 Derby (SM) - Glazebrook	13.25	4F 0-6-0	20.15	20.35 H. Mersey - Georges Rd
12.20 Glazebrook - H. Mersey	01.30	8F 2-8-0	20.35	21.25 Godley Jcn - Partington Jcn
Tiviot Dale pilot	10.30	N5 0-6-2T	22.35	Tiviot Dale pilot
11.55 Godley - H. Mersey	12.40	N5 0-6-2T	23.45	Godley pilot
H. Mersey pilot (Continuous)		J10 0-6-0		H. Mersey pilot (Continuous)
H. Mersey pilot (Continuous)		J10 0-6-0		H. Mersey pilot (Continuous)

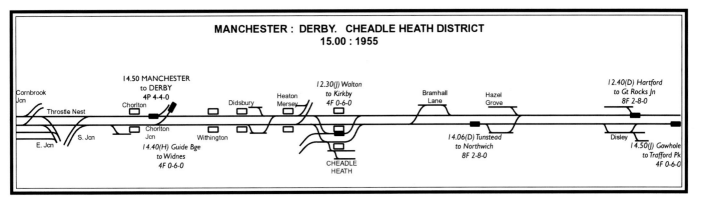

CONTROLLER'S LOG : Whilst black-mailing Barrow Hill into sending engines and men to run half a dozen trains of empties from Gowhole to Avenue sidings, 4F 0-6-0 44290 appears from the table road at Gowhole and rings out light for the Hope Valley. Could not this be used instead of one of the Hasland engines?

The short answer is no. The engine arrived in Gowhole with the 10.02 from Carlton Marshalling Yard - about ten miles south of Normanton - and the Royston men on the engine will almost certainly not sign the road between Dore and Avenue. If there is a surfeit of Sheffield traffic - and a guard can be found

which serve the immediate district. Viewed from a passing express, the trip working looks a rather secondary animal; invariably worked by a 3F or 4F 0-6-0 and seen lurking in every other station yard or siding. From the District Controller's perspective they are a dominant factor in his working life and are the principal tool by which yards and sidings are cleared of traffic and supplied with empties. The trips are the key link between the marshalling yard and the consumer.

Different parts of the railway have different policies applicable to trip working but on the Midland they are shown in the working timetable in the same way as any other train

there is insufficient traffic generated to warrant the running of through trains as is done from Peak Forest, there is enough to call for five trip workings although not all their work is done within the Rowsley area.

Different controllers have different approaches to trip workings. Some, especially those who have come from the LNER where trip timings are not published, prefer to regard them as 'as required' from start to finish; rattling off a list of instructions "... *two trips engine and brake to Matlock, load Rowsley then empties to High Peak, load Rowsley*...." to the guard as he signs on whilst others will stick to the timetabled arrangements so far as they can,

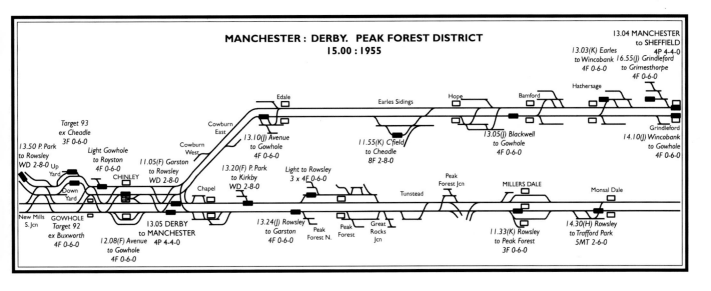

- it could be used for a special to Wincobank but it would mean a devil of a row with the enginemen whose day would be up long before they got to Sheffield. It would also mean losing a brakevan and a guard.

All trains are of course equal but, like Orwell's pigs, some are more equal than others and if there is one category of train that receives a greater share of attention than any other, it is the service of local trip workings

and in fact it is only the allocation of a reporting (or target) number which distinguishes them from the rest of the pack. The path shown reflects what the timing office assume the trip workings will do but in actual fact the District Controller will manipulate each working according to the needs of his local stations.

Appearances suggest that the southern part of the district - Millers Dale to Ambergate - is rather a barren area industrially and although

making minor adjustments as the day wears on. Train crews much prefer the latter method since it usually involves much less tender-first running - always a source of contention - and it is a mystery why the railway have never produced a large goods tank-engine which can be run equally well in any direction for trip workings. As it is, crews have to spend half their day in one of the wettest parts of the country with very little protection from the elements.

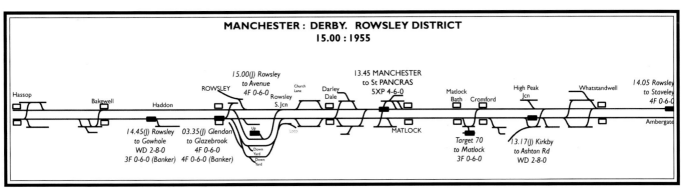

Austerity 2-8-0's tended to appear on workings from the L&Y although a small number were allocated to the Midland shed at Belle Vue. One of the class - number unseen - approaches Gowhole with a Class J mineral train.

LOCOMOTIVE ALLOCATION AND DISTRIBUTION

TRAFFORD PARK

	Oct-50	Oct-51	Oct-52	Oct-53	Oct-54	Oct-55	Oct-56	Oct-57	Oct-58	Oct-59	Oct-60
8F 2-8-0 (1935)	4	3	4	4	4	4	3	4	4	4	4
7MT 4-6-2 (1951)									6	6	8
5XP 4-6-0 (1934)	6	6	6	6	6	6	6	6	2	1	
5MT 4-6-0 (1934)	1	2	2	4	6	4	3	4	5	6	6
5F : J39 0-6-0 (1926)	4										
4P 4-4-0 (1924)	10	9	7	8	15	15	8	4	1		
4MT 2-6-4T		2	5	6	6	7	8	8	12	13	19
4MT 2-6-0 (1952)								2	2	3	3
4F 0-6-0	3	2	2	4	4	5	3	6	6	7	6
4F : J94 0-6-0T (1943)	1	1	1	1							
3P 2-6-2	2	2		2	2	5	6	11	10	10	5
3P : D16 4-4-0 (1923)	8	8									
3P : D11 4-4-0 (1920)	3	9	8	6	4	1	1	1			
3P : D10 4-4-0 (1913)	7	6	6	2							
3F 0-6-0T (1924)						1				3	
3F 0-6-0											4
2F : N5 0-6-2T (1891)	10	10	10	10	10	7	5	3			
2F : J67 0-6-0T (1890)	4	4	4	3	3	1	1				
2F : J10 0-6-0 (1892)	11	11	10	15	13	11	5	4	3	1	
1P : C12 4-4-2T (1898)	2	2	2								
TOTAL	**76**	**77**	**67**	**71**	**73**	**66**	**50**	**53**	**51**	**54**	**55**

ROWSLEY

	Oct-50	Oct-51	Oct-52	Oct-53	Oct-54	Oct-55	Oct-56	Oct-57	Oct-58	Oct-59	Oct-60
9F 2-10-0 (1954)											6
8F 2-8-0 (1935)					2	2	2	5	5	6	4
5MT 4-6-0 (1951)											10
5MT 2-6-0 (1926)	5	5	6	6	6	6	6	7	7	9	
4P 4-4-0 (1924)	1	1	2	2	2	2	3	1			
4MT 2-6-4T								2	3	3	3
4F 0-6-0	25	26	24	22	26	25	19	19	19	17	15
4F : J94 0-6-0T (1943)							3	4	4	5	4
3F 0-6-0T (1924)	6	6	6	6	6	6	6	6	6	6	6
3F 0-6-0	5	4	7	9	8	8	9	10	8	5	3
2P 4-4-0	2	2	1	1	1	1					
2F 0-6-0T (1879)	4	4	4	4	4	4	3	2	1	1	
2F 0-6-0 (1878)	6	6	3	3	3	3	2		2	2	
1F 0-6-0T (1878)	1	1	1	1				1			
0F 0-4-0ST (1932)			1	1	1	1	1	1	1	1	1
0F : Diesel 0-6-0											2
TOTAL	**55**	**55**	**54**	**54**	**59**	**58**	**54**	**58**	**56**	**55**	**54**

HEATON MERSEY

	Oct-50	Oct-51	Oct-52	Oct-53	Oct-54	Oct-55	Oct-56	Oct-57	Oct-58	Oct-59	Oct-60
8F 2-8-0 (1935)	19	22	26	24	26	26	24	26	19	20	20
5MT 2-6-0 (1926)		2	2	2	2	3	2	2	2		
5F : J39 0-6-0 (1926)	2	1									
4MT 2-6-4T							2				
4MT 2-6-0 (1952)										2	2
4F 0-6-0	10	8	9	9	11	12	13	15	15	16	10
3P 2-6-2	4	4	4	4	4	6	6	11	11	10	7
3P : D11 4-4-0 (1920)	2	2	2	2	1						
3F 0-6-0	1									3	2
2P 4-4-0 (1891/1912)		1	1	1	2	1	1				
2F 0-6-0	2	2	1	1	1	1					
2F : N5 0-6-2T (1891)	6	6	6	6	6	6	4	3			
2F : J10 0-6-0 (1892)	18	17	14	7	7	7	8	7	2	1	
0F : Diesel 0-6-0										3	3
TOTAL	**64**	**65**	**65**	**56**	**60**	**62**	**58**	**64**	**51**	**55**	**44**

BELLE VUE

	Oct-50	Oct-51	Oct-52	Oct-53	Oct-54	Oct-55	Oct-56	Oct-57	Oct-58	Oct-59	Oct-60
8F 2-8-0 (1935)	6	7	1	1	1						
8F : WD 2-8-0 (1943)			7	7	7	8					
5MT 4-6-0 (1934)	7	6	4	4	3	3					
4MT 2-6-4T (1945)	1	1	1								
4F 0-6-0	9	8	7	9	9	7					
3F 0-6-0T (1924)	2	2	2	2	2	2					
3F 0-6-0 (1885)	4	4	4	4	4	4					
2F 0-6-0ST (1877/1901)		1	1	1	1						
1F 0-6-0T (1878)	3	2	2	2	2	2					
TOTAL	**29**	**29**	**29**	**30**	**29**	**27**					

ROWSLEY AREA TRIP WORKINGS

Target 70

Arr	Station	Dep
	ROWSLEY	06.00
06.35	Matlock	09.35
09.42	M. Bath	10.15
10.22	Matlock	11.21
11.35	ROWSLEY	12.13
12.28	Matlock	14.05
14.13	M. Bath	15.10
15.17	Matlock	18.13
18.33	ROWSLEY	

Target 71

Arr	Station	Dep
	ROWSLEY	07.20
07.37	Haddon	07.40
07.45	Bakewell	08.57
09.05	Hassop	11.14
11.20	Bakewell	11.33
11.40	Haddon	11.43
11.56	ROWSLEY	12.23
12.33	Darley Dale	14.00
14.13	ROWSLEY	

Target 73

Arr	Station	Dep
	ROWSLEY	07.50
08.27	Crich Jcn	08.35 E & Brake
08.37	Ambergate	10.45
11.28	ROWSLEY	

Target 45

Arr	Station	Dep
	Derby loco	07.12 Light
07.20	St Mary's Yard	07.45
08.08	Duffield	08.38
08.56	Ambergate	10.07
10.20	Whatstandwell	11.03
11.20	High Peak Jcn	12.00
12.08	Whatstandwell	12.18
12.27	Ambergate	15.05
15.18	Buckland	15.29
16.00	Ambergate	18.02
18.49	Matlock	19.01
19.20	ROWSLEY	20.15
21.32	Chaddesden	22.10 Light
22.20	Derby loco	

PEAK FOREST TRIP

Arr	Station	Dep
	ROWSLEY	11.33
11.51	Bakewell	14.15
14.48	Millers Dale	15.00
15.10	P. Forest Jcn	15.30
15.40	Gt Rocks Jcn	16.07
16.15	Peak Forest S	17.00
17.45	ROWSLEY	

Until the late 1950's, the Northwich hopper trains were piloted from Tunstead to Peak Forest North by a 3F 0-6-0. Latterly the working was altered to allow the assisting engine to push from the rear which simplified operations at Peak Forest. Northwich 8F 2-8-0 48717 passes Peak Forest Sidings, almost at the end of the climb from Tunstead. The banking engine will drop off the train at Peak Forest North.

Driver Bretherton of Buxton urges his photographic fireman to get a move on... . 2MT 2-6-0 46465 was a regular engine on the 09.39 Sheffield - Chinley, seen here at Edale, during the first half of the 1960's.

Loco	Class	Aug-52	Sep-52	Oct-52	Nov-52	Dec-52	Jan-53	Feb-53	Mar-53	Apr-53	May-53	Jun-53	Jul-53

ALLOCATION & MOVEMENTS : HEATON MERSEY

Loco	Class	Aug-52	Sep-52	Oct-52	Nov-52	Dec-52	Jan-53	Feb-53	Mar-53	Apr-53	May-53	Jun-53	Jul-53
48089	8F 2-8-0 (1935)												
48099	8F 2-8-0 (1935)												
48127	8F 2-8-0 (1935)												
48134	8F 2-8-0 (1935)						To Willesden	X	X	X	X	X	X
48135	8F 2-8-0 (1935)												
48148	8F 2-8-0 (1935)												
48154	8F 2-8-0 (1935)							To Warrington	X	X	X	Ex Warrington	To Birk'hd
48155	8F 2-8-0 (1935)												
48161	8F 2-8-0 (1935)												
48190	8F 2-8-0 (1935)												
48208	8F 2-8-0 (1935)												
48220	8F 2-8-0 (1935)												
48275	8F 2-8-0 (1935)												
48315	8F 2-8-0 (1935)												
48316	8F 2-8-0 (1935)												
48329	8F 2-8-0 (1935)												
48406	8F 2-8-0 (1935)												
48429	8F 2-8-0 (1935)												
48503	8F 2-8-0 (1935)												
48521	8F 2-8-0 (1935)	X	X	X	X	X	X	X	X	Ex Speke Jcn			
48527	8F 2-8-0 (1935)												
48528	8F 2-8-0 (1935)	X	X	X	X	X	X	X	X	Ex Speke Jcn			
48557	8F 2-8-0 (1935)												
48667	8F 2-8-0 (1935)												
48676	8F 2-8-0 (1935)												
48682	8F 2-8-0 (1935)												
48683	8F 2-8-0 (1935)												
48751	8F 2-8-0 (1935)												
42772	5MT 2-6-0 (1926)			To Longsight	X	X	X	X	X	X	X	X	X
42775	5MT 2-6-0 (1926)												
42788	5MT 2-6-0 (1926)												
42925	5MT 2-6-0 (1926)			To Longsight	X	X	X	X	X	X	X	X	X
64723	5F : J39 0-6-0 (1926)		To Spital B.	X	X	X	X	X	X	X	X	X	X
44080	4F 0-6-0 (1924)												
44090	4F 0-6-0 (1924)	Ex Longsight											
44144	4F 0-6-0 (1924)	To Longsight	X	Ex Longsight									To Mold Jcn
44178	4F 0-6-0 (1924)												
44286	4F 0-6-0 (1924)												
44407	4F 0-6-0 (1924)												
43836	4F 0-6-0 (1911)												
43854	4F 0-6-0 (1911)	X	X	Ex Spital B.									
43945	4F 0-6-0 (1911)	X	X	Ex Longsight									
40089	3P 2-6-2 (1935)												
40094	3P 2-6-2 (1935)												
40113	3P 2-6-2 (1935)												
40124	3P 2-6-2 (1935)												
62663	3P : D11 4-4-0 (1920)												
62665	3P : D11 4-4-0 (1920)												
40405	2P 4-4-0 (1891/1912)												
69262	2MT : N5 0-6-2T (1891)	X	X	X	Ex Northwich								
69276	2MT : N5 0-6-2T (1891)												
69299	2MT : N5 0-6-2T (1891)	X	Ex Gorton										
69317	2MT : N5 0-6-2T (1891)												
69328	2MT : N5 0-6-2T (1891)		To Gorton	X	X	X	X	X	X	X	X	X	X
69331	2MT : N5 0-6-2T (1891)												
69332	2MT : N5 0-6-2T (1891)								To Northgate	X	X	X	X
69359	2MT : N5 0-6-2T (1891)												
58128	2F 0-6-0 (1875)												
65132	2F : J10 0-6-0 (1892)												
65135	2F : J10 0-6-0 (1892)												
65145	2F : J10 0-6-0 (1892)						To Brunswick	X	X	X	X	X	X
65146	2F : J10 0-6-0 (1892)											To T. Park	X
65148	2F : J10 0-6-0 (1892)												
65157	2F : J10 0-6-0 (1892)											To T. Park	X
65160	2F : J10 0-6-0 (1892)												
65178	2F : J10 0-6-0 (1892)												
65181	2F : J10 0-6-0 (1892)		To T. Park	X	X	X	X	X	X	X	X	X	X
65185	2F : J10 0-6-0 (1892)										To Brunswick	X	X
65188	2F : J10 0-6-0 (1892)	W/D	X	X	X	X	X	X	X	X	X	X	X
65193	2F : J10 0-6-0 (1892)	W/D	X	X	X	X	X	X	X	X	X	X	X
65194	2F : J10 0-6-0 (1892)												
65197	2F : J10 0-6-0 (1892)											To T. Park	X
65198	2F : J10 0-6-0 (1892)											To T. Park	X
65200	2F : J10 0-6-0 (1892)												
65209	2F : J10 0-6-0 (1892)											To T. Park	X

2F 0-6-0 22929 - almost a permanent feature (see page 82) of Heaton Mersey's allocation - Heads towards Heaton Mersey station with Target 95 in 1947. Target 95 was known locally as 'Cox's shunt' after a driver who managed to make the second part of the turn his regular turn of duty for many years. The hours involved - 10.30 to 17.48 - were known as 'Gentlemen's hours'.

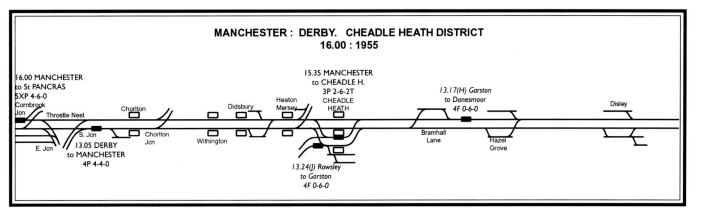

CONTROLLER'S LOG : Although there are more than enough goods trains on the move to keep one occupied, it is time to give attention to the passenger service since there are some interesting gyrations to be made on the main line with the 14.50 Manchester - Derby whilst, at the other end of the district, the Manchester peak service is about to commence.

The suburban service is a mixture of Cheadle Heath/Tiviot Dale all-stations trains worked

ex Cheadle Heath has a fair claim to kicking things off since it brings the stock of the 16.00 Manchester Central to St Pancras from Cornbrook sidings and then follows with the 16.36 local to Stockport.

Leaving eighty minutes earlier, it might be thought that the 14.50 Manchester - Derby had an ample margin ahead of the 16.00 London express but by the time the former has wound its way round the Tiviot Dale route, spent five

less.

Forty miles away, back in Manchester, the working disciplines have to be tight. The 16.00 London is closely followed by the 16.03 to Sheffield - a Trafford Park 4P 4-4-0 - and the 5MT-worked 15.30 Liverpool - Nottingham, both routed via Stockport.

All this means a savaging of freight running especially on the Hope Valley where at the present there are four goods trains and a

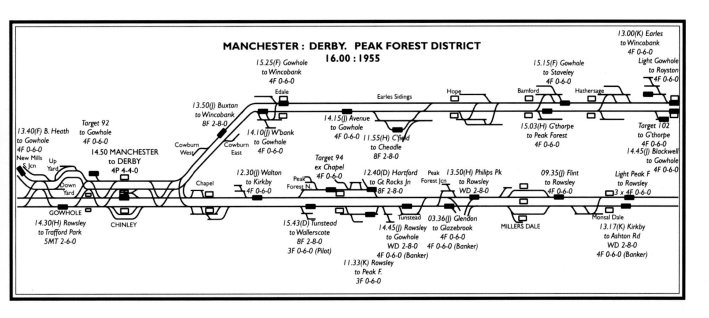

by 3P 2-6-2 tanks, the Sheffield service and a handful of Derby stoppers all of which combine to give some very interesting locomotive sightings. The suburban trains - which all but disappear between the two rush hours - are handled by 3P 2-6-2T's but the longer distance services remain, as they have done for years, in the hands of Compounds and 2P 4-4-0's.

The exact point at which the peak starts is rather difficult to determine but the Heaton Mersey 2-6-2T which arrived with the 13.55

minutes at Chinley and called at every station beyond the gap will have narrowed to such an extent that the order of running has to be reversed. This is achieved by recessing the stopping train in Church Lane loop, Darley Dale, whilst the 16.00 Manchester - St Pancras to overtakes: a piece of highly unimaginative timetabling which all very well for the express but means that the passenger from Rowsley to Darley Dale takes thirty minutes to cover the two and a half mile distance. Most walk it in

light engine making their way east. It is rather early to think about shunting trains - the 16.03 does not leave Chinley for over an hour - but some very quick mental calculations have to be done to ensure that the two trains in the Edale area will be clear in good time. On the main line one assesses the progress of the 12.30 Walton - Kirkby up the hill, wondering whether its 4F - not the most free steaming of engines - will get as far as Millers Dale without knocking the 14.50 and 16.00 passenger trains.

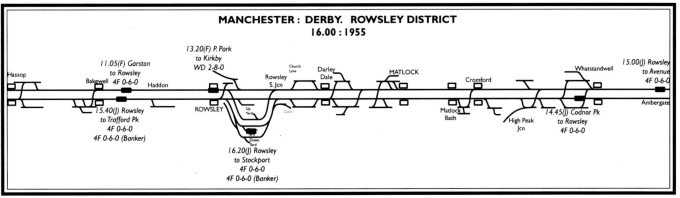

Loco	Class	Aug-53	Sep-53	Oct-53	Nov-53	Dec-53	Jan-54	Feb-54	Mar-54	Apr-54	May-54	Jun-54	Jul-54
	ALLOCATION & MOVEMENTS : HEATON MERSEY												
48089	8F 2-8-0 (1935)												
48099	8F 2-8-0 (1935)												
48127	8F 2-8-0 (1935)												
48135	8F 2-8-0 (1935)												
48148	8F 2-8-0 (1935)												
48155	8F 2-8-0 (1935)		To Northwich	X	X	X	X	X	X	X	X	X	X
48161	8F 2-8-0 (1935)												
48190	8F 2-8-0 (1935)												
48208	8F 2-8-0 (1935)												
48220	8F 2-8-0 (1935)												
48275	8F 2-8-0 (1935)												
48315	8F 2-8-0 (1935)												
48316	8F 2-8-0 (1935)												
48327	8F 2-8-0 (1935)	X	Ex Birk'hd				To Birk'hd	X	X	X	X	X	Ex Birk'hd
48329	8F 2-8-0 (1935)												
48406	8F 2-8-0 (1935)												
48429	8F 2-8-0 (1935)												
48503	8F 2-8-0 (1935)												
48521	8F 2-8-0 (1935)		To Northwich	X	X	X	X	X	X	X	X	X	X
48527	8F 2-8-0 (1935)												
48528	8F 2-8-0 (1935)												
48557	8F 2-8-0 (1935)												
48634	8F 2-8-0 (1935)	X	X	X	X	X	X	Ex Willesden				To Warrington	X
48667	8F 2-8-0 (1935)												
48676	8F 2-8-0 (1935)												
48677	8F 2-8-0 (1935)	X	X	X	X	Ex Lancaster							
48682	8F 2-8-0 (1935)												
48683	8F 2-8-0 (1935)												
48751	8F 2-8-0 (1935)		To Nuneaton	X	X	X	X	X	X	X	X	X	X
42775	5MT 2-6-0 (1926)												
42788	5MT 2-6-0 (1926)												
44080	4F 0-6-0 (1924)												
44090	4F 0-6-0 (1924)												
44144	4F 0-6-0 (1924)	X	Ex Mold Jcn										
44178	4F 0-6-0 (1924)												
44286	4F 0-6-0 (1924)												
44379	4F 0-6-0 (1924)	Ex Kirkby											
44407	4F 0-6-0 (1924)												
43836	4F 0-6-0 (1911)		To Mold Jcn	X	X	X	X	X	X	X	X	X	X
43854	4F 0-6-0 (1911)												
43945	4F 0-6-0 (1911)												
40089	3P 2-6-2 (1935)												
40094	3P 2-6-2 (1935)												
40113	3P 2-6-2 (1935)												
40124	3P 2-6-2 (1935)												
62663	3P : D11 4-4-0 (1920)												
62665	3P : D11 4-4-0 (1920)												
40405	2P 4-4-0 (1891/1912)												
40433	2P 4-4-0 (1891/1912)	X	X	X	X	X	X	X	X	X	X	Ex Buxton	
69262	2MT : N5 0-6-2T (1891)												
69276	2MT : N5 0-6-2T (1891)												
69299	2MT : N5 0-6-2T (1891)												
69317	2MT : N5 0-6-2T (1891)												
69331	2MT : N5 0-6-2T (1891)												
69359	2MT : N5 0-6-2T (1891)												
58128	2F 0-6-0 (1875)												
65132	2F : J10 0-6-0 (1892)												
65135	2F : J10 0-6-0 (1892)												
65148	2F : J10 0-6-0 (1892)												
65160	2F : J10 0-6-0 (1892)												
65178	2F : J10 0-6-0 (1892)												
65194	2F : J10 0-6-0 (1892)												
65200	2F : J10 0-6-0 (1892)												

Slowing for the 50 mph restriction at Rowsley, 5XP 4-6-0 45616 'Malta GC' heads south with the 17.50 Manchester Central - St Pancras on 1st July 1950.

Stranger in the camp.   LM Standard 5MT 4-6-0 45043 of Mold Junction, Chester, waits for relief at Derby South Junction with a Hindlow (Buxton) - Whitemoor limestone special.   The Black Five will work as far as Leicester where it will be changed for a Great Eastern engine.

Stockport may not have been everyone's idea of paradise but to the railway enthusiast it was a breath of Heaven, especially on the CLC lines which presented the unusual sight of Great Central and Midland trains running side by side. The principal traffic flows were from the Guide Bridge area (Great Central) and Gowhole (Midland), merging at Brinnington Junction, Stockport, to run either to Heaton Mersey Yard or through to Merseyside via the Cheshire Lines main line. In the above view 8F 2-8-0 48004 of Kirkby heads West at Heaton Mersey with a train of oil tanks from the Midland. In the lower picture Austerity 2-8-0 90564 (Preston, Lostock Hall) passes St Georges Road Junction, Stockport, with an Immingham - Widnes service.

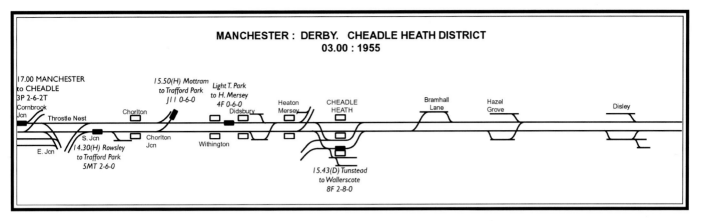

MANCHESTER : DERBY. CHEADLE HEATH DISTRICT
03.00 : 1955

CONTROLLER'S LOG : The reversal of the 16.00 Express and the 14.50 Derby slow has to be monitored carefully.

The regular signalmen can be relied upon to be familiar with the quirks of the timetable but a pair of reliefman at Rowsley South and Church Lane - perhaps on their first visit for weeks and probably ignorant of the fact that the 14.50 Manchester - Derby recesses in the loop for the 16.00 Manchester - London - can easily accept a late running goods from the up main line.

Up Yard : *Dunno.*

Controller : *South Junction? That special Chadd wants to follow the express...*

Rowsley South : *It's all right, control. It's going in the up loop to follow the London.*

Controller : *No it's not all-bloody-right. The Derby passenger uses the loop.*

Rowsley South : *No-one told me.*

Controller : *Hold the Derby passenger until I come back. Church Lane? Has that*

Darley : *What's those silly buggers at Rowsley South playing at? Doesn't he know the Derby is looped for the London.*

Controller : *Where's the Chadd now?*

Darley Dale : *It'll be up the main at oh-two.*

Controller : *Church Lane? Take the Derby from Rowsley South and PUT IT UP THE LOOP when you've had out of section for the Chadd special. Hello, Matlock? Next up to you is a Rowsley - Chadd: just leaving Darley.*

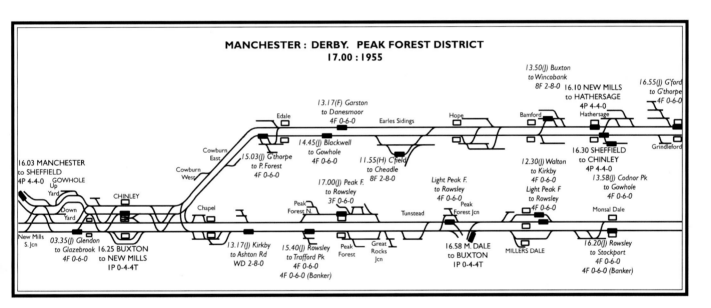

MANCHESTER : DERBY. PEAK FOREST DISTRICT
17.00 : 1955

yard and deftly turn it onto the loop on the assumption that both passenger trains ran direct to Matlock as usual.

A controller worth his salt should be a sufficient number of jumps ahead to prevent such moves from happening but...

Rowsley Up Yard : *Special Chaddesden. 48271. Toton guard 54 = 54 pools. Away at four-fifty.*

Millers Dale : *London away at fifty-two.*

Controller : *I hope that Chadd's not gone*

Chadd gone up the loop yet?

Church Lane : *In at fifty-five.*

Rowsley South : *Derby passenger at my up home. Fifty-five.*

Controller : *Keep it there. Hello, Darley? Pull off for that bloody Chadd. Get it out of the loop and up the main line - keep it going.*

Darley Dale : *Isn't this the Derby passenger coming up my loop?*

Controller : *The Derby'll be up as soon as you've got rid of that three-two.*

Put it inside for the London......"

Later comes the post-mortem. The Derby passenger stood for six minutes waiting for the loop to clear whilst the London caught nothing worse than the Rowsley South Distant; 48271 backing its train inside at Matlock in the nick of time. As soon as Matlock had given out of section for the London, the Chaddesden was allowed back onto the main line for a run to Broadholme loop. The Derby left Church Lane at five twenty-one - on time!

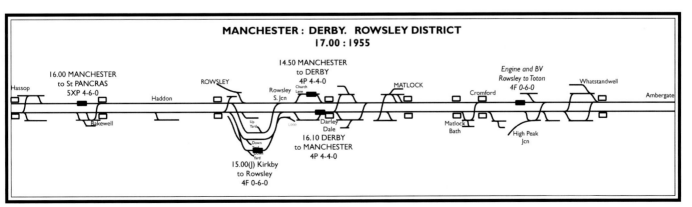

MANCHESTER : DERBY. ROWSLEY DISTRICT
17.00 : 1955

Loco	Class	Aug-54	Sep-54	Oct-54	Nov-54	Dec-54	Jan-55	Feb-55	Mar-55	Apr-55	May-55	Jun-55	Jul-55
	ALLOCATION & MOVEMENTS : HEATON MERSEY												
48089	8F 2-8-0 (1935)												
48099	8F 2-8-0 (1935)												
48127	8F 2-8-0 (1935)												
48135	8F 2-8-0 (1935)												
48148	8F 2-8-0 (1935)												
48161	8F 2-8-0 (1935)												
48190	8F 2-8-0 (1935)												
48208	8F 2-8-0 (1935)												
48220	8F 2-8-0 (1935)												
48275	8F 2-8-0 (1935)												
48315	8F 2-8-0 (1935)												
48316	8F 2-8-0 (1935)												
48327	8F 2-8-0 (1935)												
48329	8F 2-8-0 (1935)												
48406	8F 2-8-0 (1935)												
48429	8F 2-8-0 (1935)												
48501	8F 2-8-0 (1935)	X	X	X	X	X	X	X	X	X	X	Ex Longsight	
48503	8F 2-8-0 (1935)												
48527	8F 2-8-0 (1935)												
48528	8F 2-8-0 (1935)												
48557	8F 2-8-0 (1935)												
48634	8F 2-8-0 (1935)	X	Ex Warrington										
48667	8F 2-8-0 (1935)												
48676	8F 2-8-0 (1935)												
48677	8F 2-8-0 (1935)												
48682	8F 2-8-0 (1935)												
48683	8F 2-8-0 (1935)												
42775	5MT 2-6-0 (1926)												
42788	5MT 2-6-0 (1926)												
42932	5MT 2-6-0 (1926)	X	X	X	X	X	X	X	X	X	X	X	Ex Crewe (S)
44059	4F 0-6-0 (1924)	X	X	X	X	X	X	X	Ex Barrow				
44080	4F 0-6-0 (1924)												
44090	4F 0-6-0 (1924)												
44144	4F 0-6-0 (1924)												
44178	4F 0-6-0 (1924)												
44261	4F 0-6-0 (1924)	X	X	X	X	X	Ex Warrington						
44286	4F 0-6-0 (1924)												
44379	4F 0-6-0 (1924)												
44384	4F 0-6-0 (1924)	X	X	Ex Plodder L.			To Warrington	X	X	X	X	X	X
44407	4F 0-6-0 (1924)												
44421	4F 0-6-0 (1924)	X	Ex Stoke										
43854	4F 0-6-0 (1911)												
43864	4F 0-6-0 (1911)	Ex Stoke	To Stoke	X	X	X	X	X	X	X	X	X	X
43945	4F 0-6-0 (1911)												
40089	3P 2-6-2 (1935)												
40094	3P 2-6-2 (1935)												
40113	3P 2-6-2 (1935)												
40124	3P 2-6-2 (1935)												
40067	3P 2-6-2 (1930)	X	X	X	Ex Tebay								
62663	3P : D11 4-4-0 (1920)	To Lincoln	X	X	X	X	X	X	X	X	X	X	X
62665	3P : D11 4-4-0 (1920)				To Northwich	X	X	X	X	X	X	X	X
40405	2P 4-4-0 (1891/1912)								W/D	X	X	X	X
40433	2P 4-4-0 (1891/1912)												
69262	2MT : N5 0-6-2T (1891)												
69276	2MT : N5 0-6-2T (1891)												
69299	2MT : N5 0-6-2T (1891)												
69317	2MT : N5 0-6-2T (1891)												
69331	2MT : N5 0-6-2T (1891)												
69359	2MT : N5 0-6-2T (1891)												
58128	2F 0-6-0 (1875)												
65132	2F : J10 0-6-0 (1892)												
65135	2F : J10 0-6-0 (1892)												
65148	2F : J10 0-6-0 (1892)												
65160	2F : J10 0-6-0 (1892)												
65178	2F : J10 0-6-0 (1892)												
65194	2F : J10 0-6-0 (1892)												
65200	2F : J10 0-6-0 (1892)												

2F 0-6-0 22929 - later 58128 - had been venerable when the senior drivers of the 1950's had started as junior cleaners yet more than half a century later it was still working from the shed, being the regular engine for Target 95; a trip working which came off shed at 04.05 and tramped the main line between Bramhall Lane and Cheadle Heath until retiring at 17.00 each evening. Thirteen hours work a day was not bad for an engine eighty years old by the 1950's.

Although the working was taken over by a 4F 0-6-0 in 1956, it was far from being the end of the line for 58128 which spend the last four years of its working life at Newton Heath, Burton on Trent and Bushbury. It was eventually taken out of traffic in the autumn of 1962.

Loco	Class	Aug-55	Sep-55	Oct-55	Nov-55	Dec-55	Jan-56	Feb-56	Mar-56	Apr-56	May-56	Jun-56	Jul-56
48089	8F 2-8-0 (1935)												
48099	8F 2-8-0 (1935)												
48127	8F 2-8-0 (1935)												
48135	8F 2-8-0 (1935)									To Northgate	X	X	X
48148	8F 2-8-0 (1935)												
48161	8F 2-8-0 (1935)												
48190	8F 2-8-0 (1935)												
48208	8F 2-8-0 (1935)												
48220	8F 2-8-0 (1935)												
48275	8F 2-8-0 (1935)			To Longsight	X	X	X	X	X	X	X	X	X
48315	8F 2-8-0 (1935)												
48316	8F 2-8-0 (1935)												
48327	8F 2-8-0 (1935)												
48329	8F 2-8-0 (1935)												
48406	8F 2-8-0 (1935)												
48429	8F 2-8-0 (1935)												
48501	8F 2-8-0 (1935)												
48503	8F 2-8-0 (1935)												
48527	8F 2-8-0 (1935)												
48528	8F 2-8-0 (1935)												
48557	8F 2-8-0 (1935)												
48634	8F 2-8-0 (1935)												
48667	8F 2-8-0 (1935)	To Bidston	X	X	X	X	X	X	X	X	X	X	X
48676	8F 2-8-0 (1935)												
48677	8F 2-8-0 (1935)												
48682	8F 2-8-0 (1935)												
48683	8F 2-8-0 (1935)												
48693	8F 2-8-0 (1935)	X	X	X	Ex Bletchley								
48731	8F 2-8-0 (1935)	X	X	Ex Longsight									
42775	5MT 2-6-0 (1926)												
42788	5MT 2-6-0 (1926)												
42932	5MT 2-6-0 (1926)												
44059	4F 0-6-0 (1924)				To M. Lane	X	X	X	X	X	X	X	X
44080	4F 0-6-0 (1924)						To T. Park	X	X	X	X	X	X
44090	4F 0-6-0 (1924)												
44144	4F 0-6-0 (1924)												
44178	4F 0-6-0 (1924)												
44236	4F 0-6-0 (1924)	X	X	X	Ex T. Park								
44261	4F 0-6-0 (1924)												
44286	4F 0-6-0 (1924)												
44361	4F 0-6-0 (1924)	X	X	X	X	X	Ex T. Park						
44379	4F 0-6-0 (1924)												
44387	4F 0-6-0 (1924)	X	X	X	X	Ex Barrow							
44407	4F 0-6-0 (1924)												
44421	4F 0-6-0 (1924)												
43854	4F 0-6-0 (1911)												
43945	4F 0-6-0 (1911)												
40089	3P 2-6-2 (1935)												
40094	3P 2-6-2 (1935)												
40113	3P 2-6-2 (1935)												
40124	3P 2-6-2 (1935)												
40001	3P 2-6-2 (1930)	X	X	Ex Rhyl									
40067	3P 2-6-2 (1930)												
40433	2P 4-4-0 (1891/1912)												
69262	2MT : N5 0-6-2T (1891)												
69276	2MT : N5 0-6-2T (1891)												
69299	2MT : N5 0-6-2T (1891)												
69317	2MT : N5 0-6-2T (1891)							W/D	X	X	X	X	X
69331	2MT : N5 0-6-2T (1891)												
69359	2MT : N5 0-6-2T (1891)									W/D	X	X	X
58128	2F 0-6-0 (1875)									To N. Heath	X	X	X
65132	2F : J10 0-6-0 (1892)												
65135	2F : J10 0-6-0 (1892)												
65148	2F : J10 0-6-0 (1892)												
65160	2F : J10 0-6-0 (1892)												
65178	2F : J10 0-6-0 (1892)												
65187	2F : J10 0-6-0 (1892)	X	X	X	X	X	X	X	X	X	Ex Northwich		
65194	2F : J10 0-6-0 (1892)												
65200	2F : J10 0-6-0 (1892)												

5XP 4-6-0 45650 'Blake' of Kentish Town speeds an up express through New Mills South Junction. Apart from a half-mile section of level track near Disley, the train has been climbing at an average of 1 in 130 for the past nine miles and will have to complete a further eight and a half miles at 1 in 98 before the regulator can be eased. The melodious three-cylinder exhaust will be audible for a long time after the train disappears from view.

Treating its crew to the lively ride typical of the class, 7P 4-6-0 46142 'The York and Lancaster Regiment' hurries a Manchester - St Pancras express over Peak Forest Junction in September 1959 on one of its first trips after being transferred to Kentish Town from Edge Hill. Royal Scot 4-6-0's first appeared on the Midland (south of Leeds) during 1957 as an adjunct to the Britannia Pacifics which took over many of the Trafford Park diagrams. By the end of the decade the Pacifics were found to be suffering because of the tight curves north of Derby, a circumstance that led to a second batch of Scots appearing on the line. The 7P engines never completely extinguished the 5XP's from the Manchester expresses even though the extra power of the larger engines was quite apparent.

Express services over Peak Forest had never been granted anything more powerful that a class 6P (5XP) yet when the new LMS diesels were put onto the run, they were allowed to operate in multiple, giving at least twice the output of the usual Jubilee 4-6-0. 10000 and 10001 wait for the right away at Millers Dale on their first working in multiple. The train is the 16.15 St Pancras - Manchester in 1948.

Not only did they lack the romance of the branch train but they also lacked all the fascinating operating characteristics - light engine movements, empty stock workings, etc - that made railway life so interesting. For several years the London Midland stood out against multiple-unit operation before giving in to pressure from the Transport Commission. A two-car unit arrives in Millers Dale from Buxton with a trial trip on January 13th 1957.

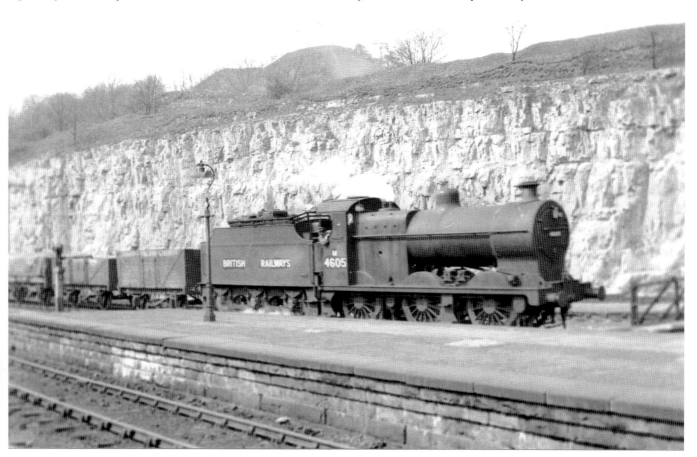

With Derby works at the end of the line and 4F 0-6-0's in near-universal use over Peak Forest, it was said that if you stood on Millers Dale long enough, you would see them all. (4)4605 of Westhouses passes Millers Dale with a train of empties for Kirkby in 1948, the prefix 'M' demonstrating the uncertainty that possessed some of the workshop staff at the time. There were several other 4605's on BR at the time and to the clerical mind, duplication was to be avoided at all costs. Finally 40,000 was added to existing LMS numbers but regarded as silent by staff. Until its last day of work 44605 was referred to as 4605.

With twenty bogies behind the tender, 8F 2-8-0 48303 of Toton - an unusual type of engine for the working - draws to a stand on the slow line at Millers Dale with a train of empty stock from Derby to Cornbrook Sidings, Manchester during the summer of 1956. With the side of a mountain to climb, only one thing matters and that is to have the water level well up the glass and the boiler well and truly hot.

One of Nottingham's best. 5XP 4-6-0 45636 'Uganda' arrives at Millers Dale with the 09.06 Nottingham - Liverpool Central in 1960. Nottingham's 5XP's were amongst the best maintained on the Midland.

Loco	Class	Aug-56	Sep-56	Oct-56	Nov-56	Dec-56	Jan-57	Feb-57	Mar-57	Apr-57	May-57	Jun-57	Jul-57
	ALLOCATION & MOVEMENTS : HEATON MERSEY												
48089	8F 2-8-0 (1935)												
48099	8F 2-8-0 (1935)												
48127	8F 2-8-0 (1935)												
48148	8F 2-8-0 (1935)												
48161	8F 2-8-0 (1935)												
48190	8F 2-8-0 (1935)												
48191	8F 2-8-0 (1935)	X	X	X	X	X	X	X	Ex Wellingbro				
48198	8F 2-8-0 (1935)	X	X	X	X	X	X	X	Ex Wellingbro				
48208	8F 2-8-0 (1935)												
48220	8F 2-8-0 (1935)												
48315	8F 2-8-0 (1935)												
48316	8F 2-8-0 (1935)												
48327	8F 2-8-0 (1935)												
48329	8F 2-8-0 (1935)												
48406	8F 2-8-0 (1935)												
48429	8F 2-8-0 (1935)												
48501	8F 2-8-0 (1935)												
48503	8F 2-8-0 (1935)												
48527	8F 2-8-0 (1935)												
48528	8F 2-8-0 (1935)												
48557	8F 2-8-0 (1935)												
48634	8F 2-8-0 (1935)												
48676	8F 2-8-0 (1935)												
48677	8F 2-8-0 (1935)												
48682	8F 2-8-0 (1935)												
48683	8F 2-8-0 (1935)		To Warrington	X	X	X	X	X	X	X	X	X	X
48693	8F 2-8-0 (1935)		To Warrington	X	X	X	X	X	X	X	X	X	X
48731	8F 2-8-0 (1935)												
73004	5MT 4-6-0 (1951)	X	X	X	X	X	Ex Leicester		To Leicester	X	X	X	X
42775	5MT 2-6-0 (1926)												
42788	5MT 2-6-0 (1926)												
42932	5MT 2-6-0 (1926)		To Crewe (S)	X	X	X	X	X	X	X	X	X	X
44090	4F 0-6-0 (1924)												
44144	4F 0-6-0 (1924)												
44178	4F 0-6-0 (1924)												
44236	4F 0-6-0 (1924)												
44250	4F 0-6-0 (1924)	X	X	X	X	X	X	Ex Rowsley					
44261	4F 0-6-0 (1924)												
44286	4F 0-6-0 (1924)												
44361	4F 0-6-0 (1924)												
44379	4F 0-6-0 (1924)												
44387	4F 0-6-0 (1924)												
44407	4F 0-6-0 (1924)												
44421	4F 0-6-0 (1924)												
44501	4F 0-6-0 (1924)	X	X	X	X	X	X	X	X	Ex Derby			
43854	4F 0-6-0 (1911)												
43945	4F 0-6-0 (1911)												
40089	3P 2-6-2 (1935)												
40094	3P 2-6-2 (1935)												
40113	3P 2-6-2 (1935)												
40124	3P 2-6-2 (1935)												
40001	3P 2-6-2 (1930)												
40004	3P 2-6-2 (1930)	X	X	X	X	X	X	X	X	X	X	Ex Northgate	
40056	3P 2-6-2 (1930)	X	X	X	X	X	X	X	X	X	X	Ex Rugby	
40057	3P 2-6-2 (1930)	X	X	X	X	X	X	X	X	X	X	Ex Rugby	
40059	3P 2-6-2 (1930)	X	X	X	X	X	X	X	X	X	X	Ex Rugby	
40061	3P 2-6-2 (1930)	X	X	X	X	X	X	X	X	X	X	Ex Rugby	
40067	3P 2-6-2 (1930)												
40433	2P 4-4-0 (1891/1912)				To Longsight	X	X	X	X	X	X	X	X
69262	2MT : N5 0-6-2T (1891)												
69276	2MT : N5 0-6-2T (1891)												
69299	2MT : N5 0-6-2T (1891)												
69331	2MT : N5 0-6-2T (1891)						W/D	X	X	X	X	X	X
65132	2F : J10 0-6-0 (1892)												
65135	2F : J10 0-6-0 (1892)												
65148	2F : J10 0-6-0 (1892)				To Darlington	X	X	X	X	X	X	X	X
65160	2F : J10 0-6-0 (1892)												
65178	2F : J10 0-6-0 (1892)												
65187	2F : J10 0-6-0 (1892)												
65194	2F : J10 0-6-0 (1892)												
65200	2F : J10 0-6-0 (1892)												

Most Midland Yards were shunted by Midland or LMS 3F 0-6-0 tanks although a number of more elderly variants were retained in stock for working in restricted locations. Midland 1F 0-6-0T was one such survivor and lasted into the 1960's. It was based at Rowsley until being transferred to Hasland in Autumn 1954.

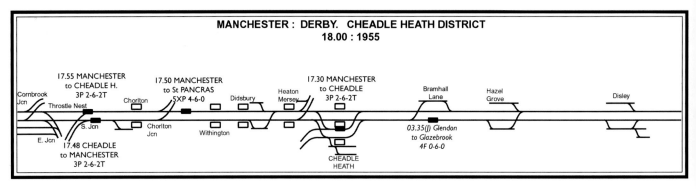

MANCHESTER : DERBY. CHEADLE HEATH DISTRICT
18.00 : 1955

CONTROLLER'S LOG : At the northern end of the district passenger trains are coming up thick and fast with the 17.22 Manchester - Buxton at Chinley, the 17.30 slow from Manchester preparing for its next trip at Cheadle Heath, the 17.50 Manchester - London getting into its stride at Chorlton and a pair of Cheadle locals passing each other at Throstle Nest. All these are worked by standard LMS types although evidence of an older generation is not far away with a Compound getting ready to leave Chinley for Sheffield whilst another of the same class approaches Buxworth

this part of the Midland - the last frontier of the small engine policy - has been fighting a not wholly unsuccessful campaign against LMS standardisation.

Any doubts in this direction can be set to rest by contemplating the 17.24 New Mills - Buxton which, anywhere else on the London Midland, would be worked by a 2-6-4 express tanks and a rake of smart suburban vehicles.

Here a different set of rules seem to apply and the working is formed of a two-coach Buxton - Millers Dale branch set and worked by either by a Midland 2P 0-4-4T or one of the

far as New Mills behind a Great Central 4-4-2T. Until one remembers that a good proportion of London season ticket holders reach Kings Cross and Liverpool Street behind pre-grouping 0-6-2T's, it seems remarkable that it is so easy to travel from England's second city behind engines of such vintage.

As can be seen from the line chart, apart from a train of empties from Walton - Kirkby, the main line is completely free of goods trains. The Hope Valley, on the other hand, has been cleared in the up direction - the double-headed 17.10 Gowhole - Avenue is about to leave the

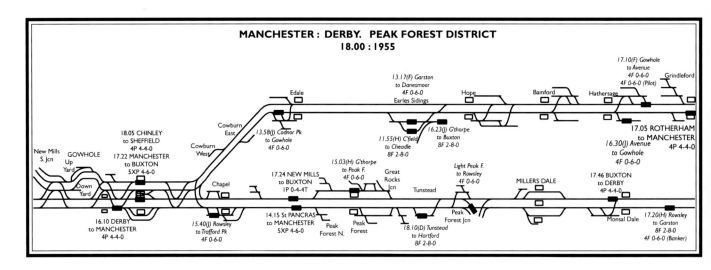

MANCHESTER : DERBY. PEAK FOREST DISTRICT
18.00 : 1955

with the 16.10 ex Derby.

In addition to providing a reasonably comprehensive service the length and breadth of the line, the rush hour also gives the inhabitants of the stations below Chinley an opportunity to sample a run behind a 5XP 4-6-0 - quite a change from the usual 4-4-0 Compound - since the 15.30 Liverpool - Nottingham (16.32 ex Manchester) is an express in name only, calling at Tiviot Dale and then all but the lowliest stations to Derby.

In spite of the taper boilers on some of the faster trains, the Compound, 2P's and 4F 0-6-0's that generally dominate the district's trains do nothing to allay suspicions that somehow

1932 LMS derivatives. Although made up of a motor-train formation, the main line has not been sanctioned as a route over which push and pull operate may work and the 17.24 therefore operates as a conventional service with the 0-4-4T running round its vehicles at New Mills after arriving as the 16.25 ex Buxton.

Not only is it the most pleasant form of anachronism imaginable but it provides a number of highly interesting ways - all pregrouping engines - of getting from Manchester to Buxton. One is to ride as far as New Mills behind the Compound 4-4-0 of the 16.03 ex Manchester whilst another is to start from Manchester, London Road and travel as

area at Grindleford - but the down road is in danger of tying itself in knots as three trains seek refuge in Earles sidings and another shunts clear of the main line at Hathersage. One of the trains 'put inside' at Earles is an eastbound working, the 13.17 Garston - Danesmoor (Clay Cross).

All this shunting is necessary to clear a path for the handful of passenger trains about to use the Hope Valley. Compound 4-4-0's abound with two of the class leaving Chinley for Sheffield with the 18.05 and 18.31 departures whilst whilst a third prepares to leave Grindleford with the 17.05 Rotherham - Manchester.

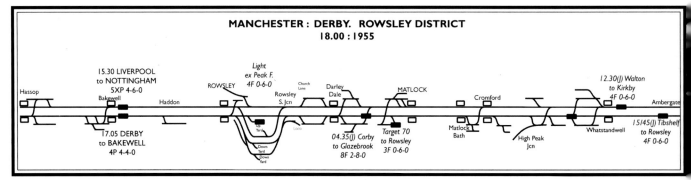

MANCHESTER : DERBY. ROWSLEY DISTRICT
18.00 : 1955

Loco	Class	Aug-57	Sep-57	Oct-57	Nov-57	Dec-57	Jan-58	Feb-58	Mar-58	Apr-58	May-58	Jun-58	Jul-58
48089	8F 2-8-0 (1935)							To Derby	X	X	X	X	X
48099	8F 2-8-0 (1935)												To Toton
48127	8F 2-8-0 (1935)							To W' houses	X	X	X	X	X
48148	8F 2-8-0 (1935)												
48161	8F 2-8-0 (1935)												
48190	8F 2-8-0 (1935)												
48191	8F 2-8-0 (1935)												
48198	8F 2-8-0 (1935)												
48208	8F 2-8-0 (1935)												
48220	8F 2-8-0 (1935)												
48315	8F 2-8-0 (1935)												
48316	8F 2-8-0 (1935)												
48327	8F 2-8-0 (1935)												
48329	8F 2-8-0 (1935)												
48406	8F 2-8-0 (1935)												
48429	8F 2-8-0 (1935)												
48501	8F 2-8-0 (1935)												
48503	8F 2-8-0 (1935)												
48527	8F 2-8-0 (1935)												
48528	8F 2-8-0 (1935)												To Kirkby
48557	8F 2-8-0 (1935)												
48613	8F 2-8-0 (1935)	X	X	X	X	X	X	X	X	X	X	X	Ex Toton
48634	8F 2-8-0 (1935)												
48676	8F 2-8-0 (1935)												
48677	8F 2-8-0 (1935)												
48682	8F 2-8-0 (1935)												
48731	8F 2-8-0 (1935)												
42775	5MT 2-6-0 (1926)												
42788	5MT 2-6-0 (1926)												
42111	4MT 2-6-4T (1945)	X	X	X	X	X	X	X	X	X	X	Ex Nottingham	
42183	4MT 2-6-4T (1945)	X	X	X	X	X	X	X	X	Ex Leicester			
44090	4F 0-6-0 (1924)												
44144	4F 0-6-0 (1924)												
44178	4F 0-6-0 (1924)											To Rowsley	X
44236	4F 0-6-0 (1924)												
44250	4F 0-6-0 (1924)												
44261	4F 0-6-0 (1924)												
44286	4F 0-6-0 (1924)												
44361	4F 0-6-0 (1924)												
44378	4F 0-6-0 (1924)	X	X	X	X	X	X	Ex Derby					
44379	4F 0-6-0 (1924)												
44387	4F 0-6-0 (1924)												
44407	4F 0-6-0 (1924)												
44421	4F 0-6-0 (1924)												
44501	4F 0-6-0 (1924)												
43854	4F 0-6-0 (1911)												
43930	4F 0-6-0 (1911)	X	X	X	X	X	Ex Leicester	To Derby	X	X	X	X	X
43945	4F 0-6-0 (1911)												
40089	3P 2-6-2 (1935)												
40094	3P 2-6-2 (1935)												
40113	3P 2-6-2 (1935)												
40124	3P 2-6-2 (1935)												
40001	3P 2-6-2 (1930)												
40004	3P 2-6-2 (1930)												
40056	3P 2-6-2 (1930)												
40057	3P 2-6-2 (1930)												
40059	3P 2-6-2 (1930)												
40061	3P 2-6-2 (1930)												
40067	3P 2-6-2 (1930)												
69262	2MT : N5 0-6-2T (1891)										To N. England	X	X
69276	2MT : N5 0-6-2T (1891)										To N. England	X	X
69299	2MT : N5 0-6-2T (1891)										To Darnall	X	X
65132	2F : J10 0-6-0 (1892)										W/D	X	X
65135	2F : J10 0-6-0 (1892)									W/D	X	X	X
65160	2F : J10 0-6-0 (1892)											To Rowsley	X
65178	2F : J10 0-6-0 (1892)												
65187	2F : J10 0-6-0 (1892)												
65194	2F : J10 0-6-0 (1892)												
65200	2F : J10 0-6-0 (1892)									W/D	X	X	X

For those in the Buxton area with a taste for adventure, one of the best alternatives to the advertised routes from Manchester was to catch a Great Central suburban suburban train London Road and connect into the 17.24 Buxton train at New Mills. The benefits included a C13 4-4-2T or A5 4-6-2T for the first part of the journey and a Midland 2P 0-4-4T for the second.
C13 67445 wheels a Macclesfield - Manchester (LR) local through the point of convergence with the line from New Mills South Junction at Marple Wharf Junction.

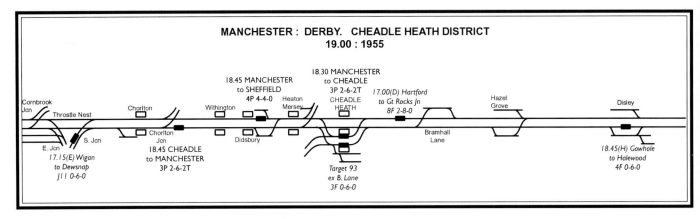

MANCHESTER : DERBY. CHEADLE HEATH DISTRICT
19.00 : 1955

CONTROLLER'S LOG : The pace of life is fast during the rush-hour; incoming reports of train movements and outgoing instructions being continuous and by the time seven o'clock arrives surprising quantities of tea and tobacco have disappeared.

The end looms into sight with the arrival of the 18.30 ex Manchester at Cheadle; its 3P 2-6-2T berthing the stock before finishing its day by running light to Heaton Mersey shed.

The class 3 tanks are rather poor tools but cope well enough with the undemanding Chea-

is better imagined than experienced. The best one can hope for is that the 2-6-2T will struggle as far as Gowhole where it can be relieved by an engine taken from a goods working.

It is generally felt that the pecking order of London Midland districts can be determined by whether or not they have been allocated 3P 2-6-2T's and it is no coincidence that many of them are based at CLC sheds which are neither flesh nor fowl.

Another motive power uncertainty is introduced by the 15.50 Toton - Trafford Park

12.10 goods from Masborough to Toton.

At Toton the engine turns again and heads north with the 15.50 empties to Trafford Park; the engine then running light to Grimesthorpe to carry on working in the Sheffield District.

When Derby turn out an ex-works engine it is not uncommon for it to be run light to Toton for the 15.50, the booked engine running light or taking a special back to Sheffield.

Not untypically someone from the traffic side will suddenly decide that the priority for empties is greater at Bristol than Manchester,

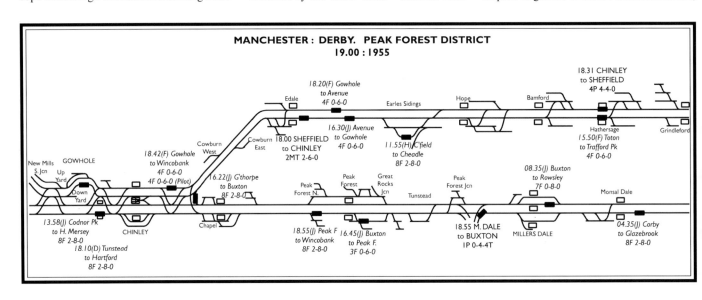

MANCHESTER : DERBY. PEAK FOREST DISTRICT
19.00 : 1955

dle Heath suburban service. The engine which has just worked the six-thirty down has done no more than four trips between Manchester and Cheadle; a day that can hardly be described as intensive although so long as the 2-6-2T's stick to their diagrammed workings, no-one complains very much. The fun starts when an up express comes to grief somewhere around Cheadle Heath and there is nothing else available to assist. It is common knowledge that the 3P's have hardly enough breath for three coaches so the delay that results from coupling one up to a dying 5XP and nine or ten coaches

which is passing Hathersage. This is a working which clears express goods empties - mainly vans - from the Nottingham district and runs them down to Trafford Park for loading; the engine then returning light to Sheffield Grimesthorpe. Lacking a return working, the engine that actually works the train as opposed to the one diagrammed could form the basis of a successful lottery.

The engine starts the day at Barrow Hill by working an early morning mineral train from Seymour Junction to Grimesthorpe before running light to Rotherham to turn and take the

diverting the 15.50 up the West of England line with the result that early the next morning several loco people at Manchester are scratching their heads, wondering where their engine has got to whilst miles away at Bristol, Barrow Road, a brand new engine sits surplus to requirements.

On the Hope Valley local enthusiasts generally turn out to catch sight of the 18.00 Sheffield - Chinley local which is booked to one of the BR standard 2MT 2-6-0s These engines have arrived at Millhouses as replacements for their Midland 2P 4-4-0's .

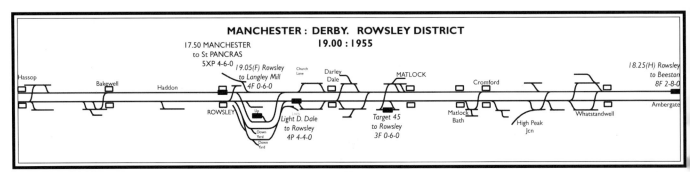

MANCHESTER : DERBY. ROWSLEY DISTRICT
19.00 : 1955

Loco	Class	Aug-58	Sep-58	Oct-58	Nov-58	Dec-58	Jan-59	Feb-59	Mar-59	Apr-59	May-59	Jun-59	Jul-59
	ALLOCATION & MOVEMENTS : HEATON MERSEY												
48148	8F 2-8-0 (1935)			To N. Heath	X	X	X	X	X	X	X	X	X
48161	8F 2-8-0 (1935)												
48190	8F 2-8-0 (1935)												
48191	8F 2-8-0 (1935)												
48198	8F 2-8-0 (1935)											To Derby	X
48208	8F 2-8-0 (1935)												
48220	8F 2-8-0 (1935)		To Annesley	X	X	X	X	X	X	X	X	X	X
48315	8F 2-8-0 (1935)		To Annesley	X	X	X	X	X	X	X	X	X	X
48316	8F 2-8-0 (1935)												
48317	8F 2-8-0 (1935)	X	X	X	X	X	Ex T. Park			To Rowsley	X	X	X
48327	8F 2-8-0 (1935)												
48329	8F 2-8-0 (1935)												
48406	8F 2-8-0 (1935)												
48429	8F 2-8-0 (1935)												
48501	8F 2-8-0 (1935)												
48503	8F 2-8-0 (1935)												
48527	8F 2-8-0 (1935)		To Hasland	X	X	X	X	X	X	X	X	X	X
48543	8F 2-8-0 (1935)	X	X	X	X	Ex W'houses							
48557	8F 2-8-0 (1935)												
48613	8F 2-8-0 (1935)												
48634	8F 2-8-0 (1935)												
48676	8F 2-8-0 (1935)												
48677	8F 2-8-0 (1935)												
48682	8F 2-8-0 (1935)												
48695	8F 2-8-0 (1935)	X	X	X	X	X	X	X	X	X	Ex Wellingbro		
48731	8F 2-8-0 (1935)												
42775	5MT 2-6-0 (1926)						To Saltley	X	X	X	X	X	X
42788	5MT 2-6-0 (1926)						To Saltley	X	X	X	X	X	X
42111	4MT 2-6-4T (1945)						To Hasland	X	X	X	X	X	X
42183	4MT 2-6-4T (1945)						To Brunswick	X	X	X	X	X	X
76085	4MT 2-6-0 (1952)	X	X	X	X	X	Ex Saltley						
76087	4MT 2-6-0 (1952)	X	X	X	X	X	Ex Saltley						
43073	4MT 2-6-0 (1947)	X	X	X	X	X	X	X	X	X	Ex Stockton		
44090	4F 0-6-0 (1924)												
44144	4F 0-6-0 (1924)												W/D
44236	4F 0-6-0 (1924)												
44250	4F 0-6-0 (1924)												
44261	4F 0-6-0 (1924)												
44286	4F 0-6-0 (1924)												
44361	4F 0-6-0 (1924)												
44378	4F 0-6-0 (1924)												
44379	4F 0-6-0 (1924)												
44387	4F 0-6-0 (1924)												
44407	4F 0-6-0 (1924)												
44421	4F 0-6-0 (1924)												
44501	4F 0-6-0 (1924)												
44554	4F 0-6-0 (1924)	X	X	X	X	Ex Coalville							
43854	4F 0-6-0 (1911)					To Coalville	X	X	X	X	X	X	X
43945	4F 0-6-0 (1911)												
43961	4F 0-6-0 (1911)	X	X	X	X	X	X	Ex Rowsley					
44015	4F 0-6-0 (1911)	X	X	X	X	X	X	Ex Brunswick					
40089	3P 2-6-2 (1935)												
40094	3P 2-6-2 (1935)												
40113	3P 2-6-2 (1935)												
40124	3P 2-6-2 (1935)												
40001	3P 2-6-2 (1930)												
40004	3P 2-6-2 (1930)									To Mansfield	Ex Mansfield		
40056	3P 2-6-2 (1930)												
40057	3P 2-6-2 (1930)												
40059	3P 2-6-2 (1930)												
40061	3P 2-6-2 (1930)												
40067	3P 2-6-2 (1930)												
43212	3F 0-6-0 (1885)	X	X	X	X	X	Ex Hasland						
43245	3F 0-6-0 (1885)	X	X	X	X	X	Ex St Albans						
43558	3F 0-6-0 (1885)	X	X	X	X	X	Ex Saltley						
43572	3F 0-6-0 (1885)	X	X	X	X	X	Ex Derby						
65178	2F : J10 0-6-0 (1892)			W/D	X	X	X	X	X	X	X	X	X
65187	2F : J10 0-6-0 (1892)							W/D	X	X	X	X	X
65194	2F : J10 0-6-0 (1892)												

Illustrating the point made several times in this book, 8F 2-8-0 48654 of Rowsley heads a northbound unbanked Class J goods through Great Longstone in April 1956; the trailing load being only a fraction of what one normally expected to see behind a 2-8-0. Because of the severity of gradients between Rowsley and Peak Forest twenty-six vehicles was the maximum permitted by any train - irrespective of the engine - unless a banker was provided.

Although the 4P Compound 4-4-0's were the booked engines for the Manchester - Derby stopping trains, the diagram specified a Class 4 tender engine and thus there was no reason why an Ivatt 'Clodhopper' should not be used at times of shortage. Although intended as a replacement for the 4F 0-6-0, the 162-strong class of 2-6-0's were too few in number and too widely distributed to make much difference to the status of the 0-6-0's. Their most significant impact was on the Midland & Great Northern where almost a third of the class was at work between Peterborough and Great Yarmouth. 43049, one of four allocated to Derby, leaves Monsal Dale whilst deputising for a Compound on a Manchester - Derby working.

Although 4-6-0's and 2-8-0's operated in large numbers elsewhere on the system, the standard engine between Derby and Manchester was the 4F 0-6-0 and larger locomotives were of rather limited benefit since the heaviest unassisted load that could be taken over Peak Forest in either direction was that of a 4F 0-6-0. Thus 5MT 2-6-0 42874, seen passing Great Longstone on the 21st April 1956 with the 14.30 Rowsley to Trafford Park goods, is limited to the 48 wagons of a 4F and not the 53 that would normally be allowed a 5MT.

A good proportion of the trains leaving Rowsley for the north were assisted in rear to either Buxton or Peak Forest and the fifteen mile section was one of the longest continuously banked stretches of line in the country. The volume of traffic south of Peak Forest was such that getting the engines back to Rowsley often posed problems and it was often found expedient to hold engines back at Peak Forest and run them coupled to reduce line occupation. To prevent lengthy cab-first running, returning bankers were routed via Buxton Junction in order to turn on the angle north of Millers Dale. In the above view 44134 which had banked the 13.24 Rowsley - Garston runs through Great Longstone in the company of two 3F 0-6-0's which had assisted the 10.30 Kirkby - Ashton Road and 10.23 Codnor Park - Agecroft services.

On the far side of the Peak, 45553 'Canada' eases the 13.45 Manchester - St Pancras through Rowsley in January 1955. As a Longsight engine, 45553 was something of a stranger to the Midland although as Trafford Park fell within the jurisdiction of Longsight, it was by no means unknown to find LNW 5XP 4-6-0's working towards St Pancras.

Although Aintree's twenty-odd Austerity 2-8-0's were mainly used across its parent L&Y to the Wakefield area, the shed did have a handful of workings up the Midland such as the 11.05 Garston - Rowsley. It appears that there was a hue and cry for mineral empties on June 27th 1957 since instead of returning northwards to Merseyside, 90343 has been utilised to work a southbound train of empties.

2-6-4T 42228 and Horwich Crab 42754 make their way towards Rowsley loco on June 27th 1957. The 2-6-0 had worked into Rowsley with a goods from the North whilst 42228 had arrived light from Bakewell after working the 17.05 passenger from Derby. 42228 was a recent transfer from Derby; having arrived as a replacement for withdrawn Compound 4-4-0 41077.

Loco	Class	Aug-59	Sep-59	Oct-59	Nov-59	Dec-59	Jan-60	Feb-60	Mar-60	Apr-60	May-60	Jun-60	Jul-60
	ALLOCATION & MOVEMENTS : HEATON MERSEY												
48161	8F 2-8-0 (1935)												
48190	8F 2-8-0 (1935)												
48191	8F 2-8-0 (1935)												
48208	8F 2-8-0 (1935)												
48316	8F 2-8-0 (1935)												
48327	8F 2-8-0 (1935)												
48329	8F 2-8-0 (1935)												
48406	8F 2-8-0 (1935)												
48429	8F 2-8-0 (1935)												
48501	8F 2-8-0 (1935)												
48503	8F 2-8-0 (1935)												
48543	8F 2-8-0 (1935)												
48557	8F 2-8-0 (1935)												
48613	8F 2-8-0 (1935)												
48634	8F 2-8-0 (1935)												
48676	8F 2-8-0 (1935)												
48677	8F 2-8-0 (1935)												
48682	8F 2-8-0 (1935)												
48695	8F 2-8-0 (1935)												
48731	8F 2-8-0 (1935)												
76085	4MT 2-6-0 (1952)												
76087	4MT 2-6-0 (1952)												
43073	4MT 2-6-0 (1947)	To Lancaster	X	X	X	X	X	X	X	X	X	X	X
44090	4F 0-6-0 (1924)												
44236	4F 0-6-0 (1924)					To Gorton	X	X	X	X	X	X	X
44250	4F 0-6-0 (1924)												
44261	4F 0-6-0 (1924)										To Hasland	X	X
44286	4F 0-6-0 (1924)												
44361	4F 0-6-0 (1924)				W/D	X	X	X	X	X	X	X	X
44378	4F 0-6-0 (1924)												
44379	4F 0-6-0 (1924)												
44387	4F 0-6-0 (1924)										To W'houses	X	X
44407	4F 0-6-0 (1924)												
44421	4F 0-6-0 (1924)												
44501	4F 0-6-0 (1924)												
44554	4F 0-6-0 (1924)												
43945	4F 0-6-0 (1911)												
43961	4F 0-6-0 (1911)				W/D	X	X	X	X	X	X	X	X
44015	4F 0-6-0 (1911)					To Gorton	X	X	X	X	X	X	X
40089	3P 2-6-2 (1935)												
40094	3P 2-6-2 (1935)												
40097	3P 2-6-2 (1935)	X	X	X	X	X	X	X	Ex T. Park				
40105	3P 2-6-2 (1935)	X	X	X	X	X	X	X	Ex T. Park				
40113	3P 2-6-2 (1935)												
40124	3P 2-6-2 (1935)												
40001	3P 2-6-2 (1930)												
40004	3P 2-6-2 (1930)				W/D	X	X	X	X	X	X	X	X
40056	3P 2-6-2 (1930)		To T. Park	X	X	X	X	X	X	X	X	X	X
40057	3P 2-6-2 (1930)								W/D	X	X	X	X
40059	3P 2-6-2 (1930)				W/D	X	X	X	X	X	X	X	X
40061	3P 2-6-2 (1930)				W/D	X	X	X	X	X	X	X	X
40067	3P 2-6-2 (1930)					W/D	X	X	X	X	X	X	X
43832	3F 0-6-0 (1906)	X	X	X	Ex Toton								
43212	3F 0-6-0 (1885)											W/D	X
43245	3F 0-6-0 (1885)												
43558	3F 0-6-0 (1885)	W/D	X	X	X	X	X	X	X	X	X	X	X
43572	3F 0-6-0 (1885)				To T. Park	X	X	X	X	X	X	X	X
65194	2F : J10 0-6-0 (1892)					W/D	X	X	X	X	X	X	X
D3852	0F : Diesel 0-6-0	X	NEW										
D3853	0F : Diesel 0-6-0	X	NEW										
D3854	0F : Diesel 0-6-0	X	NEW										

There were almost fourteen hundred Midland 0-6-0 goods tender engines including those built by the LMS and it is said that if you stood at Peak Forest long enough, you would see them all. Larger engines were produced from time to time but the 0-6-0 remained the standard between Derby and Manchester for almost the entire life of the line. By the 1950's the 4F had taken over most main line 0-6-0 workings but the 3F's were the preferred engine from the footplate point of view; being a far freer steaming engine than the 4F. The traffic department however were mindful of the fact that on level track the 4F could haul nine more wagons than a 3F and thus the latter tended to vanish from the main line work as more 4F's became available. In the down direction from Rowsley the mineral loading for the two classes was 22 and 26 wagons respectively. 3F 0-6-0 3710 climbs from Dove Holes to Peak Forest with an up train of empties for Rowsley in July 1930.

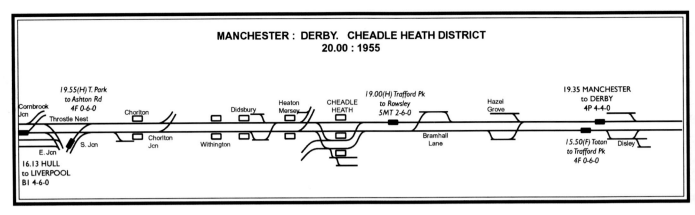

MANCHESTER : DERBY. CHEADLE HEATH DISTRICT
20.00 : 1955

CONTROLLER'S LOG : Anyone can be a Railwayman when things are running smoothly and a good pitch-in sorts the men from the boys. Indeed the best time to be a Controller is when things are running badly but even when they are not, the job is far from dull and there is a fascination to be derived from simply monitoring the movement of trains. It also keeps the telephone circuit well oiled.

Chinley : *"Down Sheffield in the down slow at fifty-nine. Where's the London?"*

Controller: *"Millers Dale. Right time."*

Chinley: *"What about the up slow?"*

Hope Valley is clear. I'll come back to you in a minute about the Glazebrook."

The train card indicates that the 04.35 Corby - Glazebrook is relieved at Chinley

Controller: " *Chinley Inspector? Have you got a set of Heaton men there for the Corby? Send 'em across to the down platform. Engine 8557 and it'll be the next on the down outside."*

Rowsley Down Yard: *"I've made up a double load for the eight-ten. I thought it was banked."*

Controller: *"Well, you'll just have to undouble it....No. Wait a minute."*

for the eight thirty-five Edgeley. 43842 is passing Bakewell. It's the banker for the eleven fifty-five but I may want it for something else first."

Ambergate: *"Blackwell empties up at ten."*

Controller: *"Down Yard? Let that Brindle Heath out."*

Rowsley Up Yard: *"Target 45. 43550 52 equal 52. 12 Wigston on the engine, 40 Chadd roughs. Away at ten. Class J."*

Peak Forest: *"London down at ten."*

Controller: *"Rowsley North? When 43842 gets to you, I want it to bank the Brindle*

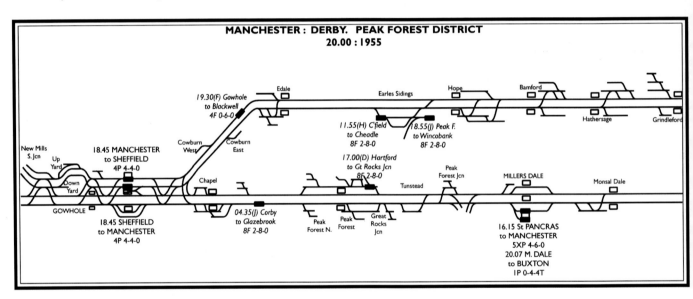

MANCHESTER : DERBY. PEAK FOREST DISTRICT
20.00 : 1955

Controller: *"Disley. Right time."*

Matlock: *"Down slow at one."*

Millers Dale: *"Down London away at one. Buxton'll be away at three."*

Rowsley Down Yard: *"The eight-ten Brindle Heath is a banker job, isn't it?"*

Controller: *"No. Single engine."*

Chinley N. Jcn: *"What's about on the down?"*

Controller: *"Glazebrook at Dove Holes.*

Bramhall: *"Rowsley goods up at four. What's this coming down to me?"*

Controller: *"Main line for Trafford Park. Chinley North? There's relief on its way for the Glazebrook. Stick it down the back outside and let it follow the London."*

New Mills S. Jcn: *"Derby slow up at six."*

Rowsley N. Jcn: *"There's two engines coming up to me..."*

Controller: *"49132 and 43278. Up yard*

Heath."

Rowsley North: *"Do the men know?"*

Controller: *"It'll be a surprise for them.*

Rowsley Down Yard: *"90389. 45 equal 45 L&Y rough for Brindle Heath. Class J, away at ten."*

Controller: *"Rowsley loco? I'm using the eleven fifty-five banker for the eight-ten. You might need to relieve it when it gets back in about two hours......"*

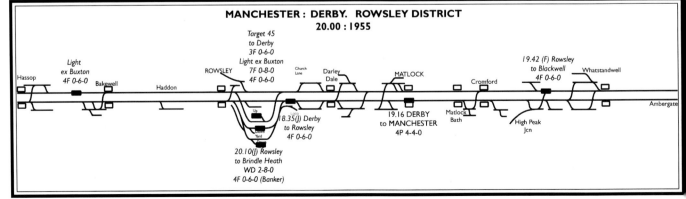

MANCHESTER : DERBY. ROWSLEY DISTRICT
20.00 : 1955

Loco	Class	Aug-50	Sep-50	Oct-50	Nov-50	Dec-50	Jan-51	Feb-51	Mar-51	Apr-51	May-51	Jun-51	Jul-51
42760	5MT 2-6-0 (1926)												
42768	5MT 2-6-0 (1926)												
42873	5MT 2-6-0 (1926)												
42874	5MT 2-6-0 (1926)												
42902	5MT 2-6-0 (1926)												
41049	4P 4-4-0 (1924)												
44046	4F 0-6-0 (1924)												
44050	4F 0-6-0 (1924)												
44134	4F 0-6-0 (1924)												
44163	4F 0-6-0 (1924)												
44168	4F 0-6-0 (1924)												
44172	4F 0-6-0 (1924)												
44246	4F 0-6-0 (1924)												
44327	4F 0-6-0 (1924)												
44429	4F 0-6-0 (1924)												
44540	4F 0-6-0 (1924)					To Derby	X	X	X	X	X	X	X
44564	4F 0-6-0 (1924)												
44565	4F 0-6-0 (1924)	X	X	X	X	Ex Derby							
44566	4F 0-6-0 (1924)	X	X	X	X	Ex Derby							
44588	4F 0-6-0 (1924)												
43835	4F 0-6-0 (1911)												
43865	4F 0-6-0 (1911)												
43872	4F 0-6-0 (1911)												
43881	4F 0-6-0 (1911)												
43882	4F 0-6-0 (1911)												
43894	4F 0-6-0 (1911)												
43918	4F 0-6-0 (1911)												
43921	4F 0-6-0 (1911)												
43925	4F 0-6-0 (1911)												
43929	4F 0-6-0 (1911)												
44017	4F 0-6-0 (1911)												
44018	4F 0-6-0 (1911)												
44024	4F 0-6-0 (1911)												
47447	3F 0-6-0T (1924)												
47457	3F 0-6-0T (1924)												
47459	3F 0-6-0T (1924)												
47460	3F 0-6-0T (1924)												
47461	3F 0-6-0T (1924)												
47679	3F 0-6-0T (1924)												
43779	3F 0-6-0 (1906)										To Kirkby	X	X
43273	3F 0-6-0 (1885)												
43290	3F 0-6-0 (1885)												
43342	3F 0-6-0 (1885)												
43370	3F 0-6-0 (1885)												
40499	2P 4-4-0 (1891/1912)												
40520	2P 4-4-0 (1891/1912)												
58850	2F 0-6-0T (1879)												
58856	2F 0-6-0T (1879)												
58860	2F 0-6-0T (1879)												
58862	2F 0-6-0T (1879)												
58189	2F 0-6-0 (1878)												
58219	2F 0-6-0 (1878)												
58224	2F 0-6-0 (1878)												
58226	2F 0-6-0 (1878)												
58228	2F 0-6-0 (1878)												
58254	2F 0-6-0 (1878)												
41875	1F 0-6-0T (1878)												

ROWSLEY YARD. STOCK POSITION AT :

	UP YARD	On Hand		DOWN YARD	On Hand
Road					
1	-		1	Buxton	
2	Chaddesden		2	Brunswick	
3	Washwood Heath		3	Ashton Road	
4	Nottingham		4	Brewery	
5	Toton up		5	Heaton Mersey	
6	Toton Down		6	Ancoats	
7	Leicester		7	Walton	
8	London		9	Gowhole	
9	Derby rough		10	Down Road local	
10	Peterborough		11	Cheadle Exchange	
11			12	Agecroft	
			13	Longsight	
			14	Garston	
			15	Trafford Park	
			16	Brindle Heath	
			17	Edgeley	
			18	Belle Vue	
			19	Edge Hill	
			20		
			21		
			22	Cripple Road	

On the left is a representation of the stock report which was telephoned several times a shift from the Yard Inspectors to the Controller. Each row in the report corresponded to a specific siding and each siding was reserved for traffic bound for a particular destination.

When the report had been received the Controller would use it to assess the loadings for departures, taking into account traffic that was about to arrive (pipeline traffic) at Rowsley.

Ancient and Modern.   Whilst its fireman fiddles with a camera, 4F 0-6-0 44169 of Buxton blows off as its waits for the road at Bakewell with an up goods. Midland 0-6-0's and their derivatives were as much a piece of the line as the stations and lasted in the area until 1966.   BR 4MT 4-6-0 75033 represented a very different kettle of fish; the class arrived at the very end of steam and went largely unnoticed.

LM Standard 5MT 4-6-0 emerges from Willersley tunnel and rockets through Cromford with the 13.45 Manchester Central - St Pancras on 24th May 1952.

Gradients were not steep in the Southern part of the district but the 1 in 584 rise between Ambergate and Rowsley required enough steam to keep the couplings taut as the incline steepened the nearer one got to Rowsley. 8F 2-8-0 48379 approaches Whatstandwell with the 15.00 Kirkby - Rowsley on 24th May 1952; the load of seventy wagons of coal making a considerable contrast with what could be taken north of Rowsley. The route taken was Kirkby to Riddings Junction and over the Butterley branch to Ambergate; the train being banked between Ironville Junction and Swanwick.

Deputising for the usual 5MT 2-6-0, 8F 48331 of Saltley passes Whatstandwell in May 1952 with the 15.15 Rowsley - Wahwood Heath Class H goods.

In a move typical of the London Midland, in 1960 it was decided that the region had a shortage of class 6 locomotives. The deficit was neatly resolved by regrading the Crab 2-6-0 engines from 5MT to 6P/5F and making them thus - on paper - the equal of a Jubilee 4-6-0. 42818 of Burton, one of the examples fitted with rotary motion, celebrates its promotion by working a Derby - Manchester slow train, seen running into Ambergate station, on 27th August 1960.

Loco	Class	Aug-51	Sep-51	Oct-51	Nov-51	Dec-51	Jan-52	Feb-52	Mar-52	Apr-52	May-52	Jun-52	Jul-52
42760	5MT 2-6-0 (1926)												
42768	5MT 2-6-0 (1926)												
42792	5MT 2-6-0 (1926)	X	X	X	X	X	X	X	X	Ex Leicester		To Spital B.	X
42873	5MT 2-6-0 (1926)												
42874	5MT 2-6-0 (1926)												
42902	5MT 2-6-0 (1926)												
41049	4P 4-4-0 (1924)												
44046	4F 0-6-0 (1924)												
44050	4F 0-6-0 (1924)												
44134	4F 0-6-0 (1924)												
44163	4F 0-6-0 (1924)												
44168	4F 0-6-0 (1924)												
44172	4F 0-6-0 (1924)												
44246	4F 0-6-0 (1924)												
44327	4F 0-6-0 (1924)												
44429	4F 0-6-0 (1924)												
44564	4F 0-6-0 (1924)												
44565	4F 0-6-0 (1924)												
44566	4F 0-6-0 (1924)												
44588	4F 0-6-0 (1924)												
43835	4F 0-6-0 (1911)												
43865	4F 0-6-0 (1911)									To Saltley	X	X	X
43872	4F 0-6-0 (1911)												
43881	4F 0-6-0 (1911)												
43882	4F 0-6-0 (1911)												
43894	4F 0-6-0 (1911)												
43918	4F 0-6-0 (1911)												
43921	4F 0-6-0 (1911)												
43925	4F 0-6-0 (1911)												
43929	4F 0-6-0 (1911)												
44017	4F 0-6-0 (1911)												
44018	4F 0-6-0 (1911)									To Derby	X	X	X
44024	4F 0-6-0 (1911)												
47447	3F 0-6-0T (1924)												
47457	3F 0-6-0T (1924)												
47459	3F 0-6-0T (1924)												
47460	3F 0-6-0T (1924)												
47461	3F 0-6-0T (1924)												
47679	3F 0-6-0T (1924)												
43776	3F 0-6-0 (1906)	X	X	X	X	Ex Derby							
43273	3F 0-6-0 (1885)												
43290	3F 0-6-0 (1885)												
43342	3F 0-6-0 (1885)												
43370	3F 0-6-0 (1885)												
43724	3F 0-6-0 (1885)	X	X	X	Ex Nottingham								
43759	3F 0-6-0 (1885)	X	X	X	Ex Saltley								
40499	2P 4-4-0 (1891/1912)												
40520	2P 4-4-0 (1891/1912)												
58850	2F 0-6-0T (1879)												
58856	2F 0-6-0T (1879)												
58860	2F 0-6-0T (1879)												
58862	2F 0-6-0T (1879)												
58189	2F 0-6-0 (1878)												
58219	2F 0-6-0 (1878)					To Derby	X	X	X	X	X	X	X
58224	2F 0-6-0 (1878)					To Derby	X	X	Ex Derby				
58226	2F 0-6-0 (1878)						W/D	X	X	X	X	X	X
58228	2F 0-6-0 (1878)												
58254	2F 0-6-0 (1878)				To Burton	X	Ex Burton		W/D	X	X	X	X
41875	1F 0-6-0T (1878)												
47000	0F 0-4-0ST (1932)	X	X	X	X	X	X	X	X	Ex Burton			

ALLOCATION & MOVEMENTS : ROWSLEY

Snow, steam and smoke as 48060 of Westhouses takes advantage of a clear road through Chapel-en-le-Frith during the winter of 1955 with a special goods from the Cheshire lines to Rowsley.

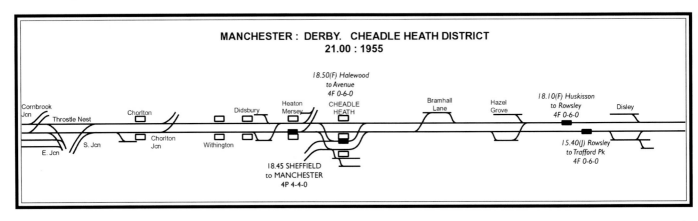

MANCHESTER : DERBY. CHEADLE HEATH DISTRICT
21.00 : 1955

CONTROLLER'S LOG : An hour later it is still going on...

Rowsley Down Yard: *"Gowhole away at fifty-eight. 44101, 45 equal 50, all for Gowhole. Class J, Banker load."*

Millers Dale: *"Goods on the down at fifty-nine."*

Controller : *"Rowsley North? Banker load drawing down to you. 44046 is the banker."*

Rowsley North: *"How far's the banker going?"*

Controller: *"Peak Forest North and back for anything?"*

Controller: *"No. Send it home light."*

Peak Forest Sth: *"Light to Buxton at three."*

Dove Holes: *"Seven Bells to Peak Forest North for the Trafford Park - Rowsley. Passed me at three. Axlebox glowing about third from the brake."*

Controller: *"Have you put on against it?"*

Dove Holes: *"Yes."*

Controller: *"Chinley South? Put the Buxton stock in the up loop. We could have the up*

to you is the Huskisson - Walton. Put it up the slow. I've got an ABR 17 in Dove Holes tunnel."

New Mills Sth: *"What's happened?"*

Controller: *"He's sent stop and examine to Peak Forest North for the Trafford Park. Seems to be a hot box - I hope it doesn't fall to bits in the tunnel."*

Dove Holes: *"Hello, Control. The Trafford saw my starter go back and he managed to pull up just inside the tunnel. The guard's gone back to examine the train."*

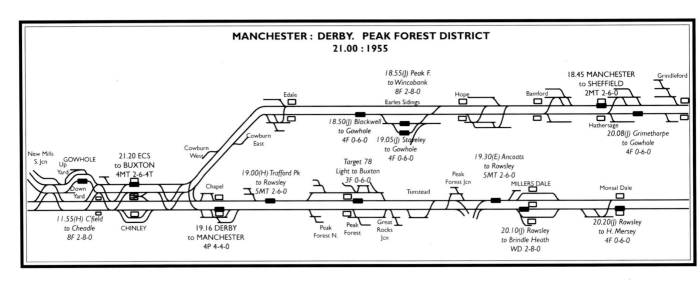

MANCHESTER : DERBY. PEAK FOREST DISTRICT
21.00 : 1955

light."

Bakewell: *"Up slow away at two."*

Controller: *"Peak Forest North? Coming down: Brindle Heath at Millers Dale, Banker off at you and back light to Rowsley. Followed by a Heaton Mersey, no banker. A Gowhole is just leaving Rowsley - it might get to you ahead of the London, I'll let you know. Somewhere in that lot will be the ICI hoppers for Hartford."*

Chinley: *"Buxton stock up at two."*

Peak Forest South: *"D'you want Target 78*

main blocked for a time."

Chinley S.: *"Will do. Derby passenger down at four. The stock'll be inside at seven."*

Controller: *"Great Rocks? Target 78 engine should be passing you in a minute or two. Don't let it go until I tell you. I may need it to examine the line between Peak Forest and Chapel."*

Great Rocks: *"It'll be here in a couple of minutes. I'll keep it here."*

Controller: *"New Mills South? Next up*

Rowsley Nth: *"Up passenger away at nine."*

Millers Dale: *"Heaton Mersey down at nine."*

Ambergate W: *"Kirkby Goods up at ten."*

Dove Holes: *"Control? The Trafford Guard can't find nothing. He's checked and all his boxes are cool. I must be seeing things. Shall I pull off."*

Controller: *"Yes."*

Never a dull moment.

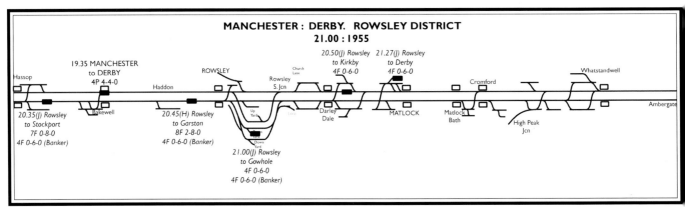

MANCHESTER : DERBY. ROWSLEY DISTRICT
21.00 : 1955

Loco	Class	Aug-52	Sep-52	Oct-52	Nov-52	Dec-52	Jan-53	Feb-53	Mar-53	Apr-53	May-53	Jun-53	Jul-53
						ALLOCATION & MOVEMENTS : ROWSLEY							
42760	5MT 2-6-0 (1926)												
42768	5MT 2-6-0 (1926)												
42792	5MT 2-6-0 (1926)	X	X	Ex Spital B.									
42873	5MT 2-6-0 (1926)												
42874	5MT 2-6-0 (1926)												
42902	5MT 2-6-0 (1926)												
40929	4P 4-4-0 (1924)	X	X	X	Ex Bedford								
40931	4P 4-4-0 (1924)	X	X	Ex K. Town									
41049	4P 4-4-0 (1924)				To Bedford	X	X	X	X	X	X	X	X
44028	4F 0-6-0 (1924)	X	X	Ex C' wood									
44046	4F 0-6-0 (1924)												
44050	4F 0-6-0 (1924)												
44101	4F 0-6-0 (1924)	X	X	X	X	X	X	X	X	X	Ex Derby		
44134	4F 0-6-0 (1924)												
44163	4F 0-6-0 (1924)												
44168	4F 0-6-0 (1924)												
44172	4F 0-6-0 (1924)												
44246	4F 0-6-0 (1924)										To Stoke	X	X
44327	4F 0-6-0 (1924)												
44429	4F 0-6-0 (1924)												
44564	4F 0-6-0 (1924)												
44565	4F 0-6-0 (1924)												
44566	4F 0-6-0 (1924)												
44588	4F 0-6-0 (1924)												
43835	4F 0-6-0 (1911)												
43872	4F 0-6-0 (1911)												To Canklow
43881	4F 0-6-0 (1911)												
43882	4F 0-6-0 (1911)			To Sheffield	X	X	X	X	X	X	X	X	X
43894	4F 0-6-0 (1911)												
43918	4F 0-6-0 (1911)												
43921	4F 0-6-0 (1911)												
43925	4F 0-6-0 (1911)												
43929	4F 0-6-0 (1911)												
44017	4F 0-6-0 (1911)												
44018	4F 0-6-0 (1911)	X	X	X	X	X	X	X	X	X	Ex Derby		To Derby
44024	4F 0-6-0 (1911)										To Stoke	X	X
47447	3F 0-6-0T (1924)												
47457	3F 0-6-0T (1924)												
47459	3F 0-6-0T (1924)												
47460	3F 0-6-0T (1924)												
47461	3F 0-6-0T (1924)												
47679	3F 0-6-0T (1924)												
43776	3F 0-6-0 (1906)												
43273	3F 0-6-0 (1885)												
43290	3F 0-6-0 (1885)												
43342	3F 0-6-0 (1885)												
43370	3F 0-6-0 (1885)												
43400	3F 0-6-0 (1885)	X	X	X	X	Ex C' wood							
43496	3F 0-6-0 (1885)	X	X	X	X	X	X	X	X	X	X	Ex Derby	
43658	3F 0-6-0 (1885)	X	X	X	X	X	X	X	X	X	X	Ex Derby	
43724	3F 0-6-0 (1885)					W/D	X	X	X	X	X	X	X
43759	3F 0-6-0 (1885)												
40499	2P 4-4-0 (1891/1912)	W/D	X	X	X	X	X	X	X	X	X	X	X
40520	2P 4-4-0 (1891/1912)												
58850	2F 0-6-0T (1879)												
58856	2F 0-6-0T (1879)												
58860	2F 0-6-0T (1879)												
58862	2F 0-6-0T (1879)												
58189	2F 0-6-0 (1878)												
58224	2F 0-6-0 (1878)												
58228	2F 0-6-0 (1878)												
41875	1F 0-6-0T (1878)												
47000	0F 0-4-0ST (1932)												

Midland 2P 4-4-0 532 blows off as it reduces speed at Rowsley North Junction with a four-coach up relief express in April 1932.

North of Derby, four-line running extended as far as Duffield; the slow lines straddling the up and down main rather than the usual Midland practice of separating them into pairs. In the upper view 5XP 4-6-0 45557 'New Hebrides' streaks through Duffield with an up express whilst, lower, 8F 2-8-0 48088 fails to get through the station with a Chaddesden - Buxton goods and is held back by signals to let the 16.15 Derby - Manchester proceed. The fireman passes the time by jumping off the engine and aiming his camera.......

The same fireman had time to walk back and take a shot of 8F 2-8-0 48532 after it had been brought to a stand at Derby North Junction with the 13.07 Buxton - Rowsley extended to Chaddesden.   Moving in the opposite direction, lower, is 9F 2-10-0 92208 as it runs light from Derby loco to Chaddesden Yard.

ALLOCATION & MOVEMENTS : ROWSLEY													
Loco	Class	Aug-53	Sep-53	Oct-53	Nov-53	Dec-53	Jan-54	Feb-54	Mar-54	Apr-54	May-54	Jun-54	Jul-54
48432	8F 2-8-0 (1935)	X	X	X	X	X	X	X	X	X	X	Ex Derby	
48654	8F 2-8-0 (1935)	X	X	X	X	X	X	X	X	X	X	Ex Derby	
42760	5MT 2-6-0 (1926)												
42768	5MT 2-6-0 (1926)												
42792	5MT 2-6-0 (1926)												
42873	5MT 2-6-0 (1926)												
42874	5MT 2-6-0 (1926)												
42902	5MT 2-6-0 (1926)												To Kettering
40929	4P 4-4-0 (1924)												
40931	4P 4-4-0 (1924)												
44028	4F 0-6-0 (1924)												
44046	4F 0-6-0 (1924)												
44050	4F 0-6-0 (1924)												
44101	4F 0-6-0 (1924)												
44134	4F 0-6-0 (1924)												
44163	4F 0-6-0 (1924)												
44166	4F 0-6-0 (1924)	X	X	X	X	X	X	X	X	X	X	X	Ex Burton
44168	4F 0-6-0 (1924)												
44172	4F 0-6-0 (1924)												
44241	4F 0-6-0 (1924)	X	X	X	X	X	X	X	X	X	X	Ex Stourton	
44327	4F 0-6-0 (1924)												
44334	4F 0-6-0 (1924)	X	X	X	X	X	X	X	X	X	X	X	Ex Sheffield
44429	4F 0-6-0 (1924)												
44556	4F 0-6-0 (1924)	X	X	X	X	X	X	X	X	X	X	X	Ex Sheffield
44564	4F 0-6-0 (1924)												
44565	4F 0-6-0 (1924)												
44566	4F 0-6-0 (1924)												
44588	4F 0-6-0 (1924)												
43835	4F 0-6-0 (1911)												
43881	4F 0-6-0 (1911)												
43894	4F 0-6-0 (1911)												
43918	4F 0-6-0 (1911)												
43921	4F 0-6-0 (1911)												
43925	4F 0-6-0 (1911)	To Derby	X	X	X	X	X	X	X	X	X	X	X
43929	4F 0-6-0 (1911)												
44017	4F 0-6-0 (1911)												
44018	4F 0-6-0 (1911)	Ex Derby											
47447	3F 0-6-0T (1924)												
47457	3F 0-6-0T (1924)												
47459	3F 0-6-0T (1924)												
47460	3F 0-6-0T (1924)												
47461	3F 0-6-0T (1924)												
47679	3F 0-6-0T (1924)												
43776	3F 0-6-0 (1906)												
43273	3F 0-6-0 (1885)												
43290	3F 0-6-0 (1885)												
43342	3F 0-6-0 (1885)												
43370	3F 0-6-0 (1885)												
43400	3F 0-6-0 (1885)												
43496	3F 0-6-0 (1885)												
43658	3F 0-6-0 (1885)								To Coalville	X	X	X	X
43759	3F 0-6-0 (1885)												
40520	2P 4-4-0 (1891/1912)												
58850	2F 0-6-0T (1879)												
58856	2F 0-6-0T (1879)												
58860	2F 0-6-0T (1879)												
58862	2F 0-6-0T (1879)												
58189	2F 0-6-0 (1878)												
58224	2F 0-6-0 (1878)												
58228	2F 0-6-0 (1878)												
41875	1F 0-6-0T (1878)												
47000	0F 0-4-0ST (1932)												

A down goods pulls away from Ambergate behind 3F 0-6-0 3294 in April 1932. 3294 remained in traffic for almost another thirty years, being withdrawn from Sutton Oak in November 1959.

Loco	Class	Aug-54	Sep-54	Oct-54	Nov-54	Dec-54	Jan-55	Feb-55	Mar-55	Apr-55	May-55	Jun-55	Jul-55
	ALLOCATION & MOVEMENTS : ROWSLEY												
48432	8F 2-8-0 (1935)												
48654	8F 2-8-0 (1935)												
42760	5MT 2-6-0 (1926)												
42768	5MT 2-6-0 (1926)												
42792	5MT 2-6-0 (1926)												
42873	5MT 2-6-0 (1926)												
42874	5MT 2-6-0 (1926)												
42902	5MT 2-6-0 (1926)	X	Ex Kettering										
40929	4P 4-4-0 (1924)												
40931	4P 4-4-0 (1924)												
44028	4F 0-6-0 (1924)												
44046	4F 0-6-0 (1924)												
44050	4F 0-6-0 (1924)												
44101	4F 0-6-0 (1924)												
44134	4F 0-6-0 (1924)												
44163	4F 0-6-0 (1924)												
44166	4F 0-6-0 (1924)				To Coalville	X	X	X	X	X	X	X	X
44168	4F 0-6-0 (1924)												
44172	4F 0-6-0 (1924)												
44241	4F 0-6-0 (1924)												
44327	4F 0-6-0 (1924)												
44334	4F 0-6-0 (1924)				To Derby	X	X	X	X	X	X	X	X
44429	4F 0-6-0 (1924)												
44556	4F 0-6-0 (1924)												
44564	4F 0-6-0 (1924)												
44565	4F 0-6-0 (1924)												
44566	4F 0-6-0 (1924)												
44588	4F 0-6-0 (1924)												
44602	4F 0-6-0 (1924)	X	X	X	X	X	X	X	Ex Derby				
43835	4F 0-6-0 (1911)												
43881	4F 0-6-0 (1911)												
43894	4F 0-6-0 (1911)												
43918	4F 0-6-0 (1911)												
43921	4F 0-6-0 (1911)												
43929	4F 0-6-0 (1911)												
44017	4F 0-6-0 (1911)												
44018	4F 0-6-0 (1911)						To Nottingham	X	X	X	X	X	X
47447	3F 0-6-0T (1924)												
47457	3F 0-6-0T (1924)												
47459	3F 0-6-0T (1924)												
47460	3F 0-6-0T (1924)												
47461	3F 0-6-0T (1924)												
47679	3F 0-6-0T (1924)												
43776	3F 0-6-0 (1906)												
43273	3F 0-6-0 (1885)												
43290	3F 0-6-0 (1885)												
43342	3F 0-6-0 (1885)												
43370	3F 0-6-0 (1885)												
43400	3F 0-6-0 (1885)												
43496	3F 0-6-0 (1885)												
43750	3F 0-6-0 (1885)	X	X	X									
43759	3F 0-6-0 (1885)												
40520	2P 4-4-0 (1891/1912)												
58850	2F 0-6-0T (1879)												
58856	2F 0-6-0T (1879)												
58860	2F 0-6-0T (1879)												
58862	2F 0-6-0T (1879)												
58189	2F 0-6-0 (1878)												
58224	2F 0-6-0 (1878)												
58228	2F 0-6-0 (1878)												
41875	1F 0-6-0T (1878)		To Hasland	X	X	X	X	X	X	X	X	X	X
47000	0F 0-4-0ST (1932)												

4P Compound 4-4-0 41150 waits to leave Sheffield Midland with a Hope Valley service in 1955. Displaced from Llandudno Junction by BR standard locomotives in Spring 1954, 41150 spent its final three years working from Trafford Park and was withdrawn in September 1957.

"On the 4th of April 1966 Harry Moss - my driver - and I had worked into Gowhole with 8F 2-8-0 48495 on the 06.25 goods from Buxton - Gowhole. We turned and watered the engine for the return working and were just starting our breakfasts when the Inspector ordered us light to Disley all speed. He told us that the 07.25 Manchester - London express had failed and that we were to give assistance.

Although Harry was the driver, it was his turn to fire and, credit were it is due, he stuck to his part of the agreement without a murmur.

We rocketed off towards Disley in a cloud of black smoke and arrived to find the express dormant behind a very dead 2500hp Sulzer diesel. Because of the position the train was in we were unable to remove the failed engine and therefore had to assist not only the 11 vehicles of the express but 118 tons of diesel as well.

We set off with gusto hoping to get a good start before hitting the 1 in 98 gradient which runs for the eight and a half miles between New Mills South and Peak Forest. Fortune was not with us and no sooner had 48495 got hold of the train than we were sent slow road from New Mills South to Chinley North Junction to allow the Blue Pullman to overtake us. With the 8F barking like a dog, Harry working like a black and the footplate rolling like the bridge of a ship we stormed through Chapel-en-le-Frith and into Dove Holes tunnel where we must have tripled the density of the atmosphere. God help any passengers who had the window open.

Eventually we struggled over the top at Peak Forest where Harry was able to put the shovel down and put his feet up. If he had had a rough time of it so far, the tables were about to turn as we accelerated downhill. 48495 had been rough at normal speeds but as we rose through the fifties and got close to the 60's, every turn of a wheel confirmed how run down it was.

I wondered if control would pull us up at Rowsley for a change of engines but the boards were off and so I kept going with 48495 rolling so much that the risk of injury was not far away.

Just as matters were starting to become severely uncomfortable, the diesel came to life and started to give us such a violent push that it became difficult to remain on the engine. Fortunately after a few minutes effort it failed again but not before pushing us to a speed that, given our condition, was dangerous. We rolled into Derby, uncoupled and ran the diesel to the shed. We examined the bearings and motion on 48495 and found them to be quite cool - certainly in better shape than its crew." : Author.

ROWSLEY MPD : ENGINE ARRANGEMENTS 1960								
Inward working	On Shed	Engine	Off Shed	Train	Inward working	On Shed	Engine	Off Shed	Train
09.15 Walton - Rowsley	14.48	4F 0-6-0	02.25	02.45 Rowsley - Walton	Light ex Peak Forest		3F 0-6-0	12.00	Bank 12.25 Rowsley - P. Forest
19.02 Trafford Pk - Rowsley	21.10	BR5 4-6-0	02.50	03.10 St Pancras	Light ex Matlock (Target 70)	10.40	4F 0-6-0	12.30	12.55 Rowsley - Matlock (Target 70)
Light ex Peak Forest	23.15	8F 2-8-0	04.30	04.51 Buxton	Up Yard Pilot	06.05	3F 0-6-0T	13.55	Up Yard Pilot
20.00 Huskisson - Rowsley	00.40	4F 0-6-0	04.45	Bank 04.51 Rowsley - Buxton	22.45 Cricklewood - Rowsley	03.50	BR5 4-6-0	14.10	14.30 Rowsley - Trafford Park
Light ex Dove Holes (LNW)	03.30	3F 0-6-0	04.49	Bank 20.35 Corby - Glazebrook	Light ex Peak Forest	08.00	4F 0-6-0	14.20	Bank 14.45 Rowsley - Gowhole
Light ex Peak Forest	01.52	3F 0-6-0	05.10	Bank 05.35 Roiwsley - Buxton	12.15 Ambergate - Rowsley (Target 7	13.00	4F 0-6-0	14.25	14.45 Rowsley - Gowhole
Light ex Peak Forest	01.16	4F 0-6-0	05.44	Bank 03.50 Pinxton - Partington	12.12 Derby (SM) - Rowsley	13.20	4F 0-6-0	14.40	Bank 13.25 Derby (SM) - Shotwick
Light ex Peak Forest	00.20	4F 0-6-0	05.55	06.20 Rowsley - Matlock (Target 70)	Light ex Bibbington	11.50	3F 0-6-0	15.07	Bank 15.32 Rowsley - Stockport
Down Yard Pilot	02.05	3F 0-6-0T	05.55	Down Yard Pilot	Light ex Peak Forest	10.39	4F 0-6-0	15.30	15.50 Rowsley - Stockport
18.20 Gowhole - Rowsley	20.18	4F 0-6-0	06.10	06.30 Rowsley - Crich Jcn (Target 73)	Light ex Peak Forest	14.18	8F 2-8-0	15.44	Bank 13.10 Kirkby - Gowhole
Light ex Peak Forest	18.10	4F 0-6-0	06.30	06.50 Rowsley - Chaddesden	13.00 Gowhole - Rowsley	14.28	9F 2-10-0	17.20	17.45 Beeston
Light ex Peak Forest	23.15	4F 0-6-0	07.00	07.19 Rowsley - Bakewell (Target 71)	Yard transfer engine (Target 72)	16.45	3F 0-6-0T	19.55	Up Yard Pilot
Light ex Peak Forest	23.20	4F 0-6-0	07.05	Bank 06.05 L. Eaton - Bruunswick	Light ex Buxton	13.15	4F 0-6-0	20.15	Bank 20.40 Rowsley - St Helens
Engineers working as require	16.00		08.00	Engineers working as required	14.15 Darley Dale (Target 71)	14.40	4F 0-6-0	20.28	Bank 20.53 Rowsley - Garston
Light ex Peak Forest	23.15	3F 0-6-0	08.20	Bank 08.45 Rowsley - Stockport	09.30 Garston - Rowsley	13.35	9F 2-10-0	20.40	20.53 Garston
Up Yard Pilot	06.10	3F 0-6-0T	09.20	Yard transfer engine (Target 72)	18.53 Matlock - Rowsley (Target 70)	19.15	4F 0-6-0	20.50	Bank 21.15 Rowsley - Gowhole
20.55 Beeston - Rowsley	11.35	9F 2-10-0	09.21	09.26 Gowhole (07.00 ex Kirkby)	17.23 Peak Forest - Rowsley	18.19	9F 2-10-0	21.40	22.00 Garston
23.40 Moston - Rowsley	04.40	8F 2-8-0	09.21	Bank 07.00 Kirkby - Gowhole	Up Yard Pilot	20.05	3F 0-6-0T	21.55	Up Yard Pilot
Light ex Buxton	09.10	3F 0-6-0	11.22	Bank 11.47 Rowsley - Garston	Light ex Peak Forest	20.40	4F 0-6-0	22.15	Bank 22.40 Rowsley - Buxton
Light ex Buxton	08.18	4F 0-6-0	11.40	12.02 Rowsley - Walton	00.10 Cricklewood - Rowsley	05.20	BR5 4-6-0	22.20	22.45 Brent
00.05 Garston - Rowsley	06.20	9F 2-10-0	12.00	12.25 Peak Forest	Pilot 17.23 Peak F - Rowsley	18.19	3F 0-6-0	23.30	Bank 23.30 Rowsley - Longsight

ALLOCATION & MOVEMENTS : ROWSLEY

Loco	Class	Aug-55	Sep-55	Oct-55	Nov-55	Dec-55	Jan-56	Feb-56	Mar-56	Apr-56	May-56	Jun-56	Jul-56
48432	8F 2-8-0 (1935)												
48654	8F 2-8-0 (1935)												
42760	5MT 2-6-0 (1926)												
42768	5MT 2-6-0 (1926)												
42792	5MT 2-6-0 (1926)	To Kettering	X	Ex Kettering									
42873	5MT 2-6-0 (1926)												
42874	5MT 2-6-0 (1926)												
42902	5MT 2-6-0 (1926)												
40929	4P 4-4-0 (1924)												W/D
40931	4P 4-4-0 (1924)												
41077	4P 4-4-0 (1924)	X	X	X	X	X	X	X	X	Ex Derby			
41185	4P 4-4-0 (1924)	X	X	X	X	X	X	X	X	X	X	X	Ex Nottingham
44028	4F 0-6-0 (1924)						To Stourton	X	X	X	X	X	X
44046	4F 0-6-0 (1924)												
44050	4F 0-6-0 (1924)												
44101	4F 0-6-0 (1924)												
44134	4F 0-6-0 (1924)												
44163	4F 0-6-0 (1924)												
44168	4F 0-6-0 (1924)												
44172	4F 0-6-0 (1924)												
44241	4F 0-6-0 (1924)												
44250	4F 0-6-0 (1924)	X	X	Ex Toton									
44327	4F 0-6-0 (1924)												
44429	4F 0-6-0 (1924)												
44556	4F 0-6-0 (1924)												
44564	4F 0-6-0 (1924)												
44565	4F 0-6-0 (1924)												
44566	4F 0-6-0 (1924)												
44588	4F 0-6-0 (1924)												
44602	4F 0-6-0 (1924)												
43835	4F 0-6-0 (1911)			W/D	X	X	X	X	X	X	X	X	X
43881	4F 0-6-0 (1911)												To Derby
43894	4F 0-6-0 (1911)		W/D	X	X	X	X	X	X	X	X	X	X
43918	4F 0-6-0 (1911)						To Nottingham	X	X	X	X	X	X
43921	4F 0-6-0 (1911)												
43925	4F 0-6-0 (1911)	Ex Derby											To Derby
43929	4F 0-6-0 (1911)												To W'boro
43982	4F 0-6-0 (1911)	X	X	Ex Nottingham									
44017	4F 0-6-0 (1911)						To Derby	X	X	X	X	X	X
47447	3F 0-6-0T (1924)												
47457	3F 0-6-0T (1924)												
47459	3F 0-6-0T (1924)												
47460	3F 0-6-0T (1924)												
47461	3F 0-6-0T (1924)												
47679	3F 0-6-0T (1924)												
43776	3F 0-6-0 (1906)												
43273	3F 0-6-0 (1885)			W/D	X	X	X	X	X	X	X	X	X
43290	3F 0-6-0 (1885)												
43342	3F 0-6-0 (1885)												
43370	3F 0-6-0 (1885)												
43400	3F 0-6-0 (1885)												
43429	3F 0-6-0 (1885)	X	X	X	Ex Derby								
43496	3F 0-6-0 (1885)												
43750	3F 0-6-0 (1885)												
43759	3F 0-6-0 (1885)												
40520	2P 4-4-0 (1891/1912)									To Royston	X	X	X
58850	2F 0-6-0T (1879)												
58856	2F 0-6-0T (1879)												
58860	2F 0-6-0T (1879)												
58862	2F 0-6-0T (1879)								W/D	X	X	X	X
58189	2F 0-6-0 (1878)												
58224	2F 0-6-0 (1878)												
58228	2F 0-6-0 (1878)												
41536	0F 0-4-0T (1907)	X	X	X	X	X	X	X	X	X	Ex Burton		
47000	0F 0-4-0ST (1932)												

LOADINGS FOR MINERAL TRAINS DERBY - MANCHESTER

Engine	3F	3FB	4F	4FB	5F	5FB	7F	7FB	G2a	G2aB	8F	8FB	WD	WDB	G	GB
Derby - Rowsley (70)	40		48		53		64		64		70		70		70	
Kirkby - Rowsley (Via Butterley) (70)	29	58	35	64	38	67	46	70	46	70	51	70	51	70	56	70
Rowsley - P. Forest (58)	22	48	26	52	26	55	26	58	26	58	26	58	26	58	26	58
P. Forest - Gowhole (60)	37		45		49		49		45		49		45			
Rowsley - Gowhole (58)	37	26	45	26	49	26	49	26	45	26	49	26	45	45	45	
Gowhole - Cheadle (Via Disley) (60)	37		45		49		49		45		49		45			
Gowhole - Cheadle (via H. Mersey) (60)	24		29		32		38		38		42		42			
Cheadle - CLC (90)	42		50		55		67		67		74		74			

4FB - 4F 0-6-0 Banked, etc

Unit of loading = loaded 13 ton mineral wagon or 2.5 empty wagons or 2 wagons of goods

Figures in brackets indicate maximum number of standard wagons permitted on each service. G = Garratt, WD = Austerity 2-8-0

CLASSIFICATION OF GOODS TRAINS

Class	Details	Max Speed
C	Fully fitted fixed loads (5MT 4-6-0 = 45 wagons) worked by passenger or mixed traffic engines	55
D	Partially (one-third) fitted fixed loads (5MT 4-6-0 = 50 wagons) worked by passenger, 9F or mixed traffic engines	50
E	Unfitted express for selected oil-axle wagons. Loads vary by route. (5MT = 55 wagons on level track)	45
F	Unfitted express for selected oil-axle wagons unsuitable for class E. Loads vary by route. (5MT = 63 wagons on level track)	40
H	Through goods with grease axle vehicles. Loads vary by route (5MT = 76 vehicles on level track)	35
J	Mineral service. Mineral service Loads vary by route (5MT = 57 loaded mineral/100 vehicles on level track)	30
K	Local trip Loads vary by route (5MT = 100 vehicles on level track)	30

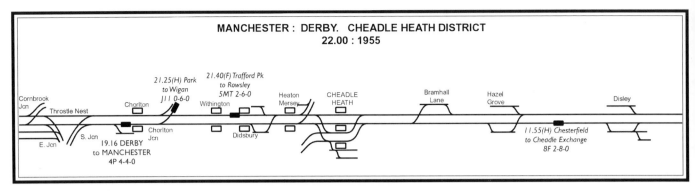

MANCHESTER : DERBY. CHEADLE HEATH DISTRICT
22.00 : 1955

CONTROLLER'S LOG: A certain amount of tension attaches itself to the running of all the London expresses, it is not only necessary for obvious reasons that they receive a clear path and run punctually but any slackness in the working arrangements inevitably invites a considerable amount of paperwork.

In the case of the 18.40 from St Pancras - now approaching Rowsley - the tension can border on anxiety since it arrives in Manchester Central only just in time for passengers to connect with the last buses and trams. Late running results in the Inspector's office being besieged by irate passengers, angrily demanding free taxi travel to their homes.

Only the Controller has the authority to sanction such expenditure and liberality with

still, Kentish Town may have had to take the booked engine out of the working and when this happens a 5MT is often all that is available to take over the diagram. The mixed traffic 4-6-0's are a very fine engine but they have a job to keep up with the faster Midland expresses and reports that the 18.40 is a minute late at Bedford, three down at Leicester and five adrift at Derby suggest a Black 5 that is going to drop even more time on the climb to Peak Forest. In the meantime calculations have to be made regarding the progress of the 21.00 Rowsley - Gowhole and the 22.00 Hoppers from Tunstead to Hartford to determine whether or not they have sufficient margin to be allowed down the main line in advance of the London. If the express is on time, the Gow-

the case via Rowsley. Its opposite number is approaching Edale and the two trains will pass each other at Earles Sidings.

The lines around Chinley and Gowhole are in their usual state of maelstrom and - ever conscious of the down London - clear instructions have to be given to make certain that once the 20.10 and 20.20 trains from Rowsley to Brindle Heath and Heaton Mersey have gone round the corner to the Joint line at New Mills South, the down line to Disley and Cheadle is kept clear.

In addition to the points mentioned, not the least of the reasons for giving the London a clear run is because one is likely to be held accountable for any delay and it is not much of a defence to state that it was knocked by the

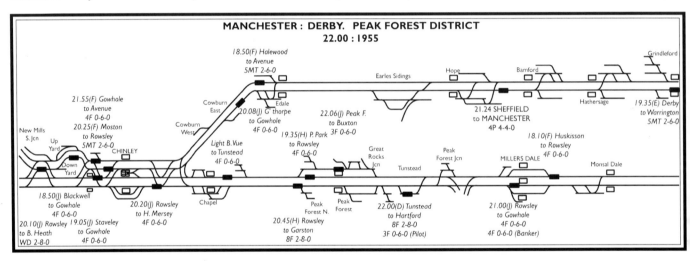

MANCHESTER : DERBY. PEAK FOREST DISTRICT
22.00 : 1955

taxis has to be justified to the District Superintendent at a later date. Older hands tend to the rather archaic legalistic view that the contract between the railway and a passenger requires the former to provide transport from London to Manchester without actually stating how long it will take. Younger hands see the timetable as a promise rather than a hope and tend to be rather more sympathetic.

The answer is to see that the train runs to time although this is sometimes easier said than done. Frequent heavy fog and a heavy line occupation do not help whilst the 5XP engines have very little margin for recovery. Worse

hole will remain at Millers Dale whilst the Hoppers will be allowed to come as far as Peak Forest.

Over on the Hope Valley, things are uncharacteristically quiet; the line having been cleared to allow a succession of fast trains to pass, one of which is the curiously routed Chaddesden to Warrington express goods which instead of running via Peak Forest takes the North Midland line through Clay Cross and Chesterfield to turn west at Dore for the Hope Valley. The advantage of the longer route is that its class 5 locomotive can be loaded to 53 vehicles without having to be banked as would be

20.20 Rowsley - Heaton Mersey because the preceding train was steaming badly. The response is that you should have seen the problem before it happened and done something about it - that is one of the things you are paid for....

On a brighter note and one in harmony with the national obsession with boiled barley, the Burton Beer is approaching High Peak Junction en route to Rowsley where its fifty wagons of ale - employment for a great many barmaids - will be broken up and distributed amongst the different services that serve the various districts of Manchester.

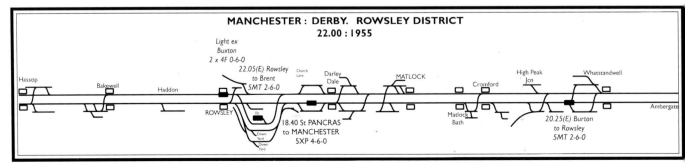

MANCHESTER : DERBY. ROWSLEY DISTRICT
22.00 : 1955

							ALLOCATION & MOVEMENTS : ROWSLEY						
Loco	Class	Aug-56	Sep-56	Oct-56	Nov-56	Dec-56	Jan-57	Feb-57	Mar-57	Apr-57	May-57	Jun-57	Jul-57
48056	8F 2-8-0 (1935)	X	X	X	X	X	Ex W'houses						
48063	8F 2-8-0 (1935)	X	X	X	X	X	X	Ex W'houses					
48192	8F 2-8-0 (1935)	X	X	X	Ex C' wood								
48432	8F 2-8-0 (1935)												
48654	8F 2-8-0 (1935)												
42754	5MT 2-6-0 (1926)	X	X	X	X	X	X	X	X	X	Ex Saltley		
42760	5MT 2-6-0 (1926)												
42768	5MT 2-6-0 (1926)												
42792	5MT 2-6-0 (1926)												
42873	5MT 2-6-0 (1926)												
42874	5MT 2-6-0 (1926)												
42902	5MT 2-6-0 (1926)												
40931	4P 4-4-0 (1924)												
41077	4P 4-4-0 (1924)									W/D	X	X	X
41185	4P 4-4-0 (1924)												
42053	4MT 2-6-4T (1945)	X	X	X	X	X	X	X	X	X	X	X	Ex Saltley
42228	4MT 2-6-4T (1945)	X	X	X	X	X	X	X	X	X	X	Ex Derby	
44046	4F 0-6-0 (1924)												
44050	4F 0-6-0 (1924)												
44101	4F 0-6-0 (1924)												
44134	4F 0-6-0 (1924)												
44163	4F 0-6-0 (1924)												
44168	4F 0-6-0 (1924)												
44172	4F 0-6-0 (1924)												
44241	4F 0-6-0 (1924)						To Walton	X	Ex Walton				
44250	4F 0-6-0 (1924)							To H. Mersey	X	X	X	X	X
44327	4F 0-6-0 (1924)												
44429	4F 0-6-0 (1924)												
44556	4F 0-6-0 (1924)												
44564	4F 0-6-0 (1924)												
44565	4F 0-6-0 (1924)												
44566	4F 0-6-0 (1924)												
44588	4F 0-6-0 (1924)												
44602	4F 0-6-0 (1924)												
43921	4F 0-6-0 (1911)									To T. Park	X	X	X
43950	4F 0-6-0 (1911)	X	X	X	X	X	X	X	X	Ex Canklow			
43982	4F 0-6-0 (1911)												
44013	4F 0-6-0 (1911)	X	X	X	X	X	X	X	X	Ex Canklow			
68006	4F : J94 0-6-0T (1943)	Ex Bidston											
68013	4F : J94 0-6-0T (1943)	Ex Bidston											
68030	4F : J94 0-6-0T (1943)	Ex Bidston											
47447	3F 0-6-0T (1924)												
47457	3F 0-6-0T (1924)												
47459	3F 0-6-0T (1924)												
47460	3F 0-6-0T (1924)												
47461	3F 0-6-0T (1924)												
47679	3F 0-6-0T (1924)												
43776	3F 0-6-0 (1906)												
43290	3F 0-6-0 (1885)												
43323	3F 0-6-0 (1885)	X	X	X	Ex Derby								
43342	3F 0-6-0 (1885)												
43370	3F 0-6-0 (1885)												
43400	3F 0-6-0 (1885)												
43429	3F 0-6-0 (1885)												
43496	3F 0-6-0 (1885)												
43750	3F 0-6-0 (1885)												
43759	3F 0-6-0 (1885)												
58850	2F 0-6-0T (1879)												
58856	2F 0-6-0T (1879)												
58860	2F 0-6-0T (1879)										W/D	X	X
58189	2F 0-6-0T (1878)												
58224	2F 0-6-0 (1878)		W/D	X	X	X	X	X	X	X	X	X	X
58228	2F 0-6-0 (1878)												
41536	0F 0-4-0T (1907)		To Burton	X	X	X	X	X	X	X	X	X	X
47000	0F 0-4-0ST (1932)												

41097, one of the LMS-built 4P Compound 4-4-0's stands on Derby loco shortly before its withdrawal in May 1956.

Loco	Class	Aug-57	Sep-57	Oct-57	Nov-57	Dec-57	Jan-58	Feb-58	Mar-58	Apr-58	May-58	Jun-58	Jul-58
48056	8F 2-8-0 (1935)												
48063	8F 2-8-0 (1935)												
48192	8F 2-8-0 (1935)												
48432	8F 2-8-0 (1935)												
48654	8F 2-8-0 (1935)												
42754	5MT 2-6-0 (1926)												To Kettering
42760	5MT 2-6-0 (1926)												
42768	5MT 2-6-0 (1926)												
42792	5MT 2-6-0 (1926)												
42873	5MT 2-6-0 (1926)												
42874	5MT 2-6-0 (1926)												
42902	5MT 2-6-0 (1926)												
40931	4P 4-4-0 (1924)												To Lancaster
41185	4P 4-4-0 (1924)	To Derby	X	X	X	X	X	X	X	X	X	X	X
42053	4MT 2-6-4T (1945)												
42228	4MT 2-6-4T (1945)												
42486	4MT 2-6-4T (1935)	X	X	X	X	X	X	X	X	X	X	X	Ex N. Heath
44046	4F 0-6-0 (1924)												
44050	4F 0-6-0 (1924)												
44101	4F 0-6-0 (1924)												
44122	4F 0-6-0 (1924)	X	X	X	X	X	X	X	X	Ex Kettering			
44134	4F 0-6-0 (1924)												
44163	4F 0-6-0 (1924)												
44168	4F 0-6-0 (1924)												
44172	4F 0-6-0 (1924)												
44178	4F 0-6-0 (1924)	X	X	X	X	X	X	X	X	X	X	Ex H. Mersey	To Toton
44241	4F 0-6-0 (1924)												
44278	4F 0-6-0 (1924)	X	X	X	X	X	X	X	X	Ex Kettering			
44327	4F 0-6-0 (1924)												
44429	4F 0-6-0 (1924)												
44556	4F 0-6-0 (1924)												
44564	4F 0-6-0 (1924)												
44565	4F 0-6-0 (1924)												
44566	4F 0-6-0 (1924)												
44588	4F 0-6-0 (1924)												
44602	4F 0-6-0 (1924)												
43950	4F 0-6-0 (1911)												
43961	4F 0-6-0 (1911)	X	X	X	X	X	X	X	X	X	X	X	Ex Toton
43982	4F 0-6-0 (1911)												
44013	4F 0-6-0 (1911)												
68006	4F : J94 0-6-0T (1943)												
68013	4F : J94 0-6-0T (1943)												
68030	4F : J94 0-6-0T (1943)												
68034	4F : J94 0-6-0T (1943)	Ex Bidston											
47447	3F 0-6-0T (1924)												
47457	3F 0-6-0T (1924)												
47459	3F 0-6-0T (1924)												
47460	3F 0-6-0T (1924)												
47461	3F 0-6-0T (1924)												
47679	3F 0-6-0T (1924)												
43776	3F 0-6-0 (1906)				W/D	X	X	X	X	X	X	X	X
43778	3F 0-6-0 (1906)	X	X	X	X	X	Ex Burton						
43290	3F 0-6-0 (1885)					W/D	X	X	X	X	X	X	X
43323	3F 0-6-0 (1885)											W/D	X
43342	3F 0-6-0 (1885)												
43370	3F 0-6-0 (1885)												
43400	3F 0-6-0 (1885)												
43429	3F 0-6-0 (1885)												
43496	3F 0-6-0 (1885)												
43750	3F 0-6-0 (1885)												
43759	3F 0-6-0 (1885)												
58850	2F 0-6-0T (1879)												
58856	2F 0-6-0T (1879)				W/D	X	X	X	X	X	X	X	X
58189	2F 0-6-0 (1878)	W/D	X	X	X	X	X	X	X	X	X	X	X
58228	2F 0-6-0 (1878)												
58137	2F 0-6-0 (1875)	X	X	X	Ex Nottingham								
47000	0F 0-4-0ST (1932)												

Had the coal board worked as closely with the Railway as I.C.I. did, the type of trains operating between Northwich and Great Rocks might have been a more familiar sight. As it was ICI vacuum hopper workings and the North Eastern Consett Iron Ore workings were isolated examples of mineral block train services. 8F 2-8-0 48135 of Northwich storms up the bank to Chinley North Junction with the 08.45 Wallerscote to Great Rocks Junction in 1950. The author, who fired on these turns, finds it remarkable that when they commenced in the late 1930's, 4F 0-6-0's were the nominated power. It didn't take the LMS long to learn that a free steaming engine was required.

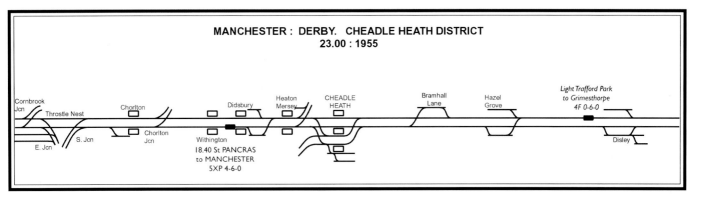

MANCHESTER : DERBY. CHEADLE HEATH DISTRICT
23.00 : 1955

CONTROLLER'S LOG : The 18.40 ex St Pancras pauses for a minute at Didsbury and with a punctual arrival at Manchester in sight we can breath a little more easily. The fireman will be running the 5XP down by raking over the fire and filling the boiler but to the reader - a regular traveller on the train - the last twenty minutes of the 18.40 is one of the most attractive of trips as it rattles through the darkened late evening Manchester suburbs, the three-cylinder exhaust chattering back from the sea of houses until the brakes are applied for the Throstle Nest curves and the cautious entry through the massive steel girders of the approach to Central station.

Late as the hour is, it is not the last Midland train to be dealt with and a path has to be maintained for the 21.24 Sheffield - Manchester Central which follows the express from Chinley, running via Stockport.

In the down direction the vacuum left by the two passenger trains is filled as usual by class J mineral trains but in the up direction attention has to be directed to the overnight express goods trains, the running disciplines of which are identical to those of passenger trains - you delay them at your peril.

Of these, the most urgent is the 22.00 Ancoats - St Pancras fitted which is passing Chinley South Junction. It will pause for five minute in Chapel-en-le-Frith station to take water after which it will run non-stop to Trent Junction, where two minutes are allowed for loco relief. The engine's next stop for water is Kettering South when the service halts for carriage & wagon examination.

With a London arrival of 04.10, the Ancoats fitted is a pretty impressive proposition but the 45 wagons conveyed are no more than a drop in the ocean given the volume of tonnage that is worked up the line to Rowsley for a wide variety of destinations that do not have through services from either Manchester or Liverpool.

During the course of the late evening seven class E and F goods trains are worked into Rowsley - five from Manchester and two from Liverpool - bringing between them a total of just over three hundred wagons. The greater part of this traffic is transferred to one of the nine night goods departures: two each for London and Birmingham and five local workings to Nottingham. Leicester, Burton and Derby.

Several of the workings are making their way up the main line. The 20.25 ex Moston, bringing traffic from the Lancashire & Yorkshire - is on the point of entering Rowsley whilst the 21.20 from Ancoats (Midland traffic from Manchester) has just come over the summit at Peak Forest. The through London is at Chinley South, followed by the 21.40 ex Trafford Park loaded with shipping traffic from the Manchester Ship Canal.

To say that these trains are important is to understate matters. When the District Superintendent reviews the night's performance in the morning, he will have some questions to ask if any passenger trains have been delay but these will be nothing like as searching as those concerning time lost by express goods trains.

So concludes our twenty-four hours as Controller of the District; a period in which over one hundred and fifty trains have passed through Millers Dale and more than one hundred at Hope. This, as near as one can calculate it, equates to about ten thousand wagon movements which - perhaps - is not a bad day's work.....

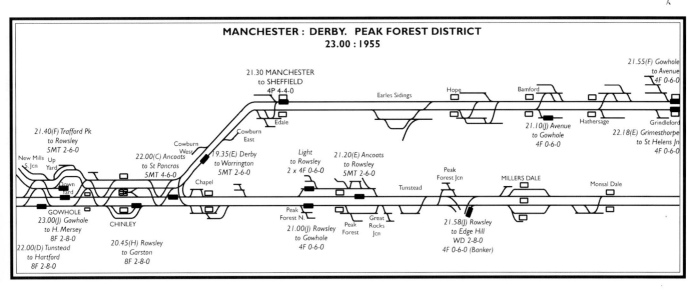

MANCHESTER : DERBY. PEAK FOREST DISTRICT
23.00 : 1955

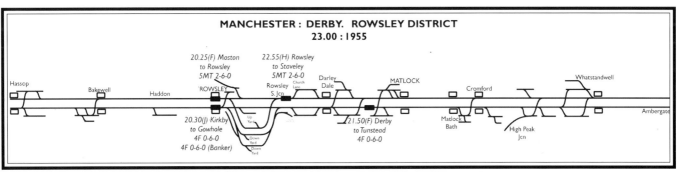

MANCHESTER : DERBY. ROWSLEY DISTRICT
23.00 : 1955

Chaddesden was the principal marshalling yard at Derby and was situated roughly parallel to the passenger station on the avoiding line between Derby North Junction and Spondon Junction. In addition to giving access to Chaddesden Yard, the avoiding line - Chaddesden Curve - permitted trains to run between the Trent and Birmingham liners without having to reverse whilst through services between the North and South could be directed away from the passenger station. In the upper view 2P 4-4-0 40552 of Derby passes Chaddesden Up Reception Yard and heads towards Derby South Junction with the 16.28 Nottingham - Derby St Mary's fitted goods. The use of a 2P 4-4-0 on such a duty was not as strange as it might appear since the class was permitted to take a load of twenty-nine vehicles which was usually as much as was required on such a short journey. In the lower view Saltley-based 4F 0-6-0 43951 passes the same spot with an excursion for Derby and Birmingham. Both pictures were taken in 1950.

ALLOCATION & MOVEMENTS : ROWSLEY

Loco	Class	Aug-58	Sep-58	Oct-58	Nov-58	Dec-58	Jan-59	Feb-59	Mar-59	Apr-59	May-59	Jun-59	Jul-59
48008	8F 2-8-0 (1935)	X	X	X	X	X	X	X	X	X	X	Ex Kirkby	
48056	8F 2-8-0 (1935)											To Hasland	X
48063	8F 2-8-0 (1935)											To Kirkby	X
48081	8F 2-8-0 (1935)	X	X	X	X	X	X	X	X	X	X	Ex Kirkby	
48128	8F 2-8-0 (1935)	X	X	X	X	X	X	X	X	X	X	Ex Toton	
48192	8F 2-8-0 (1935)											To Kirkby	X
48317	8F 2-8-0 (1935)	X	X	X	X	X	X	X	X	Ex H. Mersey		To Kirkby	X
48364	8F 2-8-0 (1935)	X	X	X	X	X	X	X	X	X	X	Ex Hasland	
48654	8F 2-8-0 (1935)												
48770	8F 2-8-0 (1935)	X	X	X	X	X	X	X	X	X	X	Ex Kirkby	
42748	5MT 2-6-0 (1926)	X	X	X	X	X	X	X	X	X	X	Ex Kingmoor	
42754	5MT 2-6-0 (1926)	Ex Kettering											
42760	5MT 2-6-0 (1926)												
42768	5MT 2-6-0 (1926)												
42792	5MT 2-6-0 (1926)												
42873	5MT 2-6-0 (1926)												
42874	5MT 2-6-0 (1926)												
42902	5MT 2-6-0 (1926)												
42053	4MT 2-6-4T (1945)												
42228	4MT 2-6-4T (1945)												
42486	4MT 2-6-4T (1935)												
44042	4F 0-6-0 (1924)	X	X	X	X	X	X	X	X	X	X	Ex Derby	
44046	4F 0-6-0 (1924)												
44050	4F 0-6-0 (1924)												
44101	4F 0-6-0 (1924)												
44122	4F 0-6-0 (1924)	To Hasland	X	X	X	X	X	X	X	X	X	X	X
44134	4F 0-6-0 (1924)												
44163	4F 0-6-0 (1924)												
44168	4F 0-6-0 (1924)						To Burton	X	X	X	X	X	X
44172	4F 0-6-0 (1924)												
44177	4F 0-6-0 (1924)	X	X	X	X	X	X	X	X	X	X	Ex Derby	To W' houses
44241	4F 0-6-0 (1924)						To Burton	X	X	X	X	X	X
44278	4F 0-6-0 (1924)	To Coalville	X	X	X	X	X	X	X	X	X	X	X
44327	4F 0-6-0 (1924)												
44429	4F 0-6-0 (1924)												
44556	4F 0-6-0 (1924)												
44564	4F 0-6-0 (1924)												
44565	4F 0-6-0 (1924)												
44566	4F 0-6-0 (1924)												
44588	4F 0-6-0 (1924)												
44602	4F 0-6-0 (1924)												
43950	4F 0-6-0 (1911)												
43961	4F 0-6-0 (1911)							To H. Mersey	X	X	X	X	X
43982	4F 0-6-0 (1911)												
44013	4F 0-6-0 (1911)	To Saltley	X	X	X	X	X	X	X	X	X	X	X
68006	4F : J94 0-6-0T (1943)												
68013	4F : J94 0-6-0T (1943)												
68030	4F : J94 0-6-0T (1943)												
68034	4F : J94 0-6-0T (1943)												
47447	3F 0-6-0T (1924)												
47457	3F 0-6-0T (1924)												
47459	3F 0-6-0T (1924)												
47460	3F 0-6-0T (1924)												
47461	3F 0-6-0T (1924)												
47679	3F 0-6-0T (1924)												
43778	3F 0-6-0 (1906)												
43342	3F 0-6-0 (1885)												
43370	3F 0-6-0 (1885)												
43400	3F 0-6-0 (1885)						To T. Park	X	X	X	X	X	X
43429	3F 0-6-0 (1885)												
43496	3F 0-6-0 (1885)												
43750	3F 0-6-0 (1885)												
43759	3F 0-6-0 (1885)												
58850	2F 0-6-0T (1879)												
58228	2F 0-6-0 (1878)												
58137	2F 0-6-0 (1875)												
47007	0F 0-4-0ST (1953)	X	X	X	X	X	Ex Derby						
47000	0F 0-4-0ST (1932)						To Derby	X	X	X	X	X	X
D3775	0F : Diesel 0-6-0	X	X	X	X	X	X	X	X	X	X	NEW	
D3776	0F : Diesel 0-6-0	X	X	X	X	X	X	X	X	X	X	NEW	

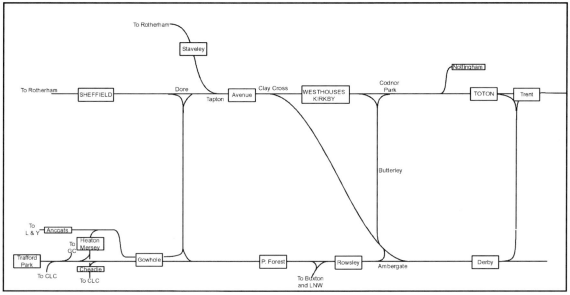

Readers will be familiar with the public map of the system but this is the network that railwaymen in the district had to work with. Goods and Passenger traffic did not always followed the same route. Passenger services consisted of occasional services from London, Derby and Sheffield whilst goods - especially mineral - tended to work across in astronomical tonnages from the Erewash Valley either via Butterley or the Hope Valley.

Rowsley 4P 4-4-0 Compound 40929 prepares to leave Derby on 6th September 1954 with the 17.05 passenger to Bakewell; one of Rowsley's two passenger workings. The diagram started with the 06.25 Darley Dale to Nottingham and concluded with the 17.05 to Bakewell. The 4-4-0 did an intermediate light engine run to St Mary's Yard with relief train crews for goods trip workings. 40929 came from Bedford in November 1952 and remained at Rowsley until being taken out of traffic in July 1956.

Loco	Class	Aug-59	Sep-59	Oct-59	Nov-59	Dec-59	Jan-60	Feb-60	Mar-60	Apr-60	May-60	Jun-60	Jul-60
					ALLOCATION & MOVEMENTS : ROWSLEY								
92008	9F 2-10-0 (1954)	X	X	X	Ex Saltley								
92009	9F 2-10-0 (1954)	X	X	X	Ex Saltley								
92048	9F 2-10-0 (1954)	X	X	X	Ex Saltley								
92049	9F 2-10-0 (1954)	X	X	X	Ex Saltley								
92050	9F 2-10-0 (1954)	X	X	X	Ex Toton								
92051	9F 2-10-0 (1954)	X	X	X	Ex Saltley								
48008	8F 2-8-0 (1935)												
48081	8F 2-8-0 (1935)												
48128	8F 2-8-0 (1935)				To Toton	X	X	X	X	X	X	X	X
48364	8F 2-8-0 (1935)												
48654	8F 2-8-0 (1935)												
48770	8F 2-8-0 (1935)				To Toton	X	X	X	X	X	X	X	X
73135	5MT 4-6-0 (1951)	X	X	X	Ex Derby								
73136	5MT 4-6-0 (1951)	X	X	X	Ex Derby								
73137	5MT 4-6-0 (1951)	X	X	X	Ex Derby								
73138	5MT 4-6-0 (1951)	X	X	X	Ex Derby								
73139	5MT 4-6-0 (1951)	X	X	X	Ex Derby								
73140	5MT 4-6-0 (1951)	X	X	X	Ex Derby								
73141	5MT 4-6-0 (1951)	X	X	X	Ex Derby								
73142	5MT 4-6-0 (1951)	X	X	X	Ex Derby								
73143	5MT 4-6-0 (1951)	X	X	X	Ex Derby								
73144	5MT 4-6-0 (1951)	X	X	X	Ex Derby								
42748	5MT 2-6-0 (1926)				To Gorton	X	X	X	X	X	X	X	X
42754	5MT 2-6-0 (1926)				To Gorton	X	X	X	X	X	X	X	X
42760	5MT 2-6-0 (1926)				To Gorton	X	X	X	X	X	X	X	X
42767	5MT 2-6-0 (1926)	X	X	Ex Gorton	To Gorton	X	X	X	X	X	X	X	X
42768	5MT 2-6-0 (1926)				To Gorton	X	X	X	X	X	X	X	X
42792	5MT 2-6-0 (1926)				To Gorton	X	X	X	X	X	X	X	X
42873	5MT 2-6-0 (1926)				To Gorton	X	X	X	X	X	X	X	X
42874	5MT 2-6-0 (1926)				To Gorton	X	X	X	X	X	X	X	X
42902	5MT 2-6-0 (1926)				To Gorton	X	X	X	X	X	X	X	X
42053	4MT 2-6-4T (1945)								To Neasden	X	X	X	X
42228	4MT 2-6-4T (1945)												
42486	4MT 2-6-4T (1935)												
42568	4MT 2-6-4T (1935)	X	X	X	X	X	X	X	Ex Neasden				
44042	4F 0-6-0 (1924)												
44046	4F 0-6-0 (1924)												
44050	4F 0-6-0 (1924)				W/D	X	X	X	X	X	X	X	X
44078	4F 0-6-0 (1924)	X	X	X	X	X	Ex T. Park						
44080	4F 0-6-0 (1924)	X	X	X	X	X	Ex T. Park						
44101	4F 0-6-0 (1924)												
44134	4F 0-6-0 (1924)												
44163	4F 0-6-0 (1924)												W/D
44172	4F 0-6-0 (1924)												
44327	4F 0-6-0 (1924)												
44413	4F 0-6-0 (1924)	X	X	X	X	X	Ex T. Park						
44428	4F 0-6-0 (1924)	X	X	X	X	X	X	X	X	X	X	X	Ex Derby
44429	4F 0-6-0 (1924)												
44556	4F 0-6-0 (1924)												
44564	4F 0-6-0 (1924)						To T. Park	X	X	X	X	X	X
44565	4F 0-6-0 (1924)						To T. Park	X	X	X	X	X	X
44566	4F 0-6-0 (1924)						To T. Park	X	X	X	X	X	X
44588	4F 0-6-0 (1924)												
44602	4F 0-6-0 (1924)												
43950	4F 0-6-0 (1911)												
43982	4F 0-6-0 (1911)				To W' houses	X	X	X	X	X	X	X	X
68006	4F : J94 0-6-0T (1943)												
68012	4F : J94 0-6-0T (1943)	X	Ex Gorton										
68013	4F : J94 0-6-0T (1943)												
68030	4F : J94 0-6-0T (1943)												
68034	4F : J94 0-6-0T (1943)												
47447	3F 0-6-0T (1924)												
47457	3F 0-6-0T (1924)												
47459	3F 0-6-0T (1924)												
47460	3F 0-6-0T (1924)												
47461	3F 0-6-0T (1924)												
47679	3F 0-6-0T (1924)												
43778	3F 0-6-0 (1906)	To Burton	X	X	X	X	X	X	X	X	X	X	X
43250	3F 0-6-0 (1885)	X	X	X	X	Ex Royston							
43342	3F 0-6-0 (1885)												
43370	3F 0-6-0 (1885)				W/D	X	X	X	X	X	X	X	X
43429	3F 0-6-0 (1885)									W/D	X	X	X
43496	3F 0-6-0 (1885)												
43750	3F 0-6-0 (1885)			W/D	X	X	X	X	X	X	X	X	X
43759	3F 0-6-0 (1885)				W/D	X	X	X	X	X	X	X	X
58850	2F 0-6-0T (1879)												
58228	2F 0-6-0 (1878)												
58137	2F 0-6-0ST (1875)												To Coalville
47007	0F 0-4-0ST (1953)												
D3774	0F : Diesel 0-6-0	X	X	X	X	X	Ex Derby						
D3775	0F : Diesel 0-6-0	To Derby	X	X	X	X	Ex Derby						
D3776	0F : Diesel 0-6-0	To Derby	X	X	X	X	X	X	X	X	X	X	X

Jubilees, Black Fives and BR Standards arrived in ever increasing numbers but still the 2P 4-4-0's survived. 40326 of Derby - one of the ex-Somerset & Dorset 1914 batch - stands in one of the carriage roads at Derby Midland in 1955. Although not having worked on the S & D for many years and having had spells at Leeds and Hellifield before arriving at Derby, the engine still retained its tablet catcher.

Arguably the most handsome class to work the line, Jubilee 45618 'New Hebrides' runs into No.6 platform with an up express.